# FOOTSTEPS THROUGH TIME

## A HISTORY OF TRAVEL AND TOURISM TO THE VICTORIA FALLS

## About the Author

Peter Roberts is a researcher and writer on the natural and human history of the Victoria Falls. Born in Wales and an ecologist by training, Peter has become drawn to the landscapes, wildlife and human history of Africa and especially the natural wonder of the Falls and its surrounds. Following publication of detailed books on the history of the Victoria Falls Bridge and Victoria Falls Hotel, Peter now presents this comprehensive overview of travel and tourism to the Falls.

## Also Available

Life and Death at the Old Drift, Victoria Falls (1898-1905)
Sun, Steel and Spray - A History of the Victoria Falls Bridge
Corridors Through Time - A History of the Victoria Falls Hotel

- - -

Footsteps Through Time - A History of Travel and Tourism to the Victoria Falls
Peter Roberts

First published 2017

Cover design and page layout by Peter Roberts

ISBN-13: 978-1534974739

Roberts, Peter (2017) Footsteps Through Time -
A History of Travel and Tourism to the Victoria Falls. First Edition,
Zambezi Book Company / CreateSpace Independent Publishing

# Footsteps Through Time

## A History of Travel and Tourism to the Victoria Falls

### Peter Roberts

# Contents

Preface 7

Introduction 9

To the Victoria Falls 10

People of the Falls 12

Livingstone's Second Expedition 15

In Livingstone's Footsteps 20

Rhodes and Rail 30

Bulawayo and Beyond 33

The Old Drift 38

Through the Wilds to Hwange 43

The Railway Arrives 48

The Victoria Falls Hotel 52

The Victoria Falls Bridge 58

A Valuable Property 62

The Zambezi Express 65

The Zambezi Regatta 67

Death of the Drift 70

Official Opening of the Bridge 71

Sykes' Guide to the Falls 72

Tickets Please! 78

Leopold Moore and The Livingstone Mail 79

To Be or Not to Be? 80

Clark's River Safaris 84

Zambezi Sculling Championship 86

The Weekender 88

Rail Connections 90

Clark's Guide to the Falls 91

Soper's Curios 93

The Hotel Rebuilt 94

On the River 96

War and Peace 97

Paradise Tamed? 98

Trolley Transport 99

From Far and Wide 101

Visit of the Prince of Wales 102

Bathing Costumes and Mackintoshes 104

Visit of Prince George                105
Livingstone Statue                    106
Flight of Angels                      108
Power from the Falls                  111
The Price of Paradise                 112
Wings of War                          114
Royal Visit                           115
The Flying Boat Service               118
Livingstone Joins the Jet-set         122
Sky Safaris                           124
Victoria Falls National Park          125
Formation of the Federation           127
Livingstone Centenary                 128
The Falls in the Fifties              130
Falls in Flood                        132
Ripples at the Landing Stage          134
Rail Overtaken                        136
Federation Folly                      137
Polarising Politics                   139
South Bank Takes Off                  140
Under a Southern Sun                  146
Seventies Struggles                   148
Eighties Independence                 154
Africa's Adrenalin Capital            157
Boom Town                             160
Visitor Highs                         163
Millennium Madness                    165
In the Spotlight                      169
Challenging Conditions                172
Tourism on the Bounce                 175
Stability and Growth                  177
Centre Stage                          178
Regeneration and Renewal              181
Expanding Horizons                    183
The Falls Today                       185
Into the Future                       189

Acknowledgements                      192
References                            193

# Preface

*The Falls from the air*

Welcome to this history of the Victoria Falls, a journey through over 150 years of travel and tourism to this great natural wonder, a destination which has caught the imagination of travellers since its existence was first promoted to the world by Dr David Livingstone in 1855.

This book expands on the author's two previous books on the Falls, 'Sun, Steel and Spray - A History of the Victoria Falls Bridge' (first published 2011, revised second edition published 2016) and 'Corridors Through Time - A History of the Victoria Falls Hotel' (first published 2015, revised second edition published 2016), providing extensive background material and additional information to the story of the human development of the Victoria Falls as a global tourism attraction.

In presenting this history, I have, wherever possible, described events directly through contemporary references and descriptions, quotations from which form a key element of the text. The names of many places and countries have changed over the years, and old names are first introduced in their original historical contexts, whilst also identified with their contemporary names for clarity, for example Rhodesia (now Zimbabwe). Alternative spellings will occasionally be found within quotations, for example Zambesi, now commonly spelt Zambezi.

For ease of reading the text often refers simply to the 'Railway Company' rather than the often changing names of the original construction and operating companies. The Bechuanaland Railway Company was originally formed in 1893 and renamed the Rhodesia Railways Limited in 1899. The operating company became the merged Beira and Mashonaland and Rhodesia Railways in 1903, changed to simply Rhodesia Railways in 1927 and becoming Rhodesia Railways, Limited in 1936. Following nationalisation in 1949 the company became a statutory body, finally evolving into the National Railways of Zimbabwe in 1980.

*View of Main Falls*

Statistics and figures relating to tourism arrivals are referenced to primary sources, such as official reports and publications, wherever possible or, where these are unavailable to secondary sources, for example news and media articles. It should be noted that figures are not always directly comparable as recording methods and criteria change over time. Reference to monetary amounts is made in either UK pounds, or more recently US dollars, at their contemporary values. Zimbabwe adopted the US dollar in 2009, replacing the struggling Zimbabwe dollar, introduced on independence in 1980 and itself replacing the Rhodesian pound (originally pegged to the British pound).

Our story occurs against a historical context of national and regional development, from the influence of European colonial powers and establishment of company administration, through self-governance and finally independence, to which reference is made but to which space does not allow full investigation or reflection.

I apologise for any errors, mistakes or omissions in the text, which I hope are few in number and small in nature. It should be noted that there is one sector of the tourism industry intentionally omitted from this book; recent decades have seen the growth of elephant-back safaris and lion-walks - captive-animal interactions which the author believes have no place in modern ethical tourism.

Comments and criticisms are welcomed, as are contributions; especially additional information, stories or photographs relating to topics covered in this book, or relating to the wider history of travel and tourism to the Falls.

*Peter Roberts, May 2017*
*peter@zambezibookcompany.com*

# Introduction

The story of tourism to the Victoria Falls follows the development of the global travel industry through the 20th century, from the early explorers and hunters travelling by horse and wagon to today's mass numbers of aviation arrivals. Ever since Dr David Livingstone first promoted the Victoria Falls to the world they have been a magnet to travellers. Livingstone hoped that the Zambezi River would be the transport corridor which would open up the central regions of Africa - his hopes of navigating the river were, however, drowned by the rough gorges and wild rapids of the middle sections of the river.

The economic development - and commercial exploitation - of the region would be realised by the financial power of Cecil John Rhodes and his dream of a railway line connecting the southern Cape with the banks of the Zambezi and beyond. The arrival of the railway in 1904 to the Falls, supported by regular steamship services to the southern Cape, brought the destination to within the reach of travellers from Britain and Europe. The opening of the Victoria Falls Hotel in the same year and landmark engineering achievement of the Victoria Falls Bridge (completed in 1905) soon established the Falls as a prestigious and fashionable destination.

After fifty years of travel dominated by rail, the development of Livingstone Airport in 1950 and Victoria Falls Airport in 1967 opened up the Falls to rapidly evolving global aviation markets. The subsequent growth of the economy air travel industry sparked a diversification in tourism services and operators on both sides of the river. The recent opening of the expanded Victoria Falls International Airport marks the beginning of another significant chapter in the development of the region, with associated pressures to further expand tourism facilities and services to accommodate dreams of ever increasing arrivals.

A visit to the Falls offers the modern-day visitor a diversity of activities, from sedate wildlife safaris and relaxing river cruises to the thrills of bungee jumping and spills of white-water rafting. But over-shadowing all these distractions is still one experience guaranteed to take your breath away - a visit to 'Mosi-oa-Tunya,' the 'Smoke that Thunders' - the Victoria Falls.

*The Falls in flood, photographed by Percy Clark*

# To the Victoria Falls

Known to the local inhabitants of the region for centuries, the majestic natural wonder of the Victoria Falls was first brought to the attention of the wider world by the famous Scottish missionary and explorer Dr David Livingstone in 1855.

On the 4th August 1851, having travelled north deep into the unmapped interior, Livingstone arrived on the banks of a large river which local inhabitants called the *Liambai*, and which he correctly identified as the upper reaches of the Zambezi, known only to Europeans by its lower stretches and great delta on the east coast. Livingstone befriended the Makalolo chief, Sebetwane, who had established power in the region, noting that some of the Makalolo wore European cloth, no doubt traded with slave traders. Livingstone was told of a great waterfall some distance downstream, although neither he or his travelling companion, William Oswell, visited them.

*Dr. David Livingstone (1813-1873)*

*"Of these we had often heard since we came into the country; indeed, one of the questions asked by Sebituane [in 1851] was, 'Have you smoke that sounds in your country?' They [the Makalolo] did not go near enough to examine them, but, viewing them with awe at a distance, said, in reference to the vapour and noise, 'Mosi oa tunya' (smoke does sound there). It was previously called Shongwe, the meaning of which I could not ascertain."* (Livingstone, 1857)

Oswell marked their rough location on a map published in 1852, but it was not until 1855, having already explored upstream and then to the west coast, that Livingstone returned to the Zambezi and finally explored downstream, escorted by Sebetwane's successor, Chief Sekeletu.

Livingstone was enchanted by the beauty of the island studded river, its forested fringes and exotic wildlife, recording emotively:

*"[N]o one can imagine the beauty of the view from anything witnessed in England. It had never been seen before by European eyes; but scenes so lovely must have been gazed upon by angels in their flight"* (Livingstone, 1857).

This last passage has often been misquoted in reference to the Falls themselves, but it was the stretches of the river upstream of the Falls which first fired Livingstone's imagination. Of the Falls themselves he would later write it *"is a rather hopeless task to endeavour to convey an idea of it in words"* (Livingstone and Livingstone, 1865).

Travelling by canoe and then along the north bank to avoid the Katombora Rapids, Sekeletu arranged a canoe and local boatman to take Livingstone the final distance downstream to the waterfall. On 16th November 1855 Livingstone was guided to a small island on the very lip of the Falls. Scrambling through vegetation to the sudden edge Livingstone struggled to understand the dramatic scene which lay before him:

*The Victoria Falls (from Livingstone's Missionary Travels)*

*"I did not comprehend it until, creeping with awe to the verge, I peered down into a large rent which had been made from bank to bank of the broad Zambesi, and saw that a stream of a thousand yards [915 m] broad leaped down a hundred feet [30.5 m]... the most wonderful sight I had witnessed in Africa."* (Livingstone, 1857)

On his explorations Livingstone carefully recorded local names for geographic landmarks. Here, however, he also named them in English - the Victoria Falls - in honour of his monarch, the reigning British Queen Victoria.

> *"Being persuaded that Mr Oswell and myself were the very first Europeans who ever visited the Zambesi in the centre of the country, and that this is the connecting link between the known and unknown portions of that river, I decided to use the same liberty as the Makololo did, and gave the only English name I have affixed to any part of the country."* (Livingstone, 1857)

Returning to the island the following day, Livingstone planting a small garden of peaches, apricots and coffee seeds. He arranged for one of the boatmen to return and make a fence to protect the plants from the wanderings of hippopotami, hoping that the eternal spray from the Falls would nourish them. In an uncharacteristic act of vanity Livingstone also cut his initials and date into the bark of a tree on the island, which he called Garden Island (now commonly known as Livingstone Island).

Livingstone continued his epic journey following the Zambezi downstream to the east coast, completing a 3,000 mile (4,828 km) trek from the west to east coasts of the continent in the process. Returning to England Livingstone's accounts of his African travels caught the imagination of Victorian Britain. His first book, 'Missionary Travels and Researches in South Africa' was published in 1857 and became an instant best-seller. Livingstone was awarded the Gold Medal of the Royal Geographical Society for his explorations and scientific observations.

# People of the Falls

The wider regions of the upper Zambezi are inhabited by the Lozi, their kingdom known as Barotseland and controlled under the Paramount Chieftainship of the Lozi king, or *Litunga*, the 'Lord of the Land.' Lozi influence stretched south to the regions of the Chobe and Zambezi confluences, and downstream to the Falls, with local chiefs paying tribute and pledging loyalty to the Litunga.

At the time of Livingstone's visits, however, the region of the Falls had fallen under the control of the Makalolo, led by Chief Sebetwane, who had invaded from the south in the mid 1830s. Sebetwane established his power-base in the Chobe-Zambezi floodlands, among the safety and security of the connecting rivers and islands. Makalolo dominion in the region was, however, eventually crushed from within by the Lozi uprising of 1864.

The area of the Chobe-Zambezi confluence is the traditional home of the Subiya, occupying both banks of the Zambezi above the Falls between Katombora and Old Sesheke (now Mwandi), some 100 kilometres upstream from the Falls.

The Leya people have inhabited the area of the Victoria Falls and river upstream for several centuries or longer, and separated under two chieftanships. Upstream of the Falls are the Leya of Chief Sekuti, with close cultural connections to the Subiya of the Chobe-Zambezi region. Sekuti and his people traditionally lived along the margins of river and the islands above the Falls, although today are settled on the north bank away from the river.

The immediate vicinity of the Falls is today home to Leya under the leadership of Chief Mukuni, whose village is located close to the Falls on the north bank. The first Chief Mukuni is said to have originated from the north, establishing his power in the region of the Falls some two or three hundred years ago.

> *"There are today two groups of Leya distinguished by political bounds. The larger group is under Chief Mukuni and the smaller under Chief Sekute. Mukuni and Sekute are hereditary titles of Leya chiefs; the incumbents of these offices may also be known by their own names."* (Mubitana, 1990)

Skilled boatmen, fishermen and hippopotamus hunters the Leya have rich cultural traditions linked to the Falls which they called *Syuungwe na mutitima,* translated by Livingstone on his later visit as 'the Place of the Rainbow' (Livingstone and Livingstone, 1865).

> *"The Leya name for the waterfall was 'Syuungwe na mutitima,' which can be translated as 'the heavy mist that resounds,' although the term 'Syuungwe' itself also implies rainbow, or the place of rainbows."* (McGregor, 2003)

The Toka are one of the largest cultural groups inhabiting the wider districts on north bank of the Zambezi in the region of the Falls, under the hereditary title of Chief Musokotwane, their language and traditions closely related to the Leya and collectively known as the Toka-Leya.

The river valley is also the adopted home of the Nambya people, displaced from their homelands in Hwange by the arrival of Mzilikazi and his Matabele, and offered sanctuary by Chief Mukuni. The Nambya know the Falls as *Chinotimba*, 'the place that thunders.'

## Sacred Secrets

The river, waterfall and even the spray itself were all part of a sacred cultural landscape for the Leya. They associated its waters with powers of healing, using the natural swimming pools on the very lip of the Falls for cleansing rituals, whilst the ephemeral spray and depths of the Eastern Cataract was home of ancestral spirits - the 'mists of the dead' - as McGregor recorded from interviews with the current Chief Mukuni in 2001:

*"For Mukuni's Leya, the most meaningful northern aspect of the waterfall is known as 'Syuungwe mufu' or 'mist of the dead,' because it is associated with the memory of ancestors and played 'a central part in the life of the people.' ... This was a place of mystery, associated with the spirits of past communities. It is said that a light used to be seen there, or that one could hear the sound of drumming, of children playing, women stamping grain and cattle lowing. Offerings could be hurled into the boiling pot over the lip of the Falls from one of the islands perched on the edge."* (McGregor, 2003)

Livingstone recorded that the islands on the edge of the Falls were used by local chiefs for traditional ceremonies and as places of worship to their deities. The French Christian missionary François Coillard, who visited Barotseland some thirty years after Livingstone, recorded:

*"*[Local inhabitants] *believe it is haunted by a malevolent and cruel divinity, and they make it offerings to conciliate its favour, a bead necklace, a bracelet, or some other object, which they fling into the abyss, bursting into lugubrious incantations, quite in harmony with their dread and horror."* (Coillard, 1897)

On his way downstream to the Falls in 1855 Livingstone was told of a mythical river spirit-serpent:

*"The Barotse believe that at certain parts of the river a tremendous monster lies hid, and that it will catch a canoe, and hold it fast and motionless, in spite of the utmost exertions of the paddlers."* (Livingstone, 1857)

In 1905 some early residents of Livingstone even claimed to have seen the great serpent writhing in the torrents of the river below the Falls. A 1930s a guidebook to the Falls expanded:

*"The Zambezi can boast of no Loch Ness monster, although there is an old tradition among the Barotse that a serpent, called by them 'Lingangole,' had*

*its habitation in the Zambezi river, which it left at night only. There are stories even today of a huge serpent, thirty feet in length, which is said to be visible occasionally at the bottom of the gorge."* (Southern Rhodesia Publicity Office, 1938)

McGregor, writing in 2003, interpreted this 'spirit-serpent' as an invisible entity:

*"Myth also told of an invisible monster that lived in the boiling pot. It was not regarded as a river god (as nineteenth century explorers assumed). Rather, the boiling pot was associated with powerful ancestral and other spirits that needed appeasement, and was a place where god (Leza) - who had no fixed place in the landscape - could be approached."* (McGregor, 2003)

# Livingstone's Second Expedition

Within a few years Livingstone returned to Africa, departing from Liverpool on 10th March 1858 aboard the S.S. Pearl and reaching the mouth of the Zambezi in May. Having severed his connections with the London Missionary Society, Livingstone was now acting under British Government auspices, having been appointed as 'Her Majesty's Counsel for the East Coast of Africa to the South of Zanzibar and for the unexplored interior.'

The aim of the Zambezi expedition was 'to survey and report on the country watered by the lower Zambezi.' Livingstone estimated it would take two years. It was to last from 1858 until the middle of 1864, failing in its initial objectives and instead exploring a major tributary, the Shire River, and becoming known as 'Livingstone's Second Expedition.' Livingstone was accompanied by Commander Norman Bedingfeld RN, naval officer, navigator and second in command; Dr (later Sir) John Kirk, botanist and medical officer; Richard Thornton, geologist; Thomas Baines, expedition artist and stock-keeper; George Rae, engineer; and Livingstone's younger brother Charles, as general assistant, photographer - a skill he was apparently still learning - and 'moral agent.'

The expedition was fraught with problems. Bedingfeld resigned soon after their arrival at the mouth of the Zambezi, and Thornton and Baines were dismissed in mid-1859 after clashing with Livingstone's brother, who appears to have been a destabilising influence on the group. Thornton later rejoined the expedition although it soon after cost him his life. Livingstone's leadership was widely criticised and his reputation tarnished by the failures of the expedition. Kirk recorded privately in his journal in 1862:

*"I can come to no other conclusion than that Dr Livingstone is out of his mind and a most unsafe leader... his head is not of the ordinary construction but what is termed cracked"* (Wright, 2008).

## *Baldwin Blunders*

William Charles Baldwin, an English hunter and the second European to visit the Falls, reached them on 2nd August 1860, travelling solo and guided only by a pocket compass. He described his arrival at the Falls in his journal:

*"I set off resolutely on the 1st* [August]*, being determined to find the Falls; walked all day and all night, and towards morning I heard the roar of them. I never rested till I threw myself down, just before daybreak, within 300 yards* [274.3 m] *of the river... The river is the finest and most beautiful I ever saw. It is rocky and rather shallow, and, just above the Falls, about one mile* [1.6 km] *wide. And now for the Falls. I heard the roar full ten miles* [16 km] *off, and you can see the immense volumes of spray ascending like a great white cloud, over which shines an eternal rainbow. The whole volume of water pours over a huge rock into an enormous chasm below, of immense depth. I counted from sixteen to eighteen, while a heavy stone of about twenty pounds weight was falling. I could not see it to the bottom, but only saw the splash in the water. I stood opposite to the Falls at nearly the same elevation, and could almost throw a stone across. The gorge cannot be more than a hundred yards* [91 m] *wide, and at the bottom the river rolls turbulently boiling."*

Through these methods Baldwin made the first reasonably accurate estimate of the size of the Falls - he considered them to be two thousand yards (1,828.8 m) wide and three hundred feet (91.5 m) high, remarkably close to the true figures and a great improvement on the conservative estimates made by Livingstone in 1855.

Baldwin spent several days exploring the Falls from the south bank, before finally accepting invitations to cross to the north bank to meet Masipootana, Sekeletu's representative at the Falls.

*"On the third day I went to see him... and made him a small present, but he was quite on the high horse and said, that now I had come across he would take care that I did not go back again; I must stay there until I had paid for the water I drank, and washed in, the wood that I burned, the grass that my horse ate; and it was a great offence that I had taken a plunge into the river on coming out of one of his punts; if I had been drowned or devoured by a crocodile or sea-cow* [hippopotamus]*, Sekeletu would have blamed him, and had I lost my footing*

*and fallen down the Falls, my nation would have said the Makololo had killed me; and, altogether I had given him great uneasiness."* (Baldwin, 1863)

## Return to the Falls

When the Livingstone brothers, together with Kirk, finally arrived at the Falls on 9th August 1860, Baldwin was still trying to resolve his misunderstanding with the chief. Livingstone's arrival helped to smooth the waters, and Baldwin left the following day, recording:

*"I had the honour yesterday of cutting my initials on a tree on the island above the Falls, just below Dr Livingstone's, as being the second European who has reached the Falls, and the first from the East Coast. Charles Livingstone says they far exceed Niagara in every respect and the Doctor tells me it is the only place, from the West coast to the East when he had the vanity to cut his initials."* (Baldwin, 1863)

On his first visit in 1855, Livingstone had been anxious not to overstate the scale of the Falls, estimating that they were 100 feet (30.5 m) deep and 1,000 yards (915 m) wide. On this second visit however, Livingstone and his team were able to make a more detailed study of the waterfall, including from the south bank. Taking many measurements they determined the total width of the Falls;

*"...to be a little over 1,860 yards [1,700 m], but this number we resolved to retain as indicating the year in which the fall was for the first time carefully examined... The depth of the rift was measured by lowering a line, to the end of which a few bullets were tied. One of us lay with his head over a projecting crag and watched until, after his companions had paid out 310 feet [95 m], the weight rested on a sloping projection,*

*Livingstone's watercolour sketch of the Victoria Falls*

*probably 50 feet* [15 m] *from the water below. On measuring the width of this deep cleft by sextant, it was found at Garden Island, its narrowest point, to be 80 yards* [73 m]." (Livingstone and Livingstone, 1865)

The detailed study of the Falls, which Livingstone undertook with John Kirk, resulted in a surprisingly accurate aerial perspective map of the Falls sketched by Livingstone in his notebook (held in the collection of the Livingstone Museum). Sadly Charles Livingstone had apparently forgotten the chemical preparations necessary to take the highly anticipated first photographs of the Falls.

## *Rocks in Gods Highway*

Livingstone envisioned the Zambezi River as the transport route by which the region would be opened up to Christian values and trade, shining the light of 'Christianity, Commerce and Civilisation' into the perceived 'Dark Continent' and describing the Zambezi as 'God's Highway into the interior.' But his dreams were dashed by the impassable Cahora Bassa rapids, blocking access upstream.

Despite severing his connections with the London Missionary Society before his Second Expedition, Livingstone still devoted himself to what he called his 'spiritual calling' - promoting Christianity and commerce in an effort stamp out the last remains of the African slave trade, abolished throughout the British Empire in 1833. Livingstone proposed that commercial cotton farming could be the solution, hoping to encourage African chiefs to adopt agriculture and giving them a valuable commodity to trade, whilst also undermining global dependence on the American cotton industry. In December 1857 Livingstone wrote to the British politician Hudson Gurney outlining his plans:

*"[M]y chief efforts will be directed to making the river Zambezi an open pathway to the interior healthy highlands in order that a centre of*

*Slaves in transit, sketched by Livingstone*

*civilisation and commerce will be formed. I shall visit all the chiefs along the banks and distribute cotton seeds - inviting the people to cultivate for our markets and I think if what I hope to begin is carried out that in the course of a dozen years Africa itself will have some material influence in diminishing the value of slave labour in America."* (Ross, 2002)

Both times Livingstone travelled the route between the Falls and the east coast, downstream in 1855 and upstream in 1860, he had left the rough, broken country through which the middle Zambezi flows and taken an easier route north of the river and across the higher, cooler Batoka Plateau. By straying from the course of the Zambezi, Livingstone failed to comprehend the character of the middle reaches, where a series of gorges force the river into long narrow and turbulent white-water stretches unnavigable to transport. Livingstone's travels and writings did, however, expose the continued activities of Arab slave traders in the heart of the continent, bringing the horrors and impacts of the trade to a wide audience and helping end the commercial trafficking and exploitation of Africa's people.

## *Death of Dr Livingstone*

In 1866, at the age of 52, Livingstone set out on his final expedition in search of the headwaters of the Nile River. His lack of contact with the outside world over a period of four years raised concerns for his welfare and prompted the New York Herald to send Henry Morton Stanley, their 'special correspondent,' to find him. Stanley eventually achieved his brief on 10th November 1871, approaching the explorer in a village on the east shore of Lake Tanganyika with the now famous greeting of *"Dr Livingstone, I presume."* Jeal, in his biography of Stanley, suggests he may have embellished the reported words of greeting for journalistic effect, as he later tore out the relevant pages from his diary (Jeal, 2007).

With Stanley's supplies Livingstone continued his explorations, but he was weak, worn out and suffering from ill health. Finally, on the morning of 30th April 1873, he was found dead, still kneeling at his bedside, apparently in evening prayer when he died. His faithful attendants, James Chuma and Abdullah Susi, buried his heart in Africa as he had requested and mummified his body, carrying it and his papers on a difficult 11-month journey to Zanzibar, a trip of 1,000 miles (1,600 kilometres). His body was then shipped to England and buried in London's Westminster Abbey on 18th April 1874, nearly a year after his death.

On hearing of his passing, Florence Nightingale commented *"God has taken away the greatest man of his generation."*

# In Livingstone's Footsteps

Many followed in Livingstone's footsteps to the Falls - explorers, missionaries, hunters, prospectors and traders - travelling via different routes and means. The names of some are forgotten, whilst others published detailed written accounts of their travels. Some returned with dramatic tales of survival against adversity - and some simply failed to return at all.

## *Chapman and Baines*

Thomas Baines and James Chapman arrived at the Falls on 23rd July, 1862, both later publishing written accounts of their travels. After failing to reach the Falls with Livingstone, Baines joined forces with Chapman, a South African hunter and trader, who was planning his own expedition to explore the middle and lower stretches of the Zambezi. Chapman had travelled far and wide in southern Africa and had previously been close to the Falls in 1853. As they approached the Falls he recorded his mixed feelings at the missed opportunity:

> *"Here the panorama first broke upon us in all its grandeur, and I could not avoid the reflection that, could I but have known of the magnificent sight I lost in August 1853 after being very near it, and how nearly I had forestalled Dr Livingstone's discovery, I should certainly have made another effort at that time to accomplish the object."* (Chapman, 1868)

On that first visit Chapman had even arranged canoes and local guides to take him downstream to the great waterfall. At the time Livingstone was exploring the Upper Zambezi with Chief Sekeletu, and their sudden return resulted in a change of heart from the boatmen. Chapman recorded:

> *"[T]hence it was that I was nearly visiting the 'Falls,' the natives having undertaken, for a consideration of beads and brass wire, to paddle my companions and myself hither; but as I was going to step into the boat with my companions, ...we heard that the chief Sekeletu had returned with Dr. Livingstone... and our payment was unceremoniously returned, with an intimation that they could not now take us."* (Chapman, 1868)

Chapman lamented the lack of descriptive powers at his disposal - *"I have never seen anything with which I can compare it"* (Chapman, 1868) - despite having a stereoscopic camera and taking the first photographs of the Falls. Whilst Chapman himself described his photographic efforts as a failure, Baines, an accomplished expedition artist, spent 12 days sketching and drawing them from every possible

*An etching by Thomas Baines (1862) from the western end of the Falls*

viewpoint. He would later develop these sketches into detailed etchings and oil paintings - regarded as some of the finest images ever executed of the Falls.

> *"I remained till near sunset sketching, and, as in all the views I had taken about here, found that the magnitude of the principal features so dwarfs everything else, as rocks, trees, etc, which in common scenes would occupy a large portion of the picture, that I could hardly bring my pencil to a point fine enough to represent them. Still, unless these accessories are minutely and distinctly painted, the vastness of the whole is much invalidated."* (Baines, 1864)

Baines and Chapman visited the 'old boatman of the rapids,' Zangurella, who had ferried Livingstone across to Garden Island in 1855, and he showed them the tree where the Livingstone brothers had cut their initials, 'D. L. 1855,' and below them 'C. L. 1860.' Baines records that the garden Livingstone established had been trampled by hippopotami and was completely overgrown. He was amazed, when standing on the very edge overlooking the chasm, facing 'a resplendent double rainbow,' to see his shadow cast in the spray, three hundred feet below. Baines named the western cataract 'the Leaping Water' and the adjoining island 'Three Rill Island' (they are now more commonly known as the Devil's Cataract and Cataract Island). His portfolio of prints, 'The Victoria Falls, Zambesi River: Sketched on the spot,' including 10 colour lithographs and eight pages of descriptive text by the artist, was first published in 1865.

Chapman recorded evidence of the wealth of wildlife residing in the dense forest supported under the everlasting spray of the Falls:

> "Before leaving this swampy spot, I must not omit to mention the fact that, to our amazement, we found numerous spoors of elephants, rhinoceroses, buffaloes, and hippopotami, besides other animals, all over the very brink of the precipice. It makes one's hair stand on end to see the numerous indications of their midnight rambles at the very verge of eternity. Here they come at the dead dark midnight hour, to drink the spray and wallow in the mire; and on asking a native how it was they were not afraid, he asked me in return, 'Didn't they grow up together?'" (Chapman, 1868)

## *Shooting Party*

Sir Richard George Glyn, with his younger brother Robert and friends, travelled to the Falls in 1863, inspired by Livingstone's Missionary Travels. Sir Richard kept a diary of his four-and-a-half month journey from Durban, and hunting played a significant role in their plans, lured by tall tales of wild animals and places where *"a man could shoot until his arm grew too tired to lift his rifle and not make a dent in their masses."* By 1863, however, the herds were rapidly declining after three decades of uncontrolled hunting, especially in the areas south of the Zambezi, Sir Richard noting in his diary that *"the country is covered with skulls of wildebeest."*

Green, writing in 1968, considered Sir Richard and his party the first tourists to the Falls, as they were neither professional hunters nor traders. Arriving at the Zambezi River two-and-a-half kilometres upriver, opposite an uninhabited island, they reached sight of the Falls in July 1863. Sir Richard recorded their arrival:

> "Started with the first light, and soon we heard a distant roar, which we knew to be the falls. Three hours toiling over thirsty sand, through forest - brought us to the edge of the plateau, and far away to the north-east we could see the tall pillars of vapour rising over the trees and marking the spot we had come so many thousand miles to see. As we stood to admire, lo! six bull elephants appeared on the opposite cliffs. Quietly they tore up a great tree and fed on the leaves. As if they knew that they had chosen the only place in southern Africa where they would not be made to feel the weight of our bullets for, for 40 miles [64.4 km] or more down, nothing with-out wings can scale the cliffs and cross the stream of the boiling Zambezi." (van Riel, 2008)

*A coloured etching by Thomas Baines (1862) showing the view
of the Falls from where the Bridge would subsequently be built*

When Sir Richard and his party arrived on Livingstone Island they found the initials of the Livingstone brothers and Baldwin were nearly grown out:

*"Livingstone's garden, though strongly fenced, has been breached in many places by the seacows [hippopotami], and is nothing but a mass of rank grass. I could only find the stump of one peach tree. We found his and Baldwin's initials nearly grown out, so re-cut them, and inscribed 'Glyn 1863' by their side."* (Glyn, 1863)

## *Fatal Attraction*

Thomas Leask, a hunter from Natal, arrived at the Falls in July 1869.

*"In his diary he tells several stories regarding Livingstone which he had heard from native sources. How Livingstone crossed the Falls with the aid of pieces if string and calico - presumably an exaggerated version of the measurement of the Falls. How Livingstone was able to make people die at will and bring them back to life again and how he was able to walk on water - all stories showing the awe in which Livingstone was held."* (Clark, 1952)

The German explorer Edward Mohr visited the waterfall in June 1870 and is credited with naming the Rainforest. Mohr was overawed by the Falls:

> "It seemed to me as if my own identity were swallowed up in the surrounding glory, the voice of which rolled on forever, like the waves of eternity... But I threw down my pen. No human being can describe the infinite; and what I saw was part of infinity made visible and framed in beauty." (Mohr, 1876)

By 1870 twenty-five Europeans are known to have visited the Falls, but there were undoubtedly others whose names have been lost. Over two years, 1874 and 1875, however, these numbers doubled, an indication of the rate at which the area was being drawn into the sphere of European activity.

Frank Oates, uncle of the heroic Lawrence Oates (member of Robert Falcon Scott's ill-fated expedition to the Antarctic), arrived at the Falls on New Year's Day 1875. Oates was one of the first European to see the Falls in full flood, but succumbed to fever on the return journey, sadly without updating his journal.

## First Guide to the Falls

George Westbeech is considered by many to be the first guide to the Falls, visiting them for the first time in 1871 and returning many times. Together with his business partner, George Arthur 'Elephant' Phillips, Westbeech had established a trading station at Pandamatenga, about 100 kilometres upstream of the Falls and a similar distance south of the Zambezi, the last stop on the 'Old Hunter's Road' before reaching the river. The trade route, which Westbeech had developed during the 1870s and '80s, soon became the main road north to the Falls and Barotseland.

Having secured exclusive rights to hunt elephant and trade ivory north of the Zambezi, Westbeech enjoyed increasing influence as an unofficial adviser to the Lozi Litunga, Lewanika. Hunters, explorers and missionaries alike came to Westbeech for advice and assistance before continuing their journeys, all requiring the permission of the Litunga before crossing the river at Kazungula, 75 kilometres upstream of the Falls.

A large party of travellers arrived at the Falls in September 1875, guided by George Westbeech, accompanied with his wife, a honeymoon couple - Mr and Mrs Frances - and the Czech explorer and ethnologist Dr Emil Holub, among others. For Holub the trip to the Falls was a diversion from his aim of exploring the Lozi heartlands of Barotseland (again directly inspired by the writings of Livingstone) whilst he awaited authorisation to proceed north. But once seen the natural wonder

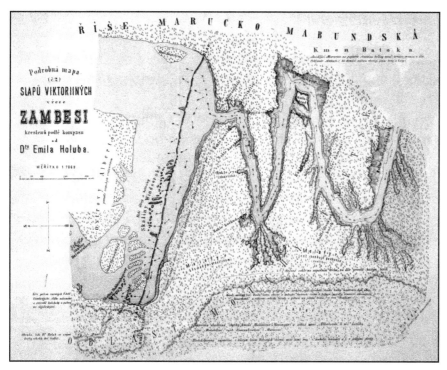

*Holub's first map of the Falls*

demanded his full attention.

*"To my mind the Victoria Falls of the Zambezi are one of the most imposing phenomena of the world... Truly it is a scene in which a man may well become aware of his own insignificance!"* (Holub, 1881)

Holub published his detailed notes on the Victoria Falls in a small booklet, the first guidebook on the Falls, written in English and printed in South Africa in 1879. He also spent time drawing a detailed map of the Falls and gorges below, which was published in the first editions of his full travelogue, published in Czech and German in 1880, but the later English edition sadly omitted this key feature.

Holub spent many years travelling extensively in the region, reflecting of the Falls:

*"Even the greatest literary masters would certainly have fallen silent facing such majestic and ever-changing scenery. A human being is totally incapable of describing Mother Nature where she performs with such might as at the Victoria Falls - there, Man just has to adore her!"*

*"I dare say, anyway, the time of removing the veil, which still covers the Falls, is not too remote. I conclude that the whole of Albert's Land* [the name which Holub unsuccessfully proposed for the region] *falls sooner or later under the British protectorate, and then the Natural Zambezian Wonder would become target not only for scholarly masters and educated travellers as it has happened with famous wonders at the Yellowstone and Missouri river basin or the valley of Yosemite in California which only 25 years ago were totally unknown."* (Holub, 1890)

# Last of the Big Game Hunters

Frederick Courtney Selous, the British explorer, hunter and pioneer conservationist, visited the Falls for this first time in June 1874, returning in October 1877.

*"One stands... on the very verge of the chasm, on a level with the river above, and only separated from the cataract by the breadth of the opening... into which it dashes, so that when a sudden puff of wind blows away the spray immediately in front one sees the beautiful blue river, studded with thickly-wooded, palm bearing islands, seemingly as still and quiet as a lake, flowing tranquilly on heedless of its coming danger, till with a crash it leaps in one splendid mass of fleecy, white foam into an abyss. At whatever part one looks the rays of the sun, shining on the descending masses of foam, form a double zone of prismatic colours, of whose depth and brilliancy no one who has only seen the comparatively faint tints of an ordinary rainbow can form any conception. Such are the Victoria Falls - one of, if not the, most transcendentally beautiful natural phenomena on this side of paradise."* (Selous, 1881)

Selous was struck by the wealth of wildlife inhabiting the Rainforest:

*"This damp and shady retreat forms (especially during the hot weather) a favourite resort of elephant and buffalo, besides water-buck, koodoo [kudu], impala, etc. The fresh spoor showed us that a herd of buffaloes had not long left before our arrival, and the huge footprints of elephants and hippopotami bore evidence that some of these animals had also been here very recently."* (Selous, 1881)

Returning to the Falls a third time from October to December 1888, Selous recorded a different scene.

*"On this occasion he rode a horse along the narrow strip of open ground between the Rain Forest and the Chasm, and he alludes to the fact that buffalo, which travellers after Livingstone, including Baldwin, Baines, Chapman and himself, had found so plentiful only a few years earlier, had now practically disappeared from the vicinity of the Falls."* (Southern Rhodesia Publicity Office, 1938)

Selous was described by Roosevelt as 'the last of the big game hunters,' but as early as 1881 even Selous was lamenting the decline of the elephant herds.

*"I had already spent ten years of my life elephant hunting in the interior and*

*Selous on safari*

*every year elephants were becoming scarcer and wilder south of the Zambezi so that it had become impossible to make a living by hunting at all."* (Selous, 1881)

He also expressed concern about the reduction in the number of white rhinoceros from his experiences on the Chobe River, where in 1874 the animal had been a common sight. In 1877 only tracks could be found and by 1879 even those had disappeared. The conclusion was inevitable; *"it must be almost extinct in that portion of the country"* (Selous, 1881). He repeated his misgivings in 1893, convinced that the species was *"upon the verge of extinction... some few white rhinoceroses no doubt still survive, but it is not too much to say that long before the close of the century the white rhinoceros will have vanished from the face of the earth"* (Selous, 1893).

## *Mixed Reactions*

Another visitor to the Falls was Richard Frewin, who arrived in August 1877 and commented that it was a great pity that so very few people would ever see them.

*"There may be a few energetic travellers who come up to visit them, but I don't think they will ever be the resort of the ordinary traveller. This part of Africa will never support a railway, and the travelling by ox-wagon, its difficulties, troubles, fatigue and endurance of hardships will never suit a Cockney or a cotton-wool traveller."* (Southern Rhodesia Publicity Office, 1938)

Many others followed, including the Portuguese explorer Major Serpa Pinto, who passed by in November 1878. Not everyone was enamoured by the wonder of the Falls, Pinto recording:

*"Mozi-oa-tunia is sublimely horrible. That enormous gulf, black as is the basalt which forms it, dark and dense as the cloud which enwraps it, would have been chosen, if known in biblical times, as an image of the infernal regions, a hell*

*View of the Falls, photographed by Frank Watson*

*of water and darkness, more terrible perhaps than the hell of fire and light."* (Pinto, 1881)

Harry Ware, a trader, appears to have been the first 'travel agent' to advertise excursions to the Falls, working in partnership with Westbeech. His announcements appeared in 'The Field,' a London weekly magazine, in 1885. Francis Harold Watson was another trader who organised expeditions to the Zambezi. Watson was also a photographer, taking a series of photographic images of the Falls in 1891 (Hoole, undated). Lionel Decle, a Frenchman who visited the Falls in 1891, wrote:

*"I expected to find something superb, grand, marvellous. I had never been so disappointed... It is hell itself, a corner of which seems to open at your feet; a dark and terrible hell, from the middle of which you expect every moment to see some repulsive monster rising in anger."* (Decle, 1898)

## Missionary Influence

In 1878 François Coillard of the Paris Evangelical Missionary Society reached Leshoma (now Lesoma), the traditional waiting place for travellers seeking the Litunga's authority to proceed north across the river. Although he soon obtained permission from the Lozi Litunga, Lewanika, to establish a mission in Barotse territory, he was forced to leave the following year by unrest in the region. Several other missionaries came and went before Coillard returned, finally helping found

*François Coillard (1834-1904)*

a mission at Old Sesheke, upstream of the Falls in 1885 (with Rev Dorwald Jeanmairet as resident). Coillard rapidly eclipsed Westbeech as the major European adviser to the Lozi Litunga, with mission stations and schools soon also established at Sefula and Kazungula. Coillard records the high-standing in which Dr Livingstone was held among local inhabitants:

*"In Europe people admired the intrepid traveller, but one must come to Sesheke where he lived, to admire the man. He has engraved his name in the very hearts of the heathen population of Central Africa. Wherever Livingstone had passed, the name of Moruti (missionary) is a passport and a recommendation. Must I confess that I have been humiliated not a little to see myself fitted with a doctor's cap by these gentlemen of Sesheke? Whether I will, or not, I am Nyaka (doctor), Livingstone's successor. Thus it is that the first missionary that comes by is invested with the boots of this giant."* (Coillard, 1897)

The Rev. Louis Jalla, head of the mission station at Old Sesheke from 1896 wrote of Livingstone (and recorded by Coillard):

*"You see legend is already beginning to mingle with history in all that concerns Livingstone. For instance, all the Batoka maintain that the Doctor entered the abyss of the Victoria Falls, that he held converse with the deity who hides there and calls the water down, and that he brought pearls up from it, with the news that whoever penetrated thither would find great treasures. In a little time, the great Doctor will not fail himself to acquire a halo of legendary divinity."* (Coillard, 1897)

Other missionaries had also made their way to the banks of the Zambezi. Father Depelchin, a French Jesuit missionary, reached the Falls on the 7th July 1880 with the intention of founding a mission, but due to illness of several members of the party, and the death of one in a boating accident, he abandoned the project. In September 1881 the Rev. Frederick Stanley Arnot left Natal to establish a mission on the Zambezi watershed. At Pandamatenga he met Edmund Selous, brother of F C Selous, and travelled with him to the Falls, reaching them on 13th August 1883.

# Rhodes and Rail

Cecil John Rhodes arrived at the Cape Colony from England in September 1870 at the age of 17. After a short unsuccessful stint cotton farming, he followed his older brother Herbert to the newly discovered diamond fields in Kimberley, where he was to make his fortune. During the 1870s and '80s Rhodes' influence grew to dominate the industry, founding the De Beers Consolidated Mining Company in 1888 and establishing a monopoly over diamond mining in the territory.

Rhodes was an ardent believer in British colonial imperialism, and as the vehicle for his ambitions he formed the British South Africa Company (BSAC), seeking British Royal approval for its activities in southern Africa. The Royal Charter, granted by Queen Victoria in 1889, gave the Company authority to administer an ill-defined area of southern Africa on behalf of the British government. The Charter bestowed wide-ranging powers of authority to the BSAC, including:

*Cecil John Rhodes (1853-1902)*

*"[T]he right to make and maintain roads, railways, telegraphs, harbours; to carry on mining or other industries; to carry on lawful commerce; to settle territories and promote immigration; to establish or authorize banking companies; to develop, improve, clear, plant and irrigate land; to establish and maintain agencies in Our Colonies and Possessions, and elsewhere; to grant lands in terms of years or in perpetuity."* (Strage, 1974)

These powers, however, were conditional on the Chartered Company acquiring appropriate, and legitimate, treaties with local rulers - merely an administrative matter for a man of Rhodes' means and methods, and all pieces of a jigsaw that he ensured would fall into place.

Rhodes became Prime Minister of the British Cape Colony in 1890 and championed the railway as the essential means by which to achieve his political and business ambitions. He is quoted as saying: *"Pure philanthropy is all very well in its way, but philanthropy plus five per cent is a good deal better."*

Rhodes profited greatly by exploiting rare mineral resources. Financed by this great wealth, Rhodes' dreams and ambitions knew no limit:

*"The world is nearly all parcelled out, and what there is left of it is being divided up, conquered and colonised. To think of these stars that you see overhead at night, these vast worlds which we can never reach. I would annex the planets if I could; I often think of that. It makes me sad to see them so clear and yet so far."* (Stead, 1902)

Rhodesia was officially named after him in May 1895, a reflection of his popularity as the territory had already become widely known as 'Zambesia.' The less appealing 'Charterland' had also been in use whilst the BSAC was consolidating its control over the vast region of central southern Africa. He is quoted to have said to a close friend: *"To have a bit of country named after one is one of the things a man can be proud of."* The territory north of the Zambezi (now Zambia), was originally divided into North-Western and North-Eastern Rhodesia, before being amalgamated to form Northern Rhodesia in 1911. The name of Southern Rhodesia (now Zimbabwe) was officially adopted in 1898 for the territory south of the Zambezi (Northern Rhodesia Journal, Jan 1956).

## Cape to Cairo

After initial successes at Kimberley, Rhodes briefly returned to Oxford to complete his studies, becoming friends with Charles Metcalfe, an engineer who in 1878 joined the London firm of Sir Douglas Fox and Partners and later travelled to South Africa as their consultant engineer for the developing Cape railway system. Sir Charles would spend three decades as the company's chief representative in southern Africa. Upon the death of his father in 1883 Charles Herbert Theophilus Metcalfe inherited the family titles, becoming Sir Charles Metcalfe, sixth baronet.

Rhodes quickly became convinced of the importance of the railway in developing the 'British sphere of influence' in Africa. As early as 1888 Rhodes and Sir Charles were planning an 'African Trunk Line' - a rail and communications route traversing the length of the continent. The grand concept soon became popularly known as the 'Cape to Cairo' railway, the 'iron spine and ribs of Africa.'

At the time several European powers were competing in their rush to claim African territories, and the Portuguese and German powers in particular looked towards the regions of the Upper Zambezi in order to connect territories on the east and west coasts. Sir Charles advised in an article he co-authored and published in London: *"There is a race for the interior of Africa, and nothing but a firm policy will maintain British interests"* (Metcalfe and Richarde-Seaver, 1889).

Although the Cape to Cairo scheme never materialised in its entirety, this period saw the rapid spread of a interconnected web of 'pioneer railways,' penetrating the subcontinent from the south and east coasts and opening up the interior to development.

## *Pauling & Company*

George Craig Sanders Pauling was the man Rhodes entrusted to build his railway. Born in England, George Pauling followed his father to the Cape in November 1875, aged 20, quickly establishing himself as an able worker and skilled engineer.

Rhodes first met Pauling in 1891, having summoned him to Cape Town to discuss plans to extend the railway from Vryburg to Mafeking (now Mahikeng) in South Africa. The Bechuanaland Railway Company was formed in May 1893 with the

backing of the Chartered Company, and with Rhodes as chairman Pauling was invited to bid for the contract. Costs were agreed and the contract signed, with Pauling's cousin, Harold, as chief construction engineer - a role he would assume all the way to the Victoria Falls.

The contracting firm of Pauling & Company Ltd. was formed in 1894, consisting of brothers George and Harry, and cousins Harold, Willy and Percy. Prior to this Pauling had operated under various company names, earning a solid reputation constructing several branch lines, and the Company traces its origins back to 1877.

*George Pauling (centre), with Harold (right), and Mr A L Lawley (left)*

Successive contracts followed for the extension of the line to Bulawayo, and eventually the Victoria Falls, which together with lines connecting Salisbury to Beira on the east coast (opened in 1899) established the core of a rail network which would transform transport in the region. Within a period of 18 years Pauling & Company constructed over 6,000 kilometres of line in southern Africa.

## Bulawayo and Beyond

The arrival of the railway line at Bulawayo in 1897 was a landmark event in the colonial development of southern Africa. The railway established a vital communication and transport route to and from the south and promised to bring an end to the pioneer town's isolation.

The first construction train, the same engine that had been used for the plate-laying of the line from Vryburg, arrived at Bulawayo on 19th October 1897. Decorated with flags it carried the banner 'Advance Rhodesia' on the front, surmounted by the arms of the Chartered Company.

*The first construction train arrives at Bulawayo*

On the 4th November hundreds of guests attended the official opening of the line. The day was declared a public holiday and for the following week of celebrations local businesses closed each afternoon to enable the townsfolk to attend the many functions, dinners and parties. A special medallion was issued to commemorate the event.

*"For the opening ceremony on the 4th November 1897 the temporary railway station was decorated with flags, bunting, greenery and a variety of slogans*

*considered suitable for the occasion. These included 'Our Two Roads to Progress, Railroads and Cecil Rhodes' and 'Change here for Zambesi.'"* (Croxton, 1982)

Henry Morton Stanley, on his last visit to Africa, commented:

*"In any other continent the opening of five hundred miles of new railway would be fittingly celebrated by the usual banquet and after dinner felicitations of those directly concerned with it; but in this instance there are six Members of the Imperial Parliament, the High Commissioner of the Cape, the Governor of Natal, scores of Members of the Colonial Legislatures and scores of notabilities, leaders of thought and action, bankers, merchants, and clergy from every Colony and State in the southern part of this continent."* (Stanley, 1898)

But one man was noticeable by his absence - Rhodes had not travelled due to ill health, although some claimed he was sulking after political defeats in South Africa. He sent a telegram to the opening ceremony announcing:

*"We are bound, and I have made up my mind, to go on to the Zambesi without delay. We have magnificent coalfields lying between here and there, which means a great deal to us engaged in the practical workings of railways. Let us see it on the Zambesi during our lifetime. It will be small consolation to me and to you to know it will be there when we are dead and gone."* (White, 1973)

## To the Banks of the Zambezi

Rhodes announced details of his grand scheme to extend the railway to the Zambezi and beyond at a meeting of the Chartered Company's shareholders in London on 21st April 1898, selling his dream of a railway connecting the length of the continent:

*"I want £2 million pounds to extend the railway to Lake Tanganyika - about 800 miles... Look at the matter. You get the railway to Tanganyika; you have Her Majesty's Government's sanction for a railway to Uganda, and then you have Kitchener [and his railway] coming down from Khartoum [in Sudan]. This is not imaginative: it is practical. It gives you Africa... the whole of it!"* (Strage, 1974)

Many in London were shocked by his ambitious plans and the Government did not respond positively, possibly because more than half of Africa was already under the control of rival European nations. City investors however were more interested, although Rhodes was a major investor in his own railway scheme.

*"Sir William Harcourt, who thoroughly detested Rhodes, thought the scheme hair-brained, and never hesitated to say so. He was staggered, therefore, to find a Welsh steel mill hard at work manufacturing rails for the Cape to Cairo railway."* (Rhodesia Railways Magazine, Nov 1957)

The consultant railway engineers Sir Douglas Fox and Partners had originally envisaged the route would pass on through to the new capital, Salisbury (now renamed Harare), and cross the Zambezi River over the Kariba Gorge, some 350 kilometres downstream of the Victoria Falls, before continuing north on to Lake Tanganyika. The country between Kariba and Lake Tanganyika, however, was found to be unfavourable terrain for the railway, and an alternative, less challenging and less expensive route was needed.

Large coal deposits had been identified in the Wankie region (now known as Hwange) in 1893 by a German prospector Albert Giese, who had heard reports from Africans of 'black stones that burn.' Coal was essential to the continued expansion of the railway network, which had until then survived on the cutting of timber from forest reserves along the route of the line and expensive imported coal from the south to feed the engine furnaces. Located only 200 miles (320 km) north-west of Bulawayo, it was claimed that the coalfields held sufficient high quality coal to last hundreds of years. A sample consignment was tested by a locomotive on the line to Bulawayo and declared to be 'equal to the best Welsh coal' (Rhodesia Railways Magazine, July 1955).

From Hwange the line would continue north to the Zambezi, crossing the river and penetrating into Northern Rhodesia. Yet it appears some were still unable to see the potential of the railway. Major Alfred St Hill Gibbons still championed Livingstone's belief that navigation of the river was the key to the development of the region.

*"No railway over the two thousand miles* [3,218 km] *separating Cape Town from the Zambezi can ever compete with a natural waterway in the conveyance of heavy goods, except where time is of course of more value than the goods themselves."* (Gibbons, 1904)

In 1898 Major Gibbons attempted to follow Livingstone's impossible route upstream to the Falls from the east coast, portaging around the Cahora Bassa rapids he was finally defeated by the sections of the Middle Zambezi known as the Kariba Gorge, now flooded under the waters of Lake Kariba. Major Gibbons used an aluminium launch to navigate the river, recording that at one point a crocodile rammed his boat with such force that he thought he had struck a rock.

## Legacy in Steel

Cecil Rhodes died on 26th March 1902, aged 49, from the heart-related illness which had limited much of his latter years. He is buried in the Matobo Hills at a place he named 'World's View,' his estate bequeathed to the nation and now the heart of the Matobo National Park. Before his death, Rhodes gave his personal approval to the preliminary design and location of the Victoria Falls Bridge, daring to cross the river just below the Falls so as to have 'the spray of the water over the carriages,' despite having never visited the Falls.

By the end of 1902, the year of Rhodes' death, the railway from the Cape to Bulawayo had been open for five years. The line from the east coast port at Beira (in Mozambique) to Salisbury was operating, and the two main centres of Salisbury and Bulawayo were also connected by rail. Bulawayo itself had grown to become a significant town, with a population of six thousand.

Rhodes has always been a polarizing figure, dividing opinion in his day, and even more so when judged by modern perspectives. The Victoria Falls Bridge is, however, Rhodes' great legacy in the commercial, industrial and economic development of southern Africa.

Construction of the Bridge would finally begin in 1904, two years after Rhodes himself had passed away, and it was left to Sir Charles Metcalfe to realise his dream of a rail crossing over the Zambezi within sight and sound of the Falls.

## Zeederberg Coach Company

Christiaan Hendrik Zeederberg, or 'Doel' as he was known, together with his three brothers Dolf, Louw and Pieter as partners, established Zeederberg & Company, Coach Proprietors in 1887, later known as the Zeederberg Coach Company. Their first regular mail-coach route, between Johannesburg and Kimberley, began operating in the same year.

In 1890 Cecil Rhodes commissioned Doel to survey the new Rhodesia territory and suggest likely transport routes, and their first regular service was opened the same year. Doel was a shrewd businessman and experienced horseman, surveying most of the routes himself over the next three years, becoming known as the 'Coaching King' of southern Africa.

The coaches were of American manufacture, lightly built with large wheels and remarkably robust. They carried up to twelve passengers with room on top for mail

*Zeederberg Mail Coach*

and baggage and were usually drawn by ten mules, which were changed at regular 10 to 15 mile (16-24 km) intervals, allowing the coaches to travel continuously without breaks.

Trade wagons pulled by upwards to twenty oxen, ferried supplies from Bulawayo north to the Zambezi. This 475 kilometre route often took up to a month or more to travel depending on season. The old hunter's road to Pandamatenga, established by Westbeech, fell into disuse during this time.

In 1901 Zeederberg introduced a regular mail coach service from Bulawayo to the Victoria Falls, with journeys taking a scheduled 10 to 12 days.

*"About 1901 the first rough survey of a coach route from Bulawayo to the Victoria Falls was undertaken jointly by Sir Charles Metcalfe and [Doel Zeederberg]... A weekly service was opened to the Wankie coal fields and the Falls, chiefly for facilitating the exploration of the mineral and other resources of the country. This... was eventually extended to Broken Hill [now Kabwe], and later was replaced by the advancing Cape to Cairo railway."* (Beet, 1923)

The Zeederberg coaches ran for a number of years across the Rhodesias, opening new routes and hailing the coming of the railway, before the advancing rails made their services redundant. Rhodes himself said that no other individual had done more to open up Rhodesia than Doel Zeederberg.

*"In his own sphere of activity Doel may be said to have been among the few who played a leading part in the development of Central South African resources. In conjunction with Cecil Rhodes, this sturdiest of pioneers recognized the potentialities of the great North Land."* (Beet, 1923)

*Travelling on the wagon road*

### *Capsizing Coaches and Drunk Drivers*

*"Zeederberg coaches ran on several sections on the north run in the early days. At intervals of ten miles [16 km] animals were changed. Due to the nature of the terrain over which coached plied, tickets carried this intimation: 'The contractors will not hold themselves responsible for loss or damage caused by the capsizing of the coach, unless this is due to the drunkenness of the driver.'"*
(Rhodesia Railways Magazine, Nov 1957)

# The Old Drift

Prior to the building of the Victoria Falls Bridge, the Zambezi River was crossed above the Victoria Falls at several established ferry points. Travellers would head for the Big Tree, the huge baobab tree close to the river above the Falls (and still standing to this day), to make arrangements to cross the river. Woods, writing in 1960, records older Livingstone residents recalling that there was more than one funeral at the Big Tree in the early days, but no sign of any graves have ever been found.

Giese's Ferry was the closest to the Falls of the three main ferry points, but suitable only for small craft. After selling his stake in the Hwange coalfields Giese had established a series of short-lived trading stores and rest huts between Hwange and Victoria Falls. Further upstream where the river bends significantly was the Palm Tree Ferry, which portered travellers across the river to two points on the north bank. The most important crossing was nine kilometres upstream of the Falls, where the river was at its narrowest, about a kilometre in width, and also at its deepest. Known as the Old Drift, a small European settlement of the same name slowly established itself on the north bank to await the arrival of the railway, which they confidently assumed would have to cross the river close by.

Mr Frederick J 'Mopane' Clarke arrived at the banks of the Zambezi in mid-1898, charged with operating the crossing and associated forwarding services on behalf of the Chartered Company. Clarke operated the crossing using an iron barge transported in sections to the Zambezi in the same year, and later also a steam launch. Passengers were taken in the barge, paddled by eight Barotse men, whilst wagons and goods were towed by the launch. A carpenter by training, Clarke built a simple general store and accommodation huts nearby, and set himself up as a trader and hotel keeper (charging 15 shillings per night). Within a couple of years several trading stores and bars had sprung up, including a Mission Station (founded in 1898 by an Italian-born cleric, Rev. Auguste Coisson, under the auspices of the Paris Missionary Society) and associated school. A Post Office was established at the Controller's Camp, a short distance downstream, and in operation during 1901, with the very scarce postmark 'Victoria Falls, S Africa' known between April and December 1901. The 'S Africa' in this context referred to the British controlled Southern African territories.

*"Life in this predominantly male settlement centred on the bars. On any given evening it often happened that virtually the whole population congregated in one bar, so the others closed. Gambling was the central attraction at Clarke's bar, notably a roulette wheel with two zeros run by a loud-voiced American. The bar-owners had their staff sieve the sandy floors each morning for coins dropped by the previous night's revellers."* (Phillipson, 1990)

*Clarke's Huts at the Drift*

*The Old Drift Mission Station*

The choice of site for the settlement, however, was not ideal. Close to the high water level, it became a flooded marshy quagmire in the wet season and proved extremely unhealthy. The death rate among the early pioneers of the small settlement was accordingly high.

Another crossing, Sekuti's Drift, was located a few of kilometres upstream of the Old Drift, and also known as Anderson's Drift:

*"Anderson was a hunchback who traded there, an unlovely character who advertised in the English papers for a wife and got one, but it is believed she did not stay long! Chief Sekuti had a village on an island close to the Drift."* (Northern Rhodesia Journal, 1950)

## Mules and Mail

By the end of 1901 the decision was made by the Chartered Company to relocate the Controller's Camp, including the Post Office, to a healthier location away from the river and on the higher sand belt. The site, known locally as Constitution Hill, soon become known as Livingstone after the new name given to the relocated Post Office - the earliest example of the postmark 'Livingstone, North Western Rhodesia' dating from 28th January 1902 (Shepherd, 2008).

*"In those days of the Old Drift the mail was supposed to run once a week. Zeederburg was contractor for the mail, and he used to bring it from the railhead*

*Early mail-runner*

*in a Scotch cart drawn by mules or oxen. In the rainy season I have known his Majesty's mails to be three weeks late from being unable to get across flooded rivers.*

*"The arrival of the mail at the Drift was announced by a bugle-call, and, whatever might be doing day or night, the whole of the inhabitants would troop down to the north bank. A dug-out or canoe would be sent across the river, and the bags brought back to a hut that served as temporary post-office. The mail would be emptied out of the bags on the hut floor, and everyone took a hand in sorting it out. There was, of course, much excitement in the process, with everybody hoping for letters from home, whether in South Africa or the Old Country. It was the great event of the week. The actual post-office was on the sand belt five miles [8 km] away, but the Postmaster rode in from there to receive or deliver the mails."* (Clark, 1936)

Mail was delivered locally by mail-runners, recruited in 1902.

*"At the Victoria Falls headquarters, which was on the north bank, a permanent staff of runners was maintained. Their uniform consisted of a long tunic of khaki smock with short sleeves and a belt, the embroidered inscription in large red letters was 'B.S.A.Co. Mail,' and to cap it all each runner wore a fez. For protection runners went in pairs, carrying a martial rifle plus a few cartridges - all of which were accounted for. For this job they earned 10/- to 15/- a month with rations."* (Watt, undated)

## *Malaria and Mosquitoes*

The major problem encountered at Old Drift was malaria, and the death rate among the early pioneers of the small settlement was extraordinarily high. It had long been known that quinine was an effective preventative, and Livingstone had been one of the first to administer it in a dose that is now considered effective. He even suggested the link between mosquitoes and malaria: *"Myriads of mosquitoes showed, as probably they always do, the presence of malaria"* (Livingstone and Livingstone, 1865).

The abundance of mosquitoes at the Old Drift caused many to succumb to malaria, with fatal complications known as 'blackwater fever' particularly common. In October 1902 Dr John Wilson, together with Nurse Chapman, arrived and set up a private clinic - thee months later he himself died of fever. At the beginning of 1904 another chemist, Dr Alexander Findlay, joined the growing list of fatalities.

> *"One settler stoically recalled that 'the Old Drift was not what one would call unhealthy, although there were plenty of mosquitoes and that sort of thing. Everyone went down with fever, though we took quinine.' However, the fact remains that in most years some twenty per cent of the settlers died. Percy Clark claimed that in one year the deaths totalled seventy per cent. But this appears to be an exaggeration."* (Phillipson, 1990)

The Administration could not let the situation continue and by the end of 1903 it was decided that the whole settlement would be relocated to a healthier location. Despite the hazards, the population had by then grown to sixty-eight Europeans, including seventeen women and six children.

## *Outspans and Drifts*

Catherine Winkworth Mackintosh visited the Zambezi in 1903 in the company of her uncle, the Rev. François Coillard ('Uncle Frank') and described in detail her stay at the Old Drift settlement.

> *"By 9 o'clock we reached the outspan which is quite close to the cataract, so close that the intervening woods quite conceal it. The noise too, strange to say, was much more audible at a distance of two or three miles than close by. After a hasty walk and a glimpse of the Falls, of which we could only see a very small part from this point, we resumed our trek... From 10 a.m. to 12 we skirted the river, but at a considerable distance. The heat was very great...*

> *"Evidently the days of untamed Nature are already gone by. 'Trespassers will be prosecuted' and 'Keep off the grass.' It was not exactly in these words, but an adaptation of the same to local exigencies; one commanding travellers and traders to camp on the south side of the road, and to abstain from cutting down palms or brushwood for fuel; the other warning them that they must, under grave penalties, 'declare' everything they bring into the country to the appointed official. No question after this, but that N.W. Rhodesia is a civilized country.*

> *"At midday precisely we reached the Zambesi at Clarke's Drift. Mr. Clarke is the trader and agent to the B.S.A. Co. and intermediary between the Northern*

*Outspan in the bush*

*Copper Mines and civilization, and seems to act as a kind of Honorary Lord Mayor, organizing festivals and everything else unofficial. He owns the steam launch which plies across the ferry. I was disappointed not to cross in a native canoe - till I saw one! The cool breeze crossing was delightful, but we had to wait for the launch an hour and a half: the most disagreeable of my existence...*

*"Delightful as our cart journey had been in many ways, it was a very pleasant change to bathe and dine and have a good rest, first under Mr Clarke's hospitable roof and then at the mission station, ten minutes away in the bush...*

*"We had two days' rest (badly needed) before going to visit the Falls. It gave me an insight into the life of a pioneer woman, of whom I saw several. 'One's life seems to slip away so uselessly,' said one. 'Oh,' I replied, 'you don't know what it looks like to us at home. We think of you as Making History and Building up Civilization.' 'To me,' she answered, 'it just seems that I am clearing away a little dust here and there and always beginning over again.'"* (Mackintosh, 1922)

## Through the Wilds to Hwange

In mid-1901 the route of the railway extension north was surveyed and agreed, the line travelling from Bulawayo to Hwange and then on to the Victoria Falls, crossing the Zambezi River below the Falls. The work was contracted in three successive

*Railway construction gangs at work*

sections, each awarded to Pauling's construction company. The first part of the route, the 161 mile (259 km) of line from Bulawayo north to Mambanje, was agreed in July 1901 and constructed at a comparatively relaxed rate, opening to traffic in March 1903.

The railway ran through sand veld, well wooded with mopane and teak, and with the exception of one river crossing was fairly easy going for Pauling and his men. The country, however, would steadily become tougher for the construction gangs.

In April 1903 the second contract was agreed for the construction of a further 46 miles (74 km) of railway terminating at the Hwange coal mines. Reporting to Sir Charles on progress of the line was Mr Charles Beresford-Fox, representative of Sir Douglas Fox and Partners (and nephew of Sir Douglas Fox). Mr Beresford-Fox would be involved with the development of the railway to the Falls and preparations for the Bridge.

Edward Rosher, surveying engineer for the line, recalled that the heavily graded section between Dett and Hwange was some of the toughest country he had ever encountered for survey work. It was often a case of crawling on hands and knees along game trails to get through the bush to reach a suitable spot where the vegetation could be cut back enough to allow surveying equipment to be set up. All this in a country rich in lion, elephant and other dangerous wildlife - causing much anxiety amongst the railway engineers.

The line to Hwange was officially opened for general traffic on 1st December 1903, with the first trainload of coal transported south in October, such was the demand. Onward passengers and mail were transferred to the Zeederberg coach service for the remaining 68 miles (109.5 km) to the Victoria Falls.

The third and final construction contract, for the section of line from Hwange to the Victoria Falls, was signed in December 1903, with a bonus of £7,500 for Pauling and his men in the event of the rails being suitable for the passage of trains by 1st April 1904. Reports record Pauling employing some 2,500 labours on the line.

Mackintosh, on her return south after visiting the Falls, described the wagon journey back toward the advancing railhead:

> "We saw quite a different country from that coming up, as now we passed places by daylight that previously we had traversed in the dark and vice versa. When the scrub widens out, vast prairies of tall grass look like fields of red wheat against the forest background. We saw no wild creatures except locusts; the traffic on the road frightens them away. We crash over all obstacles, nobody ever takes anything out of the way; young trees... lie right across the road for the next trekkers to pick up. We met many natives either coming back from the mines or coming up in gangs to work on fresh sections of the railway. But we saw none hastening south to take the places of those returning home. The latter were mostly in very poor condition, some quite starving and emaciated, with wolfish eyes, others hardly able to walk." (Mackintosh, 1922)

## Conservation of the Falls

The Chartered Company had been alerted to the need to take action to protect the natural environment of the Falls after it was rumoured in 1894 *"that some enterprising individual* [sadly un-named] *was going to 'peg out' the land around the Falls and charge gate admittance"* - an initiative they were keen to forestall.

> "The Company wanted 'immediate action' to protect the Falls - and particularly its timber resources - from 'disfigurement at the hands of transport riders, traders and others' ...A park was designated around the waterfall itself, and a Conservator was appointed... Frank Sykes, who filled this post, was also Civil Commissioner for the Livingstone area." (McGregor, 2003)

In June 1903 a brick house was being constructed for Mr Sykes at the growing Administrative camp on Constitution Hill. The house, as with his role as Conservator, was jointly funded by the administrations north and south of the river.

*"Sykes felt the landscape needed to be manipulated to 'excite the wonder of the onlooker' and to maintain its 'primitive charm.' He felt it necessary to 'open up views of the river by judiciously cutting down trees,' 'to fill up gaps by plantations' and to enlarge hippopotami tracks which were 'the only means of approach to some of the best points of view.' He also wanted to charge admission, a proposal that was dismissed by the Company as impractical and 'undignified.' Sykes was assisted by a Curator, Mr Allen (Forester to the Rhodesia Railways and former employee of Kew) who was appointed in 1904."*
(McGregor, 2003)

The regulations protecting the environment of the Falls not only restricted over-enthusiastic 'sportsmen' from shooting animals, but also limited access to the river and Falls for the local Leya people.

## Mr Clark Stakes His Claim

In May 1903 Percy Missen Clark arrived at the Victoria Falls from Bulawayo with the intention of starting a photography business.

*"I made my headquarters at the Old Drift for the time being, but my intention was to settle at Victoria Falls as soon as the railway was completed, for I believed that there would be great opportunities for those who got in early at the railhead. At the end of the year I engaged a man to build a hut for me near the spot where the railway station would be pitched, and where the hotel would be built, but I had no mind to cross the river until the railway did come up."*

A chemist by profession, Clark successfully established himself on the south bank as a photographer, selling many postcards and a popular portfolio of photographs of the Falls entitled a 'Souvenir of the Victoria Falls,' of which there were several variations produced over the years. He also developed his own guidebook to the Falls and traded in a variety of African curios and souvenirs.

*"While I lived at the Old Drift I spent a lot of my time at the Victoria Falls taking photographs, and I got together quite a good collection. I would camp out for a couple of days at a time in the hut... When that was completed I lived in it, but for most of the time I was over on the other side at the Old Drift. I liked the older haunts, and the old crowd."* (Clark, 1936)

Clark was made Fellow of the Royal Geological Society for helping Henry Balfour, on the visit of the British Association, find stone-age axe heads close to the Victoria Falls. He exhibited his photographs of the Falls at the Royal Geographical Society

*Percy Clark outside his photography hut*

and was elected Associate of the Royal Photographic Society in 1925. 'The Autobiography of an Old Drifter: The Life Story of Percy M Clark of Victoria Falls' was published in 1936. He lived in the Falls area until his death in 1937 - but is buried, however, in Livingstone Cemetery. Clark's son, Victor, himself a skilled photographer, took over the family business and continued operations for many years.

## *Christmas Party*

The earliest recorded rail tour from Bulawayo to the Falls was arranged in December 1903, six months before the railhead actually reached the Falls. The group travelled by train as far as Hwange, which had been reached earlier in the same month, before transferring to a horse-driven coach service for the remaining distance to the Falls:

> *"[T]ravellers to the Zambezi were informed that the round trip from Bulawayo would take twelve days. The management of the Grand Hotel, Bulawayo, packed attractive baskets of food, but as fresh meat would not keep indefinitely, tourists were counselled to shoot giraffe and hippo... Arrived at the Zambezi, enterprising fishermen could add to the larder by catching tigerfish - 'an appetising dish.'"* (Rhodesia Railways Magazine, December 1954)

# The Railway Arrives

The final section of the line from Hwange to Victoria Falls was begun in late 1903, financed by Rhodesia Railways Ltd, who were also responsible for the funding of the Bridge and the continuation of the line into Northern Rhodesia.

The first 68 miles (109.5 km) of line from Hwange was particularly challenging for Pauling and his railway construction gang, and included 47 miles (75.5 km) of very heavy work through difficult country covered in dense bush and supporting a full complement of Africa's 'Big Five.' Percy Clark had travelled to the Falls whilst the railway was still under construction, recording that the workmen slept in the trees for fear of attack from lion and other dangerous wild animals.

Two major river crossings were involved, one over the Deka, nine miles (14.5 km) from Hwange, and the other over the Matetsi, about half-way to Victoria Falls. For this a temporary wooden trestle bridge, 260 feet (79 m) long and 43 feet (13.1 m) high, was built to carry the line forward. It was probably the largest trestle bridge to be built by Pauling on the line and was soon after replaced by a permanent masonry and steelwork construction.

Despite the difficulties, the line to the Victoria Falls was completed on 24th April 1904, several weeks after the target date of 1st April - for once Pauling had been unable to deliver to the target date. As the last rails were laid the supporting construction train following immediately behind slowly rolled to a stop within sight of the rising spray of the Falls. Celebrations were held including a feast for all the construction workers.

*Railway construction*

*"Harold Pauling was once more in charge of this contract and, as usual, the work was speedily pushed ahead to reach Victoria Falls, where the site for the famous bridge had already been selected. On 24 April 1904, only seven months after work began, the first construction train pulled in at the site of Victoria Falls station, then to be a dead end. The train was hauled by RR 7th class no 22 and for the last lap was driven by Harold Pauling's daughter, Blanche, with the locomotive flying a Union Jack and bearing the board below the headlamp reading 'We've got a long way to go.' This referred to Cairo, as the target of Cecil Rhodes was still very present in men's minds. Blanche Pauling had already travelled on the first engine to reach Bulawayo in 1897, so she could well claim to be a pioneer engine driver. In wide-brimmed felt hat, high collared white blouse and dark skirt down to her ankles, she made an unusual figure on the footplate. As soon*

*The first construction train to reach the Falls*

*as the last sleeper was laid and the train came to rest, celebrations began, with native sports, mock battles by the tribesmen, and a feast for all the staff, white and black, engaged on the work."* (Croxton, 1982)

In his autobiography Percy Clark proudly tells of his success in selling photographs of the arrival of the first train to all the engineers, contractors and railway staff and *"did a roaring trade in prints at five shillings a time."* Presumably many of these postcards were sent home to Europe with tall tales of African adventures.

A temporary station building was quickly improvised, with Pauling operating two trains a week between Hwange and Victoria Falls from 10th May 1904, before the line was handed over to the Railway Company for official opening on 20th June 1904. A Post Office was established within the building and a regular mail service operated from 1st July 1904 with the earliest known date-stamp of 'Victoria Falls,

S Rhodesia' being the 17th July 1904. The Zeederberg mail service from the south stopped soon after, although they continued to run a short connecting mail run from the Falls to the Old Drift on Thursdays and Sundays to coincide with the train timetable (Shepherd, 2008). A permanent station building was erected and operational in the first half of 1905 with Mr John Fairlamb as Station Master.

The trains took 22 hours on the Bulawayo to Victoria Falls journey and 24 hours on the return. In advertisements it was stressed that passengers must provide their own blankets and food for their journey as there were no dining carriages, and no intermediate stations where refreshments could be obtained. Mr Pierre Gavuzzi, Manager of the Bulawayo Grand Hotel, provided hampers for the adventurous train travellers.

In late May 1904 Mr Gavuzzi would have been arranging his own hamper for the journey north, travelling by train with several truckloads of building materials destined for the construction of a modern hotel overlooking the rising spray of the Victoria Falls, and to which he had been appointed as general manager by his employers.

## *First Train Tourists*

The first group of railway tourists known to travel to the Victoria Falls from Cape Town arrived on a specially booked private train in June 1904, the first through train to the Zambezi. The trip was organised by a Mr Arderne, a businessman based in the Cape, who hired the Cape Railway's Train de Luxe, complete with refrigerator truck and dining car.

The party arrived at the Falls with the banner 'First through train - Cape Town to Victoria Falls' adorning the engine. They stayed six nights, and such was the luxury of the train that they ate and slept aboard.

Quinine was served daily at breakfast and the chef devised a special customised menu with themed names, including a Victoria Falls pudding with 'spray effect.' The women in the group were carried through the Rainforest in suspended hammocks and explored the islands on the river above the Falls by canoe and launch. On the train was a piano - the first one ever to be heard at the Falls (Green, 1968).

A descriptive and illustrated account of this inaugural tour was published privately in Cape Town as a souvenir. The trip was the first of several organised by Mr Arderne for his wealthy friends and contacts in the Cape.

*Touring the Falls*

Despite the scarcity of clientele at the Falls, Percy Clark still drove a hard bargain:

*"The first through train from Cape Town arrived with a large party. The journey was apparently a grand adventure for these good people; the train was placarded through all its length and on both sides with legends informing the world how wonderful it was. On the Sunday I was visited by many of the excursionists, who bought photographs of the Falls. One gentleman betrayed great interest in an album of views which I had made up. He asked me its price. I told him my charge was five pounds.*

*"'I never trade on Sundays,' said this pious gentleman. 'It is against my principles.'*

*"'What a pity!' I replied. 'It is the last album I have, and it is sure to be snapped up. But I have plenty of loose photographs that you can buy tomorrow.'*

*"'If it wasn't Sunday,' said he, 'I would give you four pounds for it.'*

*"'Since it is Sunday, however,' I said, 'you ought to pay more - to salve your conscience. My price is five pounds.' He hung around for some time with his 'ifs' and 'peradventures,' but I gave him no encouragement.*

*"'Well,' he sighed at last, 'I suppose I'll have to pay your price.' And pay it he did. I have often envied him his conscience - at least, as regards its flexibility."*
(Clark, 1936)

In addition to 'The Huts' Clark also established a stall at the recently opened railway station.

*"An excursion from the Cape was due to arrive late one evening and, the hotel being full, most of the passengers had to sleep in the train. I had the station bookstall, and I opened it that night with my wife and myself behind the counter. We did a roaring trade in pictorial post cards at four shillings a dozen and mahogany beans at three pence per pod. That first night we took twenty-eight pounds, and as the excursionists stopped three or four nights at the Falls our takings altogether served to put us on a fair footing."* (Clark, 1936)

# The Victoria Falls Hotel

With the line complete the Railway Company arranged in late May 1904 the transportation of materials for the construction of a 'temporary' hotel at the Falls. The Hotel was originally intended only as a short-lived structure to provide accommodation for the railway officials and chief engineers overseeing work on the erection of the Bridge and continuation of the line, to be removed from the site once the focus of railway development advanced northwards.

A simple wood and iron structure, construction of the Hotel was speedily effected once materials arrived at the Falls. The main building, essentially an extended version of the standard railway station, consisted of a cast-iron frame, wooden panels and corrugated iron roof, all raised above the ground and fronted with a wide open veranda overlooking the Batoka Gorge, the view extending down to the Bridge site in the distance. The Hotel was initially capable of hosting up to 20

*Front view of the first Victoria Falls Hotel*

guests at a time, with twelve single and four double rooms, together with a dining room, bar and administrative offices, and was equipped with modern luxuries including electric lights and fans and running hot and cold water.

The Railway Company leased the operation and management of the new Hotel to the partnership of Mr G Estran and Mr W Scott-Rodger, who were already running the Grand Hotel in Bulawayo and who sent their Manager, Mr Pierre Gavuzzi, to oversee the establishment of the new Hotel (Roberts, 2016b).

The Victoria Falls Hotel opened on 8th June 1904, the name of its first guests lost in the dusty pages of the past, along with the Hotel's first guest books. Many of the Hotel's early guests would have been linked to the Railway Company and construction of the Bridge, as well as the occasional adventurous traveller. Sir Charles Metcalfe made the Hotel his base of operations, overseeing the Bridge construction from the veranda and utilising the telegraph at the neighbouring Post Office to communicate progress to London and across the world.

The early Hotel staff were cosmopolitan in origins - Mr Gavuzzi was an Italian, the chef was French, and the barman from Chicago, with service supported by Indian waiters. The young chef, Mr Marcel Mitton, known as 'the Frenchman who became a Rhodesian,' was a well-known character in early Rhodesian history, trying his hand as a hunter and miner as well as a chef. Ever-present at that right moment, Percy Clark had the first meal served at the Hotel:

> *"I had the first meal that was served to a customer at the Victoria Falls Hotel. I ate it, I remember, in an annexe to the coal-hole near the kitchen. It was lunch I had, and I paid about four shillings for it."* (Clark, 1936)

The lowest all-inclusive tariff was twelve shillings six pence per day, and such was the demand for accommodation that within a month of opening an advert had to be placed in the Bulawayo Chronicle notifying visitors intending to stay at the Hotel that they should advise the management in advance of their arrival *"in order to ensure accommodation and to avoid disappointment"* (Bulawayo Chronicle, 9th July 1904). The rising numbers of visitors to the Falls did not go unnoticed by the Railway Company, Sir Charles Metcalfe and others soon referring to the Hotel in terms of accommodating visitors rather than engineers:

> *"[T]he line has been open right up to the Victoria Falls since June 20, and the hotel we have built there for the accommodation of visitors is a very comfortable one. It possesses every modern convenience, and from it there is obtained a beautiful view of the Zambezi Gorge."* (Metcalfe, 1904)

*The Hotel (left) and Annex buildings (right, with tennis court in foreground)*

The Livingstone Mail regularly published lists of passengers travelling by train to the Falls, showing guests arriving at the Falls Hotel from England, the United States and the Cape Colony. Arriving in large groups by train, the Hotel would often be full to overflowing during peak periods, with travellers frequently having to use train carriages as extra accommodation. Two railway engine sheds were quickly relocated to the site and converted into extra accommodation and a large dining room, and in September 1904 two further buildings added, becoming known as the Annex or Honeymoon Suites.

*"The hotel, at the beginning, was simply a long structure of wood and iron containing a dining room and bar, bedrooms and offices. Later on it was enlarged by the addition of two large engine sheds removed from railway headquarters. One of these was converted into a dining room and the other into bedrooms. Later still two annexes of wood and iron were put up, complete with bathrooms. In the hot weather the rooms were ovens, and in the cold, refrigerators - but nobody grumbled much. After all, what could one expect in the heart of Africa?"* (Clark, 1936)

The British travel agent, Thomas Cook and Sons, as an official passenger agent for the Cape Government and Rhodesia Railways, followed the progress of the railway and construction of the Hotel and Bridge in its magazine, the Travellers' Gazette and began offering excursions from Cape Town in the same year. The company anticipated a rapid expansion of business at *"Nature's greatest spectacle"* where the traveller could *"enjoy European luxury even here in the heart of Africa"* (McGregor, 2009).

## Royal Visitors

Her Royal Highnesses Princess Helena, fifth child and third daughter of Queen Victoria, known by her married title of Princess Christian of Schleswig-Holstein, and her daughter Princess Victoria, were the first members of the British Royal Family to visit the Victoria Falls in September 1904. Rickshaws were sent up from Bulawayo to convey the Royal guests to and from the Falls. Lord and Lady Roberts also visited the Falls at the same time.

*"Princess Christian and Princess Victoria were the first members of the Royal Family to see the Falls, and the two large islands were named after them to commemorate their visit on 16th September, 1904. Kandahar Island, situated about five miles [8 km] upstream, was named after Lord Roberts, on the occasion of his visit on 20th September, 1904."* (Southern Rhodesia Publicity Office, 1938)

Percy Clark recalled the visit in his autobiography:

*"The first great lady of the many I have met at the Falls was Princess Christian. She came by special train in 1904, and I was commanded to bring post cards and photographs to the royal train for her inspection. In those rough-and-ready days few of us had complete suits to our names, and I was in like case with the majority. I was in a quandary. I couldn't very well appear before her Royal Highness in khaki slacks and a shirt, so I hunted round the camp to collect what decent togs I could borrow or steal... until at last I had the complete outfit in which to present myself to Royalty, ...but when I told the aide-de-camp afterwards about my search for a rig-out he roared with laughter. He told the Princess the story subsequently, and I heard that it amused her hugely."* (Clark, 1936)

Princess Christian recorded that she was *"deeply impressed with the Victoria Falls, and that no one coming to South Africa should miss seeing them"* (BSAC, 1907).

## Rickshaw Wrangles

Clark claims to have bought the first rickshaws to the Falls, pulled by a mule and led by a young African guide, and often followed by another to help push the rickshaw through the soft sands.

*"I imported a few of those vehicles, the first to appear about the Falls, and they became very popular indeed. I made a charge of half a crown for two persons*

*to go together by rickshaw to the bridge or the boathouse - a charge which I think was eminently reasonable."*

Clark recalls that a few months after introducing the rickshaws, the Chief Clark of the Railway Company, Mr Lewis Thomas, summoned him to a meeting at the Falls Hotel.

*Rickshaw ride*

*"'Mr Clark,' he said, 'I have sent for you regarding the rickshaws. Your prices are much too high. One shilling would be enough to charge either to the boats or to the bridge...'*

*"'My price is half a crown,' I said, 'and what authority have you, in any case, for laying down the law to me?...'*

*"'I have advertised the price as one shilling,' he blustered, 'and that is the price you are going to charge!'"*

Clark refused, replying: *"If you want to charge that price you had better buy the damned rickshaws!"* A deal was promptly agreed.

*"I quoted a price, and he accepted it... I was satisfied, but the manager of the hotel wasn't. He met me right afterwards and told me that I wouldn't have got that price out of him. I told him I knew that, but that the rickshaws were worth the money."* (Clark, 1936)

## Christmas Festivities

Christmas at the Falls in 1904 would have seen a significantly different scene to the one the previous year, with the railway now at the Falls and the Hotel six month's old. Construction of the Falls Bridge was well underway, the gorge connected by means of a cable transporter system, with electric conveyor, to ferry people and materials to the northern bank, and a large number of European

*Tilting the Bucket*

engineers and railwaymen based both sides of the Falls.

*"That tourists are now making their way to this spot in Central Africa to see for themselves the eighth wonder of the world, as the Victoria Falls have been rightly termed, is made clear after a chat with the present hotel proprietor. Last Christmas there were considerably over a hundred persons staying at the hotel, many of whom had to sleep in tents and temporary annexes, so crowded was the building itself."* (Scientific American,1905)

To entertain the crowds a Christmas sports day was held, with live music provided by a band from Bulawayo and a lunchtime picnic under the shade of Palm Grove. Sport events included tug-o-war, a walking race, the very popular 'bun and treacle race' - which involved the eating of a series of buns, made by local Livingstone bakers Smith & James, covered in treacle and hung on strings - and 'tilting the bucket' (Shepherd, 2013). Clark was again present and describes the scene.

*"The tilter rode in a wheel-barrow and was provided with an assagai [spear] which he had to get through a hole in a board under a bucket of water. If he missed the hole and hit the board, of course, the bucket swung round and he was drenched."* (Clark, 1936)

## A 'Fait Accompli'

Hutchinson writing in 1905 reflects on the growing developments at the of the Falls:

*"It may be that with the advent of railways and hotels this element of romance will disappear, but at present it still survives. The Victoria Falls are now the meeting-place of civilisation and the desert, and this gives a certain charm to*

*the everyday life there. At first sight it seems to be almost too 'civilised' - the new hotel, the Canadian canoes, the crowds of camera-laden visitors, or the scene of bustle and activity at the railway station and the bridge head, all appear singularly out of place; indeed the Victoria Falls have been described by one who knew them in the old days as 'a mass of water surrounded by tourists.' But in the rainy season it is very different, for the only inhabitants then are a few officials, and enterprising traders, content to endure the feverish climate of the Zambesi valley.*

*"It is of course inevitable that the great power known as 'Civilisation' should soon extend her realm beyond the Zambesi, and it is now clear that she will set her mark upon the Falls themselves, for already there is a hotel, a railway station, cuttings and embankments, and watering-places in close proximity, and it has been necessary to surround the 'Rain Forest' with a wire fence. Within a year it is said that the passengers by the Cape to Cairo railway will cross by the new bridge, less than two hundred yards [183 m] distant from the Boiling Pot, with the spray beating on their faces, and the roar of the waters in their ears.*

*"It is the bridge that is regarded as mainly responsible for all this, for when the present site was chosen it meant not only that the Falls should be accessible, but that all the accompaniments of civilisation should be deposited at their very edge. During the past year the choice of the site has been much criticised upon these grounds, but now that the bridge is more or less a fait accompli further discussion is useless. It has, however, served to open the wider question of what is to be the future of the Falls. It is of course within the bounds of possibility that they should simply be 'exploited' as one of the commercial assets of the country; indeed, one argument used in favour of the bridge was that it would give to visitors in the future a view of the Falls which was previously unobtainable. And if this attitude is taken their fate is sealed."*
(Hutchinson, 1905)

# The Victoria Falls Bridge

The Victoria Falls Bridge was designed by Mr George Andrew Hobson of London based engineering consultants Sir Douglas Fox and Partners and the steelwork manufactured by Cleveland Bridge and Engineering Company, Darlington, England. The finished steelwork sections were shipped to Beira and transported on the railway to Bulawayo and then finally on to the Falls. The Cleveland Bridge Company appointed Georges C Imbault, a gifted young Frenchman, as their Chief Construction Engineer. Imbault established his camp on the north bank of the river a short distance above the Falls and in April 1904 was joined by a small team of skilled construction engineers, sent from England by the Cleveland Bridge Company, who would be tasked with the erection of the Bridge.

The Bridge is of a trussed arch design, the main arch a graceful parabolic curve with a rise of 90 feet (27.4 m) and span of 500 feet (152.4 m), with two short connecting side spans giving a total width of 650 feet (198.1 m). Erection of the side spans proved to be one of the biggest challenges in the construction, their positioning crucial to the alignment of the final structure. Once completed, construction of the main arch progressed rapidly, reaching outwards from each side of the gorge high over the river. The separate sides of the arch were supported as cantilevers by steel wire cables cut into the rock on either bank, and as the work proceeded daily observations were taken to see that the centre axis of the structure was maintained.

On the 31st March 1905 the main arches were ready to be joined, when it was found that the final sections overlapped by several centimetres. Imbault remained confident and the following morning, after the steelwork structure had cooled and contracted during the night, the final sections fitted perfectly.

The engineering company, Sir Douglas Fox and Partners, announced to the

world that the arch of the great Zambezi Bridge was linked up at six o'clock on Saturday 1st April 1905. An engineering report from the time detailed that there were anxious minutes as the sun rose and everyone watched to see if the effects of the heat on the steel, and tension of the whole structure, had been accurately calculated and constructed. The upper deck of the Bridge was completed in June 1905, and a temporary track was immediately laid over the open steelwork suitable for light traffic, with only the final fixed riveting of the Bridge remaining prior to the official opening in September (Roberts, 2016a).

*Bridge engineers at work*

Not everyone was in favour of the Bridge being constructed within view of the Falls, including Cecil Rhodes' brother, Frank. Mr Hobson, the Bridge designer, recalled:

> *"When at Victoria Falls* [Hotel] *last July (1905), I had many talks with one of the chief malcontents, the late Colonel Frank Rhodes... Looking at the bridge from our breakfast table, in his cheery way he said: 'Well, I have done all I could to prevent the bridge being built there; but there it is, and nothing is now left for me to do but pray daily for an earthquake.' But he confessed that he liked the thing itself very well."* (Hobson, 1923)

## *Chief Mukuni's Musings*

The chief of the local Leya, Chief Mukuni Sianyemba, reportedly came with his headmen each day to a rock vantage point to watch the construction of the Bridge. Varian, one of the engineers working on the Bridge, recorded the Chief's doubts on the design in his memoirs 'Some African Milestones' (published in 1953):

> *"Of course the white men are very clever... but as soon as all this zimbe* [iron] *gets further from the bank it will of course fall down the gorge."*

With wonder he watched the progress until the two sides were finally linked up, but still refused to relinquish his doubts.

> *"Now with great luck, they have got this thing across, the trouble will be when they try to put a train on it, which they evidently mean to do. What they should do to save it all would be to put a stick up from the bottom to hold it up, certainly it would have to be a long stick, but as they have got the bridge across, they should be able to do that as well, but it is not for me to tell them."* (Varian, 1953)

The chief's forebodings, however, did not materialise and he stood alone on his rock vantage point as the first train rumbled across the Bridge. His response was that it must be the finger of the white man's god that held the Bridge up. The impact of the Bridge on the cultural beliefs of the local Leya people is often overlooked.

> *"Old Leya people recall that ceremonies at the boiling pot ceased as the resort grew and people lost access to the waterfall: the light in the boiling pot was said to have gone out, and the sounds of past communities in the form of drumming, cattle lowing and children playing could no longer be heard... The building of the bridge over the river, for example, had defiled one of Mukuni's religious sites, as the supports for the bridge reached down into the sacred place of the boiling pot."* (McGregor, 2003)

## On the Run

Clark recalls an incident following the detention of a Bridge worker, his name and crime unrecorded, by the local police constabulary, which Clark recalled numbered only seven at the time.

*"Keeping order at the Falls did not exercise them much. Once they had to arrest a man who was working on the bridge. They had only a pole and dagga hut to put him in, so they leg-ironed him for the night. In the darkness he escaped, leg-irons and all. Next day the detachment under the corporal hunted for him all over the countryside, but without success. In the early hours of the morning that followed the corporal looked out of his window. On the fence six feet [less than 2 m] away from him dangled the leg-irons. Whether the offender was too honest a man to take away Government property or merely gifted with an acute sense of humour I cannot guess, but he was never caught."* (Clark, 1936)

By 1906 a permanent police station, consisting of traditional wattle and daub huts, had been established on the approach to the Falls from the south (Heath, 1977).

## Trayner's Rag

Mr William Trayner became, by chance rather than calculation, the publisher of the first official newspaper in Northern Rhodesia. Mr Trayner was employed by 'Mopane' Clarke to operate the boat crossing, and as such undertook regular trips to the south bank, where he would hear news of the wider world from railway and hotel staff. During 1905 Trayner started providing hand-written news updates, with information gathered from visiting travellers, for the Old Drift residents, leading to the rather informal evolution of an official newspaper. Demand for news from the 'home country' no doubt grew with the arrival of the construction engineers.

*"It was a gradual growth without any intention on my part of starting a paper. I was given the job of running the Drift (the River Crossing). To those living in the camp on the north bank in utter isolation, the southern bank was the outside world and as I was over there and at the Falls many times a day, I was regarded as a source of news when I rolled up at the bar [on the north bank] of an evening. In the very early days news was a bit scarce and had to be 'made-up' about crocs and the hippo we had seen or the lion spoor close to the drift."* (Northern Rhodesia Journal, 1964)

*"By popular request he prepared hand-written news-sheets which were passed from hand to hand or pasted up in one of the bars. These impromptu*

*'newspapers' had varying headings, examples being Trayner's Rag or The Livingstone Liar. No copies are known to survive."*

These informal notes became typewritten with the donation of a typewriter, and finally Northern Rhodesia's first 'official' newspaper was born.

*"The Administration asked Trayner to register his paper and to issue it at regular intervals with a fixed title, so that it could be used for the publication of official Administration notices. The name Livingstone Pioneer and Advertiser was suggested and agreed upon and the paper appeared at regular weekly intervals, with interruptions due to the indisposition of the editor/proprietor, from 13 January to 29 September 1906."* (Phillipson, 1990)

## A Valuable Property

The value of the Victoria Falls as a potential tourism destination was soon recognised by the Chartered Company.

*"In the Victoria Falls we possess a very valuable property, which is likely to promote materially the prosperity of the country. During the short period in which the railway to the Falls has been open, a large number of visitors has been attracted to them, and the tourist traffic which may be legitimately expected in the immediate future is likely to increase."* (British South Africa Company, 1905)

At the annual General Meeting of the Railway Company shareholders, held in London in 1905, a report was presented recording:

*"Lord Grey has told you that we have reached the Victoria Falls. We took over that line on June 20 [1904]... We have also, since then, effected what we call a temporary hotel which, however, is a very comfortable one. It has every modern convenience and accommodation for about forty people. It has most magnificent views of the bluff gorge. It has the electric light, cold storage, hot and cold water baths, and every modern luxury."*

The report also referred to the fragile nature of the Falls environment and concerns over its conservation and preservation.

*"We also have a botanist [Mr Allen] who came from Kew Gardens last year. He is looking after the two parks which have been made to preserve the beauty of*

*The Victoria Falls Station*

*the Falls from advertisement boards and other buildings, and he is making an arboretum there to grow rare plants."* (Rhodesia Railways, 1905)

The immediate area around the Falls on the south bank, known as the Victoria Falls Reserve, was fenced as part of a conservation plan in 1904. The area included the Falls Rainforest and extended upstream to the Big Tree, Palm Tree Ferry and inland to the track leading to the Old Drift crossing.

Local wildlife, especially of the larger variety, took little notice of these barriers to their movement, and a perhaps predictable problem was the nocturnal wanderings of resident hippopotamus, as one visitor, Mr Agate, recorded:

*"Our friend, the Engineer of this section of the railway, to whom we were indebted for much kindness and advice, told us that the relation of the hippo to barbed wire fencing in that neighbourhood was a problem they had failed to solve. They had put up a number of fences of the strongest barbed wire they could get, the fence being made of several strands of it fixed on stout posts, and, as far as their observations went, they had come to the conclusion that the hippos walked through it without noticing its presence."* (Agate, 1912)

The Falls Hotel was built on land within the designated Railway Reserve, together with the Railway Station and Post Office (with a telegraph line connecting to Livingstone), and Percy Clark's house and huts. All were supplied with water from a small pumping station above the Devil's Cataract.

## *Within Reach of the World*

By 1905 the Falls were being promoted as a global tourism attraction, one South African travel brochure boldly declaring:

> *"The average man in the street has hardly yet realised that the Victoria Falls are within reach of anybody having a couple of months to spare."*

From England, for example, all one had to do was catch the train from London to the port of Southampton. From there, the Union Castle mail steam-liner sailed every Saturday to Cape Town, taking 17 days. From the Cape it took three days by train to Bulawayo and a further 22 hours to reach the Falls. It was not uncommon for passengers to travel this great distance, only to stay a few nights at the Falls Hotel and then start their return journey. Travel companies offering combined travel deals included Thomas Cook, Pickfords, the German East Africa Line and the Aberdeen Line, with the last two accessing Rhodesia through the port of Beira and connected to the Falls by rail via Salisbury (now Harare).

The Union Castle Mail Steamship Company, official mail carrier from the United Kingdom to the Cape Colony in South Africa, was intrinsically linked with the early development of the Rhodesias. The lavender-coloured liners of the Union Castle were a familiar sight at the Cape, and along with other steamship companies such as Cunard, White Star and P&O becoming household names in a rapidly evolving global industry. A 1905 promotional booklet produced by Union Castle Line encouraged travel to the Zambezi, 'the World's Riviera.'

*The Union Castle Line RMS Saxon*

# The Zambezi Express

By June 1905 three passenger trains a week were running to and from Bulawayo. Also featuring on the timetable was the Zambezi Express - a special weekly service from Kimberley to the Victoria Falls, which completed the final 450 kilometres from Bulawayo in under 18 hours, and fully equipped with bedding services and dining car.

Passengers received an 'Annotated Time Table of the Zambezi Express on the Rhodesia Railways', which gave details of the times at the stops along the route in both directions, and interesting information and photographs on the places passed. A connecting train ran from Cape Town, as detailed in the following extract from the Cape Government Railways timetable of September 1906:

*"A First Class Saloon for Victoria Falls leaves Cape Town on the 11.30 a.m. train on Tuesdays, and is attached to the Zambezi Express at Kimberley. It reaches Victoria Falls Station at 7.15 a.m. on Saturday. It is luxuriously appointed, and includes showerbath, etc. The distance from Cape Town is 1,642 miles [2,650 km], and the return fare £23:16:8d. Terms at Victoria Falls Hotel, 21/-a day."*

Of particular note was the dining-saloon, allowing passengers to dine to fine standards on route.

*"In contrast to the hampers passengers had to carry on the first excursion service to the falls, those who enjoyed the comforts of the Zambesi Express could lunch in the dining-saloon... The menu consisted of: Tomato Soup; Boiled Kabaljoe with parsley sauce; Haricot Mutton; Roast Ribs of Beef; Assorted Vegetables; Cold York Ham and Roast Beef; Chicken and Tongue; Dressed*

*The Zambezi Express*

*Salad; Tapioca Pudding; Stewed Fruit; Cheese and Biscuits; and Black Coffee."*
(Croxton, 1982)

## *Travel by Train*

An unnamed travel writer recorded their journey from Cape Town to the Falls on the special 'Train de Luxe' service:

*"It is thoroughly well equipped, and our old friend Conductor McEvoy never tires of showing off its good points. One does not know which to admire and appreciate most, the brilliant electric light, not forgetting the reading lamp you get, or the cuisine. The catering at the Refreshment Rooms of the Cape Government Railways is under the management of the popular Mr R A Simmons, and he deserves great credit for all his admirable arrangements...*

*"In September and October the country is liable to look parched, and you get more than a fair share of sand in your compartment. It is warm travelling at these times, but there is always the shower bath to comfort you, and there is generally congenial companionship in the smoking or observation car...*

*"You find yourself in Bulawayo on the morning of the third day out. A refreshing bath at the Grand, a pleasant lunch at the Club, and a drive round about passes the day amenably and you join the evening train for the Falls. After a comfortable night you are awakened at Inyantue by a native who has coffee for sale. In an hour or two you reach Wankies, and as you are sitting at a good breakfast off a clean tablecloth you can hardly realise that all this was a land of mystery and romance but a few short years back...*

*"The train pulled into the [Victoria Falls] station on a Sunday afternoon, and there were several knots of men who had travelled a bit to see the event of the day, the arrival of the train from the south. We were a small party, but seemed to make quite a stir in the little community. A long path, picked out with white stone borders,*

*Aboard the Train de Luxe to the Falls*

*led to the hotel, which was a revelation and a very welcome surprise... Tired and dusty as I was, I walked at once to the best spot for a view, and stood riveted to it for some time. Away to the left were distant and constantly moving clouds of spray... All around there was verdure to gladden the jaded traveller. It was a veritable oasis in the desert."* (South Africa Handbook, 1905)

## Teachers Conference

A group of teachers from the Cape were among the first to take advantage of the Zambezi Express service, travelling to hold their annual conference at the Falls.

*"More than one hundred South African teachers held their 1905 conference at the Victoria Falls. A newspaper remarked, 'they braved the dangers of poverty and malaria, crocodiles, lions and hippos.' During the run from Bulawayo the Falls they saw a tremendous bush fire; it had been burning for two years and could not be halted. Teachers paid the usual fares to Kimberley; and the round trip to the Falls and back to Kimberley cost twenty guineas a head including full board in the dining-car. Poems, articles and photographs by these learned visitors were collected and published in book form."* (Green, 1968)

# The Zambezi Regatta

The first Zambezi Regatta was held on 13th June 1905 to celebrate the fiftieth anniversary year of Livingstone's first arrival at the Falls and the construction of the Bridge. The regatta was the highlight to three days of sporting events and celebrations aimed at promoting the accessibility of the Falls to the wider world.

The regatta was held on a mile and a half (2.4 km) straight stretch of water between Luanda Island (now known as Long Island) and the north bank, and the event attended by close to a thousand visitors, flooding the Falls, and the Hotel, with an unprecedented number of tourists. A camp site and temporary grandstand was set up at the finish line, close to where the Livingstone Boat Club would be built by Pauling the following year.

The boats were imported from Oxford especially for the event. Six teams of fours, from Cape Town, Livingstone, Kalomo, East London, Port Elizabeth and Kafue competed. The main race was the four-oared race for the Zambezi Challenge Cup, with crews from Cape Town, Port Elizabeth, and East London competing, and after a fine race East London came in winners with Cape Town a close second and Port Elizabeth third.

*Regatta grandstand*

The Rhodesia Challenge Cup was presented by Mr Lawley for competition between the Rhodesian crews. Northern Rhodesia fielded three teams of fours, from Livingstone, Kalomo (manned by Company Civil Servants) and Kafue (manned by a crew selected from Pauling's railwaymen, including Varian). The race was won by Kafue, with Livingstone second. During the race the boat of the Kalomo crew began to take on water and slowly sink. The crew and boat were rescued, and to the sombre tune of the 'Dead March' the boat was carried away.

Also included in the regatta schedule were several 'native races,' including a race of the Lozi royal barges. Local Toka and Leya people under Chief Mukuni, who had traditionally controlled the river crossings, were notable for their absence from the event, having been eclipsed by the relationship formed between their Lozi overseers and the Chartered Company. It was said that Paramount Chief Lewanika, who attended the event, told his crew that if they did not win he would leave them on an island in the Zambezi for the benefit of the crocodiles. In the event the crew of Chief Letia (Lewanika's son) were victorious - it was not recorded what happened to Lewanika's loosing team!

Visitors drank dry the stocks of beer and whisky and there were apparently ugly scenes in the 'outside bar' of the Falls Hotel when the last bottles were emptied. Percy Clark was less than impressed with the rush on local supplies:

*"By the second day the hotel was cleared of beer and whiskey, and food had almost run out. I was invited by a friend to dine there. The feast was worthy of the rude fellow's grace: 'Gawd! What a meal!' I wished I had invited my friend to my own place. The service was terrible, with a wait of twenty minutes between each of the courses. These were: soup - with the taste and appearance of weak Bovril; one bony cutlet and half a potato; biscuits and cheese with no butter. There wasn't a scrap of butter in the hotel, no joints, no poultry. For this*

*The East London crew, regatta winners*

*magnificent (!) spread we were charged seven-and-six apiece. I'd sooner have bought a marriage licence."* (Clark, 1936)

The event received much promotion and coverage back in Britain, with the London Evening News describing the Zambezi as 'Our New Henley.' The Company's annual report for the year recorded that *"thanks in a great measure to the organising ability of Sir Charles Metcalfe, Mr R T Coryndon, and Mr A L Lawley, the Regatta was a great success"* (British South Africa Company, 1906). It was hoped that the Regatta would become an established annual event, but it was held only irregularly over the following years, including 1906, 1909 and 1910.

## Hippo Hazards

Mr Jack Rose (later Colonel Rose), one of the Cape rowers, later recalled:

*"It was a wild and exciting place in those days... Fever was a constant menace and there were few amenities but we enjoyed ourselves. There was lots to talk about - a bull hippo entered the marquee near the river where the boating club dinner was being held. We all cleared out pretty quick."* (Green, 1968)

Hippopotamus have always been a hazard along the river, easily capable of capsizing a canoe and to be treated with utmost respect on the water or river bank.

*"Several bad accidents have taken place already through these ugly denizens of the river charging boats. Two or three days before I arrived, while Mr Gavuzzi and a crew were rowing about a hippo tore a hole in the bottom of the boat, which immediately began to sink. The occupants had all to swim for it, but the distance to shore being only about 20 yards [18 m], they got off with nothing worse than a ducking."* (South Africa Handbook, 1905)

## *Fire at the Falls*

Disaster struck the fragile environment of the Falls during the dry season of 1905, when a careless visitor discarded a still smouldering match or cigarette in the Rainforest and caused an intense bush fire.

> *"The havoc was sadly visible on my visit. A path through the forest formerly available was now choked by the debris of dead palms and other half-burnt trees lying across it. What had been dense shade was now a long open space, a third or half the forest having fallen a prey to the flames. But for the fact of the remainder being thoroughly wet it would, of course, have gone too."* (South African Handbook, 1905)

# Death of the Drift

It soon became apparent that the location of the Bridge and route of the railway would make the Old Drift crossing, and settlement, redundant - irrelevant of the health concerns of the Administration or the wishes of the settlers. The Chartered Company's Administration considered two possible resettlement sites along the line of the railway, one that was 'close to the Falls and the river' (known as Imabult's or the Bridge Engineer's Camp) and the other on the 'sand-belt some seven miles (11 km) north' (location of the already established Commissioner's Camp at Constitution Hill). Without consultation with the settlers, Coryndon, the Company's Administrator, decided upon Constitution Hill, where the Government Station and Post Office had already been established, believing that a town *"so close to the Falls would be bound to mar the natural beauty of the area"* (Phillipson,1990).

> *"Before Livingstone was inhabited, before even it was surveyed, its political history began in the shape of a unanimous expression of popular dissatisfaction*

*The Old Drift*

*with the site selected... The inhabitants pointed out the distance separating the new site from the Falls; its inaccessibility to tourists and others; the distance from the water supply; and the absence of any industry or enterprise in the neighbourhood to justify its existence in the event of its failing to become a resort for visitors. The danger of an opposition township springing up, in a more favourably situated position, on either the South or North bank was urged, and subsequently, the difficulty of constructing roads or of obtaining suitable foundations for brick building in the sandy soil."* (Livingstone Mail, Dec 1906)

The Old Drifters were unified in their protests that the selected site was *"too far from both the Falls and the river"* and that the ground was *"unsuitable for building and road-making, and the approaches being through heavy sand, make transport expensive"* (Arrington-Sirois, 2017). One of the settlers questioned was *"the country so beautiful that a township* [closer to the Falls] *would mar the beauty?"* and another demanded: *"Do you think people enjoy a six mile* [9.6 km] *walk or drive through heavy sand?"* (Lewis, 2018).

The Administration were unmoved by the arguments of the settlers at the end of June were instructed in writing by Sykes, as District Commissioner, to cease all trading by 23rd August and depart from the site by 23rd September. The threat of a one pound daily fine from January 1906 finally encouraged the last settlers to move, and in early 1906 the Old Drift was all but abandoned to the bush. Only the Mission Station was allowed to remain, finally closing a few years later.

# Official Opening of the Bridge

The official opening ceremony for the Victoria Falls Bridge took place on 12th September 1905. One of the newest 7th Class engines in the country at the time, decorated with two flags (that of the BSAC and the Union Jack), palm leaves and floral dressings, pulled the six coaches which then halted on the Bridge for the passengers to alight. Mr Allan Bowes is recorded as the driver. The party was met by Sir Charles Metcalfe  and Major Robert Coryndon, the Administrator of North-Western Rhodesia.

Sir Charles made a welcoming speech and invited Professor (later Sir) George H Darwin, President of the British Association for the Advancement of Science (now the British Science Association), to declare the Victoria Falls Bridge officially open.

The Association had been invited to visit the Falls and open the Bridge as an extension to their tour of South Africa. Many eminent scientists, professors and

*Opening of the Victoria Falls Bridge*

engineers were present: Sir Benjamin Baker, Sir Colin Scott-Moncrieff, Lord Ross, Sir William Crookes and Sir Richard Jebb (who died soon after returning to England) to name a few. Also among the distinguished guests at the ceremony was Mrs Agnes Bruce, wife of Colonel Bruce, and daughter of Dr David Livingstone.

Once the ceremony was complete the train slowly drew forward amid cheers. The main group of guests alighted on the northern bank where they could explore the Palm Grove, or visit Livingstone Island. The remainder of the guests visited the Rainforest, under the guidance of Mr Allen, and then back to the Hotel for lunch, by which time the train returned with the first group and collected the second group for the trip to the north bank. Guests were given voucher tickets for the train, tours and meals, issued together with a special commemorative programme.

In the evening the Falls Hotel served dinner for a several hundred guests, after which Sir Charles read a telegram from the President and Directors of the Chartered Company, congratulating all on the opening of the Bridge.

*"Very fitting that foremost representatives of science should be associated with inauguration of modern engineering. Regret the founder of country is not alive to witness realization of part of his great ideal."* (Bulawayo Chronicle, 1905)

The British archaeologist and anthropologist Henry Balfour made the first of his four visits to the Victoria Falls for the opening ceremony, staying on the train due to the Hotel being full. *"Had to dine late owing to the fearful crush. Food vile, so dined on bread and marmalade"* (Balfour, 1905).

*'A poem in steel'*

# Sykes' Guide to the Falls

As the Conservator at the Falls, Sykes authored the first 'official' tourism guide, published soon after the railway had arrived, with the Falls Hotel less than a year old and the Bridge, at the time of writing, complete but awaiting its official opening.

A fold-out map shows the original railway layout, with a dead-end and turning points extending from the Railway Station, where trains turned before passing back through the Station and then looping round in front of the Hotel and passing down to the Bridge. Early pathways from the Hotel down to the Bridge, Falls and river are also shown. Sykes introduces his guide with the arrival of Dr Livingstone at the Falls in 1855, and goes on to record interesting local names and their meanings.

> *"The Native (Sekololo) name for the Falls is Mosi-oa-tunya, meaning 'the smoke which sounds.' It is a most appropriate one, as, viewed from any of the surrounding hills, this rising columns of spray, more particularly on a dull day, bear an extraordinary resemblance to the smoke of a distant veldt fire... The native in their songs say 'how should anyone lose his way with such a land-mark to guide him?'"*

Several features of the Falls had yet to be given their common names, Danger Point being identified as Buttress Point, and the Boiling Pot as The Cauldron. The Devil's Cataract is identified as the Cascade or Leaping Water, so named by Thomas Baines in 1862. Cataract Island is given its now commonly used English name, with Boruka Island as *"the native name, signifying 'divider of the waters.'"* Of the Rainforest, Sykes notes the *"natives themselves refer to it as 'the place where the rain is born.'"*

On Livingstone Island Sykes wrote:

*"Situated on the edge of the chasm almost in the centre of the Falls is the Island named after David Livingstone. 'Kempongo' was the old native name, which means 'Goat Island.' He himself named it Garden Island. It is a curious coincidence that it should bear a similar name to that other island which occupies almost an identical position at Niagara."*

In those early days visitors to the north bank had to undertake a rather tricky scramble across the 'Knife Edge' if they wished to view the Falls from the buttress beyond:

*"Proceeding along the path down a steep declivity, one reaches a dripping grove of palms and shade trees, at the end of which is an Arête known as the 'Knife Edge,' a peculiar depression with narrowed surface, and only to be negotiated at some risk, if the end of the promontory, which faces Buttress Point across the Cauldron, is to be the objective."*

In the corner of the Eastern Cataract, known as the Eastern Recess, was a rope assisted pathway down into the gorge:

*"There is a ravine or gully at the Eastern end of the Falls, by which it is possible to descend to their base with the assistance of a rope here and there; but, on reaching the bottom, the spray is so dense that little can be seen, and a thorough wetting may be regarded as a certainty."*

Sykes offered his advice on viewing the Falls:

*"For the guidance of visitors it may be remarked that, as the line of the Falls is almost East and West, in order to obtain the best effects from a light and shade point of view - and the beauty of the Falls so much depends upon the angle at which the rays of the sun illumine the rising spray - the Eastern end should be seen before mid-day and the Western end in the afternoon. Those who come armed with a camera should especially take note of this. From 8 to 10 o'clock in the forenoon the Falls present a magnificent spectacle when viewed from the cliff top on the Eastern extremity. As the spray lifts, the long array of falling water, extending as far as Livingstone Island, breaks into view. At full flood the scene from this spot is majestic, and leaves and impression of overwhelming power on the mind."* (Sykes, 1905)

The guide included several chapters written by knowledgeable experts with

*The Falls from Cataract Island*

detailed information on aspects of the Falls, including geology, written by G W Lamplugh, FRS, notes on the flora, by C E F Allen (Sykes' assistant and botanist), and an introduction to the birds of the region by W L Slater of the South African Museum. The back pages carried several adverts for Livingstone based businesses including Smith & James, butchers and bakers, and The Victoria Falls Coach & Boating Company, operated by Mr E Goodwin, advertising his 'motor launch, boat and cart' services, with experienced guides conveying visitors to Cataract and Livingstone Islands, all of which could be booked through the Falls Hotel. 'Mopane' Clarke advertised his hotel and bar, stocking the 'finest brands of liquors, wines and cigars' and offering catering services for picnic trips and excursions. Clarke also promoted motor launch and Canadian canoe services on the river and his general merchant stores, with branches also at Sesheke and Kalomo.

## Wildlife Warnings

Sykes also writes of the dangers of encountering hippopotamus on the river:

*"Hippopotami may be seen occasionally amongst the islands above the Falls. They have been known to attack and capsize boats, and therefore should be approached with caution, or better still, avoided as much as possible."* (Sykes, 1905)

He wrote from first hand experience.

*"In 1905 at the time of the regatta, Mr F W Sykes, a government official at Livingstone, escaped when the hippo overturned his boat near the lip of the Falls. Several natives were drowned. Gavuzzi the hotel manager, was rowing about the same area with a crew of natives when a hippo tore a hole in the bottom of the boat. They all had to swim for their lives and all reached the shore safely. A journalist who was visiting the Falls at the time wrote; 'I have little sympathy with the idea of some visitors that these brutes should be allowed to multiply in the river at this place on the plea that they form picturesque adjuncts to the scenery. I should not only permit them to be shot off but I should put a reward on every hippo's head.'"* (Green, 1968)

## Rules and Regulations

At the end of the guide Sykes lists the regulations which visitors were expected to follow for the protection of the Falls environments, detailing the prohibiting of:

*"- Shooting of any and every description within a radius of five miles [8 km] of the Falls on either bank.*
*- Netting and dynamiting in the river.*
*- The cutting of initials on or other defacement of the boles of trees.*
*- Plucking of flowers and ferns, uprooting ferns, orchids or other plants.*
*- Setting fire to the grass in the park.*
*- Trespassing of animals.*
*- Washing of clothes in the river above the Falls.*
*- Picnic parties are requested to remove all traces of their presence, such as tins, bottles, paper, etc, before leaving.*

*"The importance of the above will be obvious to all visitors who are lovers of nature, and their loyal observance is confidently relied upon."* (Sykes, 1905)

Fines and punishments are not recorded, although Mackintosh commented that *"punishment for carving one's name in the neighbourhood of the Falls is to be penal servitude for life in the Wankie's Mine!"* (Mackintosh, 1922). It was estimated that by 1905 some 5,000 visitors had now travelled to view the great waterfall:

*"Five thousand people have now seen the Falls, and though that number is a long way off the 500,000 who go to Niagara every year, the ball of information about them has now been well set a rolling by the Chartered Company."* (South Africa Handbook, 1905)

# The Livingstone Tree

*The Livingstone 'Name Tree'*

Sykes records interesting details relating to the tree on Livingstone Island upon which Dr David Livingstone had carved his initials in 1855, and which were said to still be faintly visible:

*"The Name Tree upon which he cut his initials still remains. Its identity was determined two years ago by the writer... An old white-haired native, by name Namakabwa, who spent most of his time down the gorge catching fish, on being questioned said he well remembered Livingstone, whose native name was 'Monari,' coming to the Falls, and described how he (Namakabwa) a day or two after Livingstone's departure, made his way over to the island and found that a small plot had been cleared of bushes, also that he had made some cutting on a tree. When asked 'which tree?' he immediately went to the Name Tree, and put his finger on what had evidently been a cut. The authenticity of the above then is based on the evidence of 'the oldest inhabitant,' and may be accepted as genuine. The bark of the tree is so rough and the marks so nearly obliterated that one would have had some doubts on the subject, were the source of information less worthy of belief.*

*"It is to be recorded with regret that a certain class of tourists, to whom nothing is sacred, had commenced to strip and carry away pieces of the bark from this tree, and so came the necessity for a notice-board and tree-guard, in themselves a witness against the relic hunting vandal who lightly destroys what can never be replaced. Even Livingstone, the discoverer of the Falls, excuses himself for 'this piece of vanity.' Would that others were only as sensitive on this point as the great explorer, and delay carving their meaningless initials on the trunks of trees until they can boast such a world-wide fame as was his to excuse the act!"* (Sykes, 1905)

# Tickets Please!

The Railway Company required a permanent Bridge watchman and toll-master, duties which included guarding against accidental fire on the Bridge caused by falling coals from passing trains. John Walter Soper (born in London in 1876) was their appointed man, duly arriving at the Falls from the south in December 1905.

A small toll-house was built close to the southern approach, from which tickets for foot-passengers, at one shilling each, were issued. 'Jack' Soper's role ensured he met almost every visitor in those early days as nearly all crossed the Bridge to view the Falls from both banks.

*"Mr Soper had his living quarters close to the Toll House and one of the attractions for visitors was young cheetah which was kept in a cage. Thousands of photographs must have been taken of this animal as a souvenir of 'Darkest Africa' at the time. More than one of them found their way into popular overseas magazines."* (Rhodesia Railways Magazine, Aug 1967)

The toll levied on pedestrians crossing the Bridge was cancelled in March 1914 (Rhodesia Railways Magazine, Sept 1957).

*Soper's south-bank toll hut overlooking the Bridge*

# Leopold Moore and The Livingstone Mail

Leopold Frank Moore (later Sir), arrived on the banks of the Zambezi in 1904, setting up residence at the Old Drift before relocating to the new town of Livingstone (he was one of the last settlers to move from the Drift), where he would become a central figure in the early development of the frontier town. Moore had followed the advancement of the railway, firstly to Mafeking and then Bulawayo, where he established a small chemist's shop.

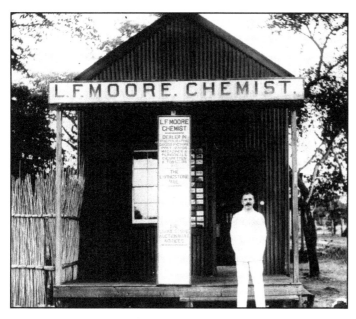

*Moore outside his chemist shop, Livingstone*

*"When his business was bankrupt, he claimed that this was caused by a boycott organized by the Chartered Company... whose intention to bring out indentured Chinese labour he had opposed."*

On arrival at the Old Drift Moore took up the vacant role of chemist. His predecessor, Mr Southurst, had 'wandered into the veld in a fit of malarial fever and been found dead some days later.'

Moore founded the Livingstone Mail in March 1906, three months after Trayner had officially launched the Livingstone Pioneer and Advertiser.

*"Leopold Moore did not take kindly to the Pioneer and on 31 March 1906 he started a rival weekly newspaper, the Livingstone Mail. It was typewritten on wax stencils and produced on foolscrap duplicating paper in purple ink. While concentrating on local settler news and views it contained a modicum of international matter: the first issue included the winner of the 1906 Grand National, run seven days previously... The Livingstone Mail survived for sixty years and is a valuable source of information on the history of the town and country, particularly from the settler point of view. By May 1908 its circulation had risen to one hundred and seventy-five copies. In October of the previous year Moore had run into trouble: it was so hot that the wax on the duplicating stencils melted on the typewriter. Nothing daunted, he ordered a printing press which was installed in August 1908."* (Phillipson, 1990)

## Falls on Film

One of the earliest known cinema films of the Falls, a silent information featurette called 'The Great Victoria Falls, Zambesi River,' was recorded by Emile Lauste during 1906 and shown in early movie cinemas in 1907. The film and Falls, which 'of fairyland-like beauty, captivated everyone,' was 'the topic of conversation in every town where it is shown' (Rice, 2008).

# To Be or Not to Be?

In May 1905 members of the Livingstone community, still dissatisfied with the location of the new town, petitioned the Administration that the Falls Hotel be demolished, arguing that all tourists should be accommodated and served from Livingstone, as had been intended when the railway and town had been originally planned. They also contended that the (then still unpainted) Bridge was a 'red monster' to reach which 'an ugly gash had been scoured across the countryside' (Rhodesia Railways Magazine, Aug 1955).

The Hotel, and indeed Percy Clark, had even been granted trading licenses to run general stores and curio shops on the south bank, causing further consternation, especially when others failed to obtain similar licenses.

The ongoing existence of the Hotel was a source of frustration for Major Coryndon, the Administrator of North-Western Rhodesia, who supported the concerns of Livingstone traders over the Hotel and did his best to have it removed, deploring the positioning of the buildings within sight of the Falls. By 1907, however, even he admitted defeat:

> "[Major Coryndon] *announced that he had failed in his endeavours to have... [the Hotel] abolished. It had originally been erected as temporary accommodation for engineers, etc. employed on the Bridge and Railway construction, and for visitors to the Falls, and was to be pulled down as soon as a new township was laid out; He could hold out no hope of this being done, however.*" (Livingstone Mail, Jan 1907)

### Livingstone on the Move?

Those who had invested in establishing the new town of Livingstone had high expectations of the development which would follow.

*"The prospect of the arrival of the railway provoked fantasies of economic growth, and global comparisons. It was confidently assumed that urban and industrial developments would be on the scale of Niagara City and Buffalo, which had grown up on the basis of power generated from the Niagara Falls... The South Africa Handbook of 1903 noted that thanks to the proximity of coal, minerals and water power, the site possessed 'all the factors for the creation of a great manufacturing centre. A new Chicago, let us call it Cecilton, will spring up near the banks of the Zambezi.' ... [In contrast] Niagara's precedent was invoked again in debates over conservation, this time offering a negative example. Lord Curzon was not alone in feeling that the Victoria Falls were more sublime than Niagara on the grounds of the 'lack of signs of civilization,' and it was widely believed that new industrial prosperity in Niagara had spoilt its aesthetic appeal."* (McGregor, 2009)

But industry, and tourism, was slow to reach Livingstone and residents in their dissatisfaction blamed the Chartered Company. Moore voiced his varied criticisms against the Company and its Administration through the pages of the Livingstone Mail, identifying the poor transport links between Livingstone and the Falls as a significant handicap to tourism.

*"Conductor Holland informs us that there were 101 passengers on board last Saturday's train de luxe. About a dozen of them managed to get as far as Livingstone. This is most unsatisfactory and it is to be hoped that some effort will be made... to provide transport facilities for our visitors."* (Livingstone Mail, April 1906).

By August 1906 rumours were in circulation concerning the ongoing campaign by the residents, led by Moore and the Livingstone Mail, to relocate Livingstone to a site closer to the Falls. It was believed that the Administration had requested £60,000 in order to move both the capital at Kalomo and the town of Livingstone to a new site in the vicinity of the Bridge Engineers Camp. A front-page headline from the Livingstone Mail in June 1907 claiming that the move had been approved turned out to be wishful thinking.

In August 1907 three of the Directors of the Board of the Chartered Company, Henry William Montague Paulet (the 16th Marquess of Winchester), Sir John Henry Birchenough (later to become President of the Company) and Mr Henry Wilson Fox, visited to review the proposals regarding the capital and address the concerns of the residents of Livingstone, who at that time numbered some 180 individuals. Sir Birchenough apparently felt that Livingstone should be relocated to the present site of the Victoria Falls town on the south bank. The other two representatives were initially in favour of a move to a new site on the north bank. In the end, however, they decided only to relocate the capital from Kalomo to Livingstone, and left to the residents to decide whether to stay in Livingstone or to move to the south bank, where the development of a small settlement was now officially accepted. Livingstone became the capital of North-Western Rhodesia in September 1907, bringing at least some life, and trade, to the struggling township. The town remained the capital after the formation of Northern Rhodesia in 1911 (following the amalgamation of the territories of North-Eastern and North-Western Rhodesia) up until 1935 when the administration was moved to Lusaka, the current capital.

Despite the commitment to develop a settlement on the south bank, several years elapsed with no signs of progress before it was announced in 1909 that the project had been abandoned for the foreseeable future.

*"The project for establishing a township at Victoria Falls has been temporarily abandoned, and it seems to us unlikely that it will be revived while the Company retains the administration."* (Livingstone Mail, Dec 1909)

## Development Dream?

The 1907 Christmas Issue of the Livingstone Mail contained an interesting fictional piece entitled 'A Peep into the Future' and imagining the Falls and Livingstone fifty years into the future. In the article Moore lets his imagination run wild with dreams of unrestrained economic growth and tourism development, with little appreciation or awareness of the need to conserve and protect the natural values of the Falls.

*"Livingstone covers an area of some 30 square miles [77.7 square km]; the banks of the river, both above and below the Falls are crowded with hotels and blocks of flats of various periods of construction and styles of architecture... On either side, for ten miles above the Falls, there are excellent terraced roads, the South side is almost covered with hotels, interspersed with palatial private residences...; the islands in mid-stream, of which there are a great numbers, have been converted to like uses, though some of the larger are utilised as pleasure grounds and are nightly crowded with holiday makers attracted thither by illuminations, music and entertainments. In the day time the river is almost covered, from bank to bank, with craft of every conceivable description, from the pre-historic rowing boat and motor launch to the more familiar surface-skimming aerostatic vessels... Bridges of fantastic pattern span the huge canon from Livingstone and Cataract Islands to the Rain Forest, and hydraulic lifts descend every few minutes through the rock to the edge of the boiling tumult of waters below."* (Livingstone Mail, Dec 1907)

## North-Western Puts Livingstone on the Map

With the relocation of the capital to Livingstone the Administration purchased the new town's most significant building, the North-Western Hotel (built by George Pauling in 1906) to become Government House. Within a few years a second, grander North-Western Hotel opened, built by 'Mopane' Clarke and managed by Fred Mills, also owner of the Livingstone Hotel (opened in 1906). In March 1909 the Livingstone Mail carried a front page advert for the new Hotel:

*"The North-Western Hotel (Proprietor F W Mills) will be opened on Thursday 1st April, Finest brands of liquors and cigars. Banquets and private dinners specially catered for. Special terms for month boarders. Livery & Bait Stables. Moderate charges. Carriages meet every train. Manager: Paul McUlenbergh, Late of Victoria Falls Hotel and Livingstone Club."* (Livingstone Mail, March 1909)

But transport around the growing settlement remained problematic.

*"Transport in and around the town remained difficult for some years, due to the deep unconsolidated sand. Mules were the only practicable draft animals as horse-sickness was very frequent. The North-Western Hotel's 'carriage' which 'met all trains' was in fact an old Zeederberg stage coach drawn by a team of mules."* (Phillipson, 1990)

## Livingstone Trolley System

*On the trolley line outside the North-Western*

In 1908 a local rail trolley system was introduced to Livingstone, running on a two-foot gauge track from the Railway Station down to the river and Livingstone Boat Club. Another line later ran to the North-Western Hotel.

*"Rickshaws were used for a short period, but were not*

*popular. Light trolleys consisting of two benches back to back and running on rails were installed in 1907-8 between the North-Western Hotel and the Boat Club. They had a hand brake but no motor, being pushed uphill by four Africans. They were popular among those passengers who were not involved in the occasional derailments."* (Phillipson, 1990)

Trains ran from Livingstone to the Falls twice a day, but only on three days of the week - highly inconvenient for visiting tourists restricted to only a few days to tour the area.

*"By 1907 there were, twice daily on three days of the week, return trains between Livingstone and the Falls. Road development was slow and expensive: in the dry season the roads were little more than a strip of deep soft sand. In 1907 a hard road was laid from the Railway Station to Government House and similar work was carried out on a small scale in most years thereafter, but it was ten years before a road was built linking Livingstone and the Falls."* (Phillipson, 1990)

## Clark's River Safaris

In 1908 Percy Clark imported nine Canadian canoes and a small motorised launch, establishing his own river safari operation on the south bank and providing a welcome excursion for guests at the Falls Hotel.

*"With these I started a boating business, and right from the start it was a good, money-making enterprise. All the bookings were made at the hotel... and I paid the hotel a percentage."* (Clark, 1936)

Clark operated from the site of Giese's Drift, seeing potential in pleasure trips on the river above the Falls. Giese himself had moved on to settle and farm in the Hwange district. Whilst several companies operated from Livingstone, being on the south side of the river would again have its advantages for Clark, who enjoyed a monopoly on bookings through the Hotel. In March 1911 Clark announced in the Livingstone Mail the arrival of a new, larger motorised launch, which he operated from the boathouse on the northern bank.

*"The new motor launch, Inyandiza, will leave the regatta boathouse every Sunday afternoon at 3 o'clock sharp, any weather, and return from the Falls at 5.30 pm on the return journey. 3s/6d single, 5/- return. P M Clark."* (Livingstone Mail, March 1911)

*Canoes and clients at the Landing Stage*

Clark promoted his river safaris in his guidebook on the Falls:

*"A whole day should be devoted to a trip up the magnificent Zambesi River. The trip may be made in Canadian canoes, paddled by expert Native boys, or in a modern, roomy and comfortable motor launch. The river trip is one of some seven miles [11 km] up the river, and above the Falls. Many picturesque islands are visited on the journey, the regatta course is negotiated, and ultimately Kandahar Island is reached, where a most enjoyable picnic can be held. After luncheon the return journey should be commenced, say at about 2.30 pm, and a break made upon one of the charming islands for tea. The return trip is perhaps the more pleasant, as one catches the gorgeous tints of the setting sun on the tree-topped islands with their wealth of palm trees and semi-tropical growths, and the multi-coloured tints of the spray from the Falls, as seen from behind."*

*"From the middle of June until the end of December is it possible to visit Livingstone Island (originally named by David Livingstone 'Garden Island'), the trip being made [from the north bank] by canoe. The tree on which he carved his initials is still to be seen, and visitors should be careful not to mutilate it in any way. The whole of the Rainbow Fall is usually visible, and the view of the Main Fall is unique."* (Clark, c1911)

### Landslide Washes Line Away

Originally the railway line ran round in front of the Falls Hotel, trains arriving at the Railway Station before turning on a special extension of track and then looping back round in front of the Hotel and passing on down to cross over the Bridge.

*The train arrives in front of the Hotel*

In late 1908 a torrential rainstorm, during which seven inches of rain fell in five hours, eroded the sandy soils in front of the Hotel and created a substantial landslide - resulting in a section of the line collapsing into the gorge. The line was re-laid in 1909 with trains passing straight through the station on a new section of track which then curved round to the Bridge, known as the 'balloon loop.'

### A Close Shave

The Livingstone Mail recorded one late-night visitor to the Falls had a lucky escape whilst waiting to witness the lunar rainbow:

*"A tourist went to view the Falls by moonlight, and, while waiting in a clearing near the Devil's Cataract for the moon to rise, he was suddenly charged by a hippopotamus. He was cut about the head with one of its tusks, but, except for a severe shaking, escaped otherwise unhurt. He climbed a tree and was ultimately rescued by a party from the hotel."* (Livingstone Mail, Dec 1908)

## Zambezi Sculling Championship

In January 1910 the Chartered Company announced that the World Professional Sculling Championship would be held on the Zambezi. In the build up to the event the New York Times reported:

*"A world's championship is to be fought out next Thursday in a spot which, within living memory, was an unexplored part of the Dark Continent. This will be the sculling championship of the world, and the scene of the contest will be the Zambesi River, close to the famous Victoria Falls discovered by Dr Livingstone, who, when he first saw them, committed, on his own confession, the only piece of vanity of which he was ever guilty. He cut his initials on a tree, and they remain to this day for the visitor to see. Since the railway to the Zambesi was completed in 1904 many thousands of visitors have been at the Falls, and next week's contest was arranged to take place there partly with the object of attracting world tourists' attention to their beauty and accessibility."*

The English sculling champion Ernest Barry, and challenger for the international title, had invited the holder, New Zealander Richard Arnst, to travel to England for the race, but he was unable to raise the funds for the trip. (Traditionally the challenger would travel to the title holder's home country at his own expense, but apparently Barry was also unwilling or unable to make the long journey.) The British South Africa Company saw an opportunity and offered to stage the race on the Zambezi, offering a £1,000 prize to the winner and covering the athletes travel expenses, believing the race would promote tourism to the region. Stakes and expenses were guaranteed by the Company and the race arranged over a three-and-a-half mile (5.6 km) course along the Zambezi River on 18th August 1910.

On arrival about two months before the race to acclimatise and train, Arnst pitched his camp near the boathouse on the Zambezi whilst Barry, who arrived later, stayed in the town, with all its distractions. Attending a dance one evening Barry unfortunately fell and sprained an ankle, resulting in a break from training for about two weeks whilst he recovered.

The race was highly competitive, with the heat and altitude affecting both men, but Arnst coped the better of the two men and crossed the line in front of Barry to retain his title. R H Christie, Secretary of the Hunyani Rowing Club in Southern Rhodesia, wrote in the early fifties;

*The finish line*

*" ...after the first three miles [4.8 km] both scullers were so overcome by the*

*unaccustomed heat and altitude that they stopped dead, unable to row another stroke. To Barry's despair, Arnst, who had a chest expansion of ten and a half inches, recovered his breath first, and paddled home the winner. Barry still regards that race as the hardest of his long career, during which he frequently won the world championship."* (Northern Rhodesia Journal, Jan 1953)

The two men would race again for the title in 1912 on the Thames, in a race which Barry won.

## *All Quiet on the River*

The author Agate and his travelling party arrived at the Falls just as preparations for the 1910 Regatta were getting into full swing. Spending a full day on the river they failed to see a single hippopotamus, *"the reason being - so our boatman told us - that it was the breeding season, at which time the hippos keep to the creeks and sludgy places, and seldom come out into the stream."*

*"We went aboard a very comfortable motor launch... [but] not without experiencing a few anxious moments, as after we had shoved off into the stream, the motor, after the habit of motors, refused to start until the fourth attempt, during which time he had begun to drift downstream towards that hideous drop... I don't suppose there was really any danger, still it was, under the circumstances, quite a pleasant sound to hear that motor begin to take an interest in things!"* (Agate, 1912)

In later years a boom was installed just below the landing stage, running across the river to a nearby island and preventing boats from potentially drifting downstream.

# The Weekender

From 1910 a weekly special passenger train service ran from Livingstone to Victoria Falls on Saturdays, known popularly as 'The Weekender' and transporting Livingstone socialites over the Bridge for Saturday night dances at the Falls Hotel. The train comprised a Nasmyth Wilson locomotive, hauling one composite first and second class coach. By 1910 the population of Livingstone was estimated to have grown to nearly 300.

*"The train was colloquially known as The Weekender and the Saturday night dances at the Falls Hotel brought good patronage from the young people, especially as the railway detached one or two carriages at Victoria Falls*

*The Weekender pauses on the Bridge*

*station into which in the small hours the tired dancers would retire for a few hours rest before the carriages were coupled up to the northbound train back to Livingstone. For a time in 1916 the steam train was replaced by the first Rhodesian railcar. This 'rail motor coach,' as it was officially described, was propelled by a 70 hp petrol engine; it was 24 ft [7.3 m] in length and seated twenty passengers with a little space at one end for light packages. Built by the Drewry Car Co in England it did not remain in service for a very long."* (Croxton, 1982)

## Act of God?

In 1910 an earthquake shook the region of the Falls, dislodging a shower of rock and stone into the gorges. The Bridge was structurally unharmed, but before sending the mail train across a pilot engine completed a test crossing.

*"On Saturday morning, May 28th, Livingstone was visited by an earthquake, which was felt over a stretch of sparsely inhabited country extending from Bulawayo to Broken Hill. The shock lasted about a minute and a half. Little damage was done, in fact the episode is remembered rather on account of the amusing incidents that occurred - several late risers being seen in the public streets in somewhat sketchy attire."* (Livingstone Mail, Dec 1910)

## Visit of Duke and Duchess of Connaught

Their Royal Highnesses the Duke and Duchess of Connaught, son and daughter-in-law of Queen Victoria, and their daughter Princess Patricia visited the Victoria Falls in November 1910, following the opening the new Union of South Africa

Parliament in Cape Town and subsequent tour of the Union. The Royal Party sailed from England on the S.S. Balmoral Castle and toured by special train, including stops at Bulawayo and Salisbury as well as the Falls and Livingstone. The Royal party did not stay at the Falls Hotel, instead crossing the Bridge and spending four nights based at Livingstone aboard their train.

*"A pilot train ran ahead of the royal train and an emergency train followed at an interval of 30 minutes, this being deemed necessary in case of breakdown between widely separated stations. A feature of the tour was the haulage of a bogie truck carrying four cows to supply fresh milk each day. These survived the three weeks' tour and must have achieved a record journey for cows. The royal party stayed four days at Livingstone, living in their train, which made short trips to the Falls for sightseeing from the bridge and elsewhere."* (Croxton, 1982)

## Rail Connections

Special connecting train services were the life-blood of early tourism to the Falls, bringing cruise liner passengers to ports from the Cape in the south to Beira on the east coast, often in groups of hundreds at a time. First class return trips from the Cape to the Falls took thirteen days, including three nights at the Falls Hotel. To gain a sense of perspective on the size of the Falls, travellers were informed that eleven Union Castle mail steamers placed end to end would just reach across their length.

One such visitor was Mrs Getcliffe, of Cheshire, England, who travelled on a special train service from Johannesburg to the Falls and wrote of her travels in the 'Macclesfield Courier & Herald' in 1910. The train carried 100 passengers, 20 staff, two dining cars, a food supply wagon and five tons of ice.

*An early Union Castle Line promotional poster*

*"There were three passengers in each compartment, the remaining berth being used for our luggage. The seats were very comfortable, being fitted with springs, and at night they were turned into beds with pillows, sheets, etc. Each compartment had a lavatory basin and a looking glass so that passengers could either dress in their compartments or, if they so preferred, in the bathrooms."*

Mrs Getcliffe and her companion stayed at the Falls Hotel and recorded they were *"not charmed with the accommodation or the service, but when we felt inclined to complain we reflected that all the food had to be brought from Cape Town or Beira, and that there are no shops nearer than Bulawayo, which is a 20 hours journey by rail."*

Mrs Getcliffe appears similarly unimpressed by having to pay Mr Soper a shilling for crossing the Bridge:

*"There is a railway bridge across the Zambesi guarded by a man in the employ of the railway company. He lives in a hut at one end of the bridge and allows foot passengers to cross on payment of one shilling. As no visitors come in the summer we asked him how he spent the time. He told us he went up country shooting game, large and small."* (Rhodesia Railways Magazine, March 1962)

A 1911 South African Railway pamphlet promoting the Falls described them as *"the most beautiful gem of the earth's scenery"* (Green, 1968).


# Clark's Guide to the Falls

Percy Clark soon published his own (sadly undated) guidebook to the Victoria Falls, the earliest (second) edition available to the author dating from soon after the 1910 visit of the Duke and Duchess of Connaught. Clark's guide, priced one shilling, offered local information, a selection of his own photographs and a guide to various walks available to the visitor over a suggested three day itinerary.

*"The Native name of 'Mosi-oa-Tunya' (which means 'The Smoke which Sounds') is most appropriate, for the huge column of spray has been distinctly seen at a distance of 28 miles [45 km] from the Falls; and the roar heard 16 miles [35 km] away."* (Clark, c1911)

Among the features of the Falls, Danger Point and the Boiling Pot are now both named. Clark himself named a local kopje after the Native Commissioner, Andrew Dale.

*"Andrew Dale's district was a large one, but very sparsely populated. The natives trusted him and came to him with their troubles. It was his custom to visit the Zambesi every second or third month; he did the journey on horseback, and habitually made his camp on a kopje only two miles* [3 km] *from the Victoria Falls. I have immortalized him by naming the kopje on which he used to camp 'Dale's Kopje'... Anyone who comes to see the Falls will find a visit to Dale's Kopje well worth while. It gives a really magnificent view of the Zambesi, with its beautiful stretches of lake-like water and its islands studded with palms."* (Clark, 1936)

Clark also uses the guide to promote his own specialist services and those of the Falls Hotel, knowing that he would also see the benefits to his businesses:

*"Amateur photographers can have their plates and films developed at the Falls. Every care is used in handling same. View albums, photographs, pictorial postcards, and enlargements of all kinds are kept in stock at the picturesque Huts opposite the Station. Visitors desiring to take longer time over the different trips than has been shown herein can easily do so by obtaining from the hotel, luncheon hampers for the day. Any enquiry at the hotel office will be answered if possible, and every assistance will be afforded to make the stay here as pleasant as possible."*

Clark refers to the near eradication of malaria and blackwater fever, and a rather ambitious scheme to introduce trout into the Zambezi above the Falls.

*The Falls from the Rainforest*

*"Large and ever-increasing numbers of visitors journey to the Falls during the wet season, the bogey of fever having almost effectually been dispelled, in fact it is a most rare occurrence for an visitor to suffer from fever, and with proper safeguards, such as one would take in any portion of the world, there is no danger of illness to be feared.*

*"In addition to the fishing in the Gorge, there is a good sport to be had in the upper reaches of the River, and it will not be long ere followers of Isaak Walton will have their fill of enjoyment, as trout spawn is being put into the river, and should provide in course of a short time most excellent sport."* (Clark, c1911)

The scheme did not account for the highly predatory Zambezi tigerfish, native to the river, and which would have made this a rather short-lived introduction attempt.

Prior the 1910s there was still very little development on the southern bank, the main focus of the small settlement being the Hotel, Railway Station and Percy Clark's Huts, all situated on a plot of land identified as the Railway Reserve. The Police Camp was located outside the Railway Reserve a short distance up the hill.

The limited water and electricity supply on the south bank may well have been significant in limiting its early expansion.

*"A factor which may have restricted development in the township... [however] was the lack of piped water and electricity. Buildings outside the Railway Reserve had been dependent upon water obtained from a pump near the railway station and transported in drums by donkey cart."* (Heath, 1977)

# Soper's Curios

In 1911 Jack Soper established Soper's Curios next to Clark's Huts, and set about giving Clark some healthy competition in the growing tourism souvenir trade.

Soper, together with another resident, is recorded as being the first to descend the face of the Falls down into the gorge. Soper described the first part of the descent, from Livingstone Island and made during the dry season with the aid of ropes, as precipitous, but the lower part as moderately easy climbing. Apparently it was not altogether a pleasure trip, and they are recorded as having no desire to repeat the attempt (Varian, 1953). Soper became an expert crocodile hunter, and was known amongst locals as the 'Crocodile King' for his skills and abilities in catching these dangerous predators.

*"His recreation was killing crocodiles, due to one of them taking his dog, and his favourite point of vantage was above the Silent Pool from which point he shot many hundreds of them... [He also] made crocodile traps which he placed in the Maramba River, again catching and killing many hundreds of these reptiles. There was, however, no demand for crocodile skins at that time so Mr Soper sometimes exported them live. His workshop, where he manufactured curios from local products, was something out of the Ark. Low-roofed, with no electricity, he had natives lying on their backs on tables pedalling cycle wheels to apply power for the lathes!"* (Rhodesia Railways Magazine, July 1958)

Realising the curious attraction of the tourist to these ancient reptiles, Soper established a small pool beside his shop were he kept one captive:

*"At one of the curio shops at the Victoria Falls, for a very small sum you will be able to see quite a large crocodile. When caught in the Zambezi in 1932, 'Sam' as he is called was 5 feet 6 inches [1.6 m] long. After 25 years in captivity he measured nearly 11 feet [3.3 m] and like all reptiles he will never cease to grow until the day of his death."* (Woods, 1960)

Soper's Curios traded for over 100 years, having changed hands after Soper's death in 1953 and relocating from its original site in 1975 to a new location behind the Post Office. The store closed its doors in May 2016, relocating to its current location within the adjoining Elephant's Walk Shopping and Artists Village complex.


# Falls Hotel Rebuilt

By 1912 plans were well advanced for the redevelopment of the Falls Hotel. Having secured the future of the Hotel on the site, the Railway Company now planned to expand and erect permanent brick buildings. Preliminary drawings were supplied by Sir Charles Metcalfe but the final designs, dated April 1912, were executed in Bulawayo by the Railway Company's chief architect Frank Scott.

The new buildings were constructed from 1914, with completion of the work postponed by several years due to the impacts of the First World War. The final furnishing and fitting further delayed the opening of the new Hotel until mid-1917, at an approximate construction cost of £40,000.

The cool and spacious single-storey building, consisting of a central wing and two flanking side wings, housed twenty-four bedrooms and two private suites. Two observation towers, either side of the main wing, gave panoramic views

*The new Victoria Falls Hotel*

over the gorges to the Bridge and rising spray of the Falls. Guests could relax in the Lounge, find time for quiet reflection in the Writing Room, or socialise in the Drawing and Music Rooms, Smoking Room or small private bar. A darkroom was provided for the use of amateur photographers. The spacious new Dining Room was designed with echoes of features from the original railway shed which had served as the Hotel's first dining room, an example being the high oval windows, also a feature of the Lounge. Another short wing housed the Hotel's kitchens. The Hotel laundry was steam operated from the customised boiler of a Kitson-Meyer railway engine, decommissioned in 1912 after service at Hwange Colliery, and which remained on site and operational for over eighty years.

Period photographs show the old hotel building situated alongside the new buildings, suggesting that the Hotel remained open and operating throughout the extended building period. It remained on site for several decades, serving to accommodate overflow during the busy season.

## Brick by Brick

*"The first permanent building outside the Railway Reserve was erected in 1914 when the police camp acquired a brick building which was used both as an office and for accommodation... In 1916 six acres were surveyed and set aside for the police camp and a rifle range. This was the first official government land to be surveyed and was located north of the proposed township and some distance west of the Railway Reserve, around the existing police camp buildings; an example of planning following rather than preceding development."* (Heath, 1977)

# On the River

The growth of Percy Clark's boating business on the river above the Falls had not gone unnoticed by the Falls Hotel. Recognising the potential profits if managed 'in-house' the General Manager of the Railway Company, Colonel Birney, eventually made Clark an offer for his boating business.

*"As I refused to sell, the hotel bought a launch for itself. This cooked my goose, for... all the bookings were made at the hotel office. I had about as much chance of carrying on in opposition as I would have of coughing effectually against thunder."* (Clark, 1936)

The Falls Hotel promptly purchased the launch boat 'Diana,' named after Colonel Birney's daughter, and carrying up to 30 passengers. Two huts and a boat shelter were developed at the launch site, with boat trips operating upstream to Kandahar Island, where passengers would alight for a picnic, and the canoes downstream to Cataract Island, on the very lip of the Falls. In 1928 the Hotel invested in a second launch, the 'Daphne,' and soon after a third, the 'Dorothy.' The Hotel's boat and canoe service was managed by Mr Victor Pare, who appears to have had more than the occasional close encounter on the river.

*"Soon after World War I, the Victoria Falls Hotel launch set out full of visitors and a vindictive hippo appeared. It made an unprovoked rush for the boat, tore a piece from the stern, dived underneath and holed the boat amidships. Mr Pare was injured but the boat reached the river bank without sinking."* (Green, 1968)

*The Landing Stage*

# War and Peace

During the period of the First World War (1914-8) the Falls Bridge was a strategically important transport link for the movement of British South African and Rhodesian troops - and a potential target for German saboteurs, with German South West Africa (now Namibia) only 80 kilometres away. To prevent attack the Bridge was defended with a military guard, observation blockhouses and a rail mounted searchlight.

After the war the fashion slowly returned for luxury cruise liner trips to distant destinations. Union Castle reintroduced the 'Round Africa' cruise service in October 1919 and during the early 1920s visitors to the Victoria Falls numbered around three thousand per year.

Many of the Union Castle line's vessels had been requisitioned by the British government for national service as troop or hospital ships during the War, and eight were sunk by mines or German U-boats. During the late 1920s and early '30s Union Castle dominated the route with a new generation of 20,000-ton steam liners, including the Carnarvon Castle, Winchester Castle and Warwick Castle, sailing weekly from Southampton to the Cape in only 14 days.

In August 1923 a cenotaph was erected on the northern bank close to the Eastern Cataract, honouring the names of the men from Northern Rhodesia who lost their lives to the War. It was unveiled by His Royal Highness Prince Arthur of Connaught, grandson of Queen Victoria and Governor-General of the Union of South Africa (1920-4).

*The Carnarvon Castle*

# Paradise Tamed?

Following her first visit to the Falls shortly before the arrival of the railway, Catherine Mackintosh returned to the Zambezi in 1920. Travelling to the Cape on the Union Castle Line S.S. Saxon, she recorded of her journey:

*"There were only two drawbacks, the excessive overcrowding of the decks, especially with children, who, poor little things, had not nearly enough space to play about; and the fact that I knew no one on board. However, one makes acquaintance somehow, and it is surprising how in chance talk some illuminating word may light up a wholly new point of view."*

After travelling by train to Bulawayo and then on to the Falls, Mackintosh compared the journey to her previous trek in 1903 and contrasted the many changes at the Falls since her earlier visit.

*"We reached Victoria Falls station, near the hotel, on the south side of the Zambesi gorges, at 8.15 am on Friday, June 11, having left Bulawayo at 1pm the day before. In 1903, our light spring cart (not a waggon) took us from before dawn on August 24, Monday, till mid-day on the following Saturday. Now there is a little station at the Falls, and the hotel is seen through the forest, as if standing in its own park. My companions alighted here, as did most of the passengers... After a long halt, the train started again and we were summoned to breakfast (and glad of it!). Another halt; the train whistled to warn foot-passengers and waited for them to clear off the bridge, and then we*

*By the river*

*found ourselves crossing it, lashed by the spray from the Falls, at that moment thundering down in fullest flow."*

On exploring the Falls Mackintosh noted:

*"All is now tidied up, paths constructed and marked with white stones, rustic seats pavilioned with thatch placed at the right view-points. One can't say that, in this respect, the change is for the better; one feels no more the thrill of the wilderness, but... the custodians jealously guard the natural beauties, and certainly all these changes make for the greatest happiness of a greater number, including the fairly numerous tourists who had come up in our train and were already (some of them) walking about with cameras. No shooting is allowed for five miles [8 km] round, so that baboons and hippos disport themselves audaciously and sometimes alarmingly. The very next week the latter attacked a boat full of tourists and bit a piece out of it!"* (Mackintosh, 1922)

## Trolley Transport

Always on the lookout for a new business opportunity, Percy Clark claims to have been the first to see the potential of a local rail transport system, along the lines of that already established in Livingstone, to take tourists from the Hotel to the river:

*"I now got another idea of making money, and I took a trip home on the strength of it. My notion was to run a trolley-line down to the bridge and the landing-stage. I was very kindly received by the BSAC office in London, ...but after exhibiting details of my scheme I was told that the whole thing was in the province of the railway company... Then years went by, however, before the trolley-line came into being. I have always believed that I got the idea first, and believing that I think I ought to have shared the profit."* (Clark, 1936)

The local rail trolley system was finally developed by the Railway Company in 1920, at a cost of £4,000, with the operation of the service managed by the Hotel.

*"The trolley system had three sections, not physically connected. From the hotel, a double track ran one mile northward to 'Trolley Junction,' where passengers changed to two single track lines leading to the various points of interest. One line (the longest) ran eastward beside the Rain Forest to the Victoria Falls Bridge, and was later paralleled by a road; the other ran northward to the Landing Stage and Boat House...*

*"From the terminus of this line, three-quarters of a mile upstream from the Falls, tourists could join launch or canoe trips to the islands in the river. Photographs show two types of vehicle, a four-seat trolley with cross seats pushed by two Africans, and a knifeboard*

*Trolley tours*

*eight-seat trolley pushed by three or four. Each trolley had a roof and canvas awning, and a screw handbrake applied from either end."* (Price, 1966)

Telephone boxes were installed at each terminus and junction so that a trolley could be summoned when required. The fare was one shilling each way. The trolleys were available during the hours of daylight only, although special arrangements could also be made with the Hotel Manager each month on the full-moon for night-time trips to see the lunar rainbow.

## *End of the Charter*

In the early 1920s the BSAC and British Government began negotiations over the future of the Rhodesias following the end of the period of the Company's Royal Charter. Many expected that Southern Rhodesia would become part of the Union of South Africa, and detailed proposals were drawn up in Johannesburg (even including the drafting of postage stamps showing the Victoria Falls). A referendum was held in Southern Rhodesia on 27th October 1922, giving a choice of establishing responsible government or joining the Union. With 59 percent voting in favour Southern Rhodesia was granted self-governing status on 1st October 1923. Northern Rhodesia became a British Protectorate in on 1st October 1924, setting the two countries on very different paths to eventual independence.

# From Far and Wide

In 1925 American South African Lines (renamed Farrell Lines in 1948), initiated a regular transatlantic cruise service from New York to South Africa stopping at Cape Town, Port Elizabeth and Durban. A growing North American market developed with the launch of round-the-world cruises, such as the 96-day 'Great African Cruise' undertaken from New York in 1926, including stops in South America, South Africa and Europe.

*"Efforts were being made to foster the tourist trade and in 1926, in conjunction with the SAR* [South African Railways]*, two special trains carrying 350 American tourists from a world-cruise liner included visits to Bulawayo and Victoria Falls, the parties staying at the Falls Hotel for a couple of nights. The success of this tour, to be the forerunner of many more, led to the enlarging of the hotel. Another fifty bedrooms were built, with bathrooms and other facilities, along with modern station offices in a style to harmonise with the hotel."* (Croxton, 1982)

Between 1926 and 1939 more than thirty North American cruise liners were met by fifty luxury special train services, transporting some 5,000 wealthy tourists from ports into southern Africa, with the Victoria Falls on nearly everybody's schedule (Pirie, 2011). Victor Pare, manager of the Falls Hotel's tourism services, described the reactions of transatlantic voyagers, often drawing comparisons with Niagara Falls.

*"Tourists from the United States, when asked what they thought of the Victoria Falls, have time and again declared that they found them beyond all description. Some said they were the most transcendently beautiful natural phenomenon on this earth. Another said: 'They sure make Niagara look like a trickle of sweat.' One prominent American cabled to Buffalo: 'Scrap Niagara. It's out of date.'"* (Pare, 1926)

*The Zambezi Express arrives at Bulawayo Station*

# Visit of The Prince of Wales

In June 1925, His Royal Highness The Prince of Wales (who in 1936 would become King Edward VIII, before abdicating in less than a year), visited the Victoria Falls and stayed overnight in Livingstone during his extensive tour of southern Africa.

The South African Railways provided two special trains, one of which was specially built for the tour and comprised several luxurious saloons for the Prince and his party. The Royal Train was painted white with gold lining and lettering and became known as the White Train. A guiding pilot train was again used throughout the tour (Clark, 1952).

The Prince toured the Falls for several hours guided by Sir Herbert Stanley, Governor of Northern Rhodesia, and was then taken upriver by motor-launch for lunch on Kalai Island. Victor Pare recalled:

*The Prince of Wales views the Falls*

*"His Royal Highness the Prince of Wales, when asked what he thought of our Rhodesian wonder, replied with a twinkle in his eye, 'Damned wet.' But I knew how it had impressed him. I had watched his eyes. He had seen most things worth seeing in the world and, perhaps for the first time, he was wonderstruck."* (Para, 1926)

In the evening an African themed open-air dinner was held at the Livingstone Golf Club (opened in 1909) in his honour.

*"[The] band of the native Northern Rhodesia Police, commanded by a band-master who was formerly of the first cornet of the Irish Guards, was conspicuous at the ceremony."* (Ward Price, 1926)

*The Prince of Wales on the river*

One source recorded that the Prince enjoyed his evening so much he called for the clocks be put back an hour to allow it to continue!

*"The Prince left the dance towards midnight and drive down the long straight road that leads to the Victoria Falls. A great honey-coloured half-moon was hanging low among the stars, and as the Prince's car stopped by the edge of the eastern falls, a lunar halo could be seen, wan and pale, on the curtain of spray that hangs as a permanent pillar of cloud over the thundering abyss. It looked like the ghost of a lost rainbow haunting the gloomy chasm."* (Ward Price, 1926)

## Road Routes

During the period 1925 to 1928 the route to the Falls was upgraded with a compacted dirt road constructed between Bulawayo and Victoria Falls, providing access to the area for the growing number of regional travellers journeying by motor-car.

*"Only a limited amount of growth occurred in the decade between 1920 and 1930. Further additions were made to the Police Camp in 1921 and to the existing hotel buildings. Within the Railway Reserve, additional housing, government buildings and an African location were constructed west of the railway line and, towards the end of this period, a garage was built by the Railways in the north east portion of the Reserve... a curator's cottage was constructed* [in 1926] *between the Railway Reserve and the Police Camp. At the same time, land was set aside for an African village to the west of the surveyed township."* (Heath, 1977)

# Bathing Costumes and Mackintoshes

*Bathers at the Falls*

With the 1930s defined by the Great Depression, the longest and most severe worldwide economic depression of the twentieth century, global tourism growth slowed significantly. Regional travel to the Falls was encouraged by the Railway Company with the offer of inclusive travel and accommodation fares, with passengers staying at the Hotel. Special fares were not available for the public holiday periods when the Hotel often had a long waiting list. A 1930s Southern Rhodesian government guide to the Victoria Falls contained the following advice for visitors to the Falls:

*"Visitors are advised to provide themselves with mackintoshes and galoshes (boots) when traversing the Rain Forest, or when exposed to the spray-clouds. Oilskins and sou'-westers can be hired from the hotel... When spray from the Falls is heavy, visitors will find it an advantage to wear a bathing costume only underneath the mackintosh."* (Martin, 1997)

Clothing advice for tourists recommended sunshades for the ladies and wide-brimmed felt hats for gentlemen. Swimming, golf, tennis, and fishing were all listed as available leisure and sports activities. The pioneering travel agent Thomas Cook promoted the Falls in 1930 as a fashionable destination:

*"There is a splendid and comfortable hotel at the Falls and during the season the fashionable throngs in the grounds and on the verandas are more reminiscent of a European spa than of a retreat in the interior of Africa."* (McGregor, 2009)

*The Hotel Courtyard*

The Falls Hotel was significantly expanded during the late 1920s and early 1930s, with the addition of the 'hammerheads,' courtyard and western wings, which even included a small chapel.

## Bridge Reconstruction

In 1929 urgently required alterations were carried out to the Falls Bridge, involving the complete removal and replacement of the top deck, which was raised and widened to include a roadway and sidewalks alongside one line of rails (instead of the previous two). The increasing popularity of motorcar travel was not the only reason for the upgrades, the structure needing reinforcing to address short-comings in the original design, and works included measures to strengthen the main arches and cross-bracing of the Bridge to cope with increasing loads. The works took several years to complete, with the road finally opening in 1931.

# Visit of Prince George

In 1934 His Royal Highness Prince George the Duke of Kent visited the Falls, arriving by overnight train from Bulawayo and staying at the Falls Hotel. The Prince spent the Easter weekend exploring the Falls.

*"[T]he Falls presented an inspiring sight when the Prince, changing into a vest and shorts soon after his arrival, hurried from the hotel to have a first look at them. The Zambesi was coming down in flood, and enormous quantities of*

*water were hurtling over the falls, estimated to amount to one hundred million gallons [455 million litres] every minute. During the weekend the river steadily rose as the result of rain in the heart of Africa, and when the Prince left the Falls two days later, it had reached a new record high level. Because of the vast volume of water pouring into the chasm the spray was very dense, and somewhat obscured the view but the Prince spent so much time around the Falls that he saw every possible aspect of them. Declining to use a waterproof coat, His Royal Highness thoroughly explored the wonders of the Rain Forest, in which he wandered about opposite the Main cataract until he was drenched to the skin. The Prince spent many hours energetically visiting every vantage point, despite the uncomfortable heat. He was particularly impressed by the lunar rainbow...*

*"The Prince did a lot of walking in the countryside around the hotel, the whole area being a game reserve and abounding with animals and birds. But the Prince unfortunately did not see any crocodiles, which thrive on the Zambesi River. The flood waters had driven the reptiles way."* (Frew, 1934)

*The Prince at the Falls*

# Livingstone Statue

The famous bronze statue of David Livingstone, sculpted by Scottish artist William Reid-Dick, RA (later Sir), was unveiled overlooking the western view on the south bank of the Victoria Falls on 5th August 1934 by Mr Howard Unwin Moffat, CMG, ex-Prime Minister of Southern Rhodesia (1927-33), and nephew of David Livingstone's wife, Mary Moffat. The bronze statue, ten-and-a-half feet (3.2 m) high stands on a 37-ton rough hewn solid granite base, at the time claimed to be the largest block of stone quarried in Africa. News reports of the unveiling of the statue recorded Livingstone's initials were apparently still faintly visible on the tree he had originally carved them into in 1855, although by now some doubts were being expressed as to the authenticity of marks and identification of the tree.

## Rhodes-Livingstone Museum

The town of Livingstone added a significant tourism attraction with the development of the David Livingstone Memorial Museum, opened in 1934. The museum was originally envisaged to preserve the material culture of local ethnic groups but was expanded to include the life of Dr David Livingstone. In 1939, following the addition of collections on Cecil Rhodes, the museum was renamed the Rhodes-Livingstone Museum (and is now known as the Livingstone Museum).

## Protection and Preservation

The Victoria Falls Executive Committee was established on the north bank in 1934 under the Victoria Falls Reserve Preservation Ordinance, with the primary objective to foster tourism. Developments in 1935 included the first chalets at the North Bank Rest Camp and establishment of the Game Park, later to become the Mosi-oa-Tunya National Park.

On the south bank the Victoria Falls Reserve Preservation Act (1928) had been drawn up establishing the Victoria Falls Reserve, a zone extending upstream and downstream of the Falls. In 1931 the Victoria Falls Game Reserve was established under the Game and Fish Preservation Act (1929), later to become the Zambezi National Park.

*"In 1931 the Victoria Falls was declared a 'protected area' and the use of the environs of the Falls became more strictly controlled... In 1932... the piped water supply was extended to the Police Camp and to the remainder of the village in the following year."*

*"To the north of the curator's cottage... five stands had been occupied by Messrs. Spencer, Gibson and Lloyd, and further north, by a Mr. J. Picken. It was decided to accept the status quo and to re-plan the township incorporating these five stands, the curator's cottage and the police camp... Little major development took place between 1930 to 1939."* (Heath, 1977)

The Victoria Falls Special Area, a zone extending upstream and downstream of the Falls, was proclaimed a National Monument by Government Notice 318 on the 14th May 1937, under the Southern Rhodesia Monuments and Relics Act (1936). Government Notice 317 approved the bylaws which were to be enforced within the protected area, which now fell under the control of the Commission for the Preservation of Natural and Historical Monuments and Relics.

# Flight of Angels

*The Victoria Falls Bridge from the air*

In the late 1920s aviation advances gave visitors a new and breath-taking way to experience the Falls - from the above. The short-lived Rhodesian Aviation Company was established with the aim of tapping the tourism potential of the Falls, with their first aircraft, an Avro Avian, operating commercial 'flips' over the Victoria Falls from June 1929 (McAdams, 1969). A 15 minute flight over the Falls cost £1. Henry Balfour, on the last of his visits to the Falls in 1929 recorded:

> *"Great changes since 1910. A large and very fine stone hotel has replaced the wood and tin shanties which used to serve as* [the] *hotel. Many new houses have been built... I went down to the Aerodrome and... went up with Major Smith in an Avro-Avian plane. Flew over the Falls, down to beyond the Masui River and up as far as Kandahar Island. Wonderfully interesting. We flew at about 1,500 ft.* [457.2 m] *Made a very good take-off and landing."* (Balfour, 1929)

## Spencer's Airways

Edward Herbert ('Ted') Spencer was initially posted to the Falls in 1923 after joining the British South Africa Police. He soon saw the potential of a motor garage and car hire business, establishing Spencer's Garage and Service Station, strategically located on the corner of the Falls Hotel's access road, to service the growing numbers of visitors arriving by motor vehicle.

*Puss Moth VP-YBC above the Falls*

In July 1935 Spencer purchased a second-hand de Havilland Puss Moth aircraft, ZS-ACB (re-registered as VP-YBC), and employed the services of a recently qualified young pilot Jack McAdam, to offer game viewing and charter flights. Operating under the name of Spencer's Garage and Air Service (later simply Spencer's Airways) flights were serviced from the Victoria Falls Aerodrome, which Spencer himself cleared out of the bush. In early 1936 Spencer acquired a DH83 Fox Moth biplane (VP-YBD), in which he trained and soon also qualified as a pilot. Spencer is recorded practising aerobatics and amazing his ground-bound African spectators - so much so that 'Spensaar!' became a locally adopted exclamation of amazement (Whitehead, 2014).

Details from McAdam's log books, flight notes and diary were posthumously collected and published in 1982 as 'On Wings of Fabric,' reproduced in Stirling and House (2014).

*"These game-viewing flights, of about two hours' duration, were a popular attraction. Leaving the Victoria Falls, the route generally followed the Zambezi to Kazungula where the boundaries of four territories meet at a single point and a 360° turn would carry the aircraft in rapid succession over South West Africa [Namibia]... and the countries then known as Bechuanaland [Botswana], Southern Rhodesia [Zimbabwe] and Northern Rhodesia [Zambia]. Then, flying in a westerly direction, roughly parallel to the Chobe River, the aircraft flew across the eastern extremity of the Caprivi Strip where a variety of wild animals, particularly lechwe, could usually be seen. Then, turning south and crossing the Chobe River near Kasane, the route continued to Kazuma Pan and thence back to the Falls. (Sometimes, by way of variety, the reverse direction would be flown.) So plentiful was the wildlife that Ted Spencer would offer prospective customers a guarantee: 'No game - no pay.' Never, to the author's knowledge, was a refund claimed."* (Stirling and House, 2014)

McAdam records many interesting aviation adventures and incidents during his time flying for Spencer's Airways. Not all flights were pleasure trips, with McAdam assisting in the unsuccessful search for a missing American visitor in September 1935:

*"The body of Mrs Mary McKee, a 70 year old American visitor, was found two days later under a tree with dense foliage (which probably explained the failure of the air search). She had evidently wandered off into the scrub, lost her way, and died of exposure, not more than half a mile from the boathouse on the south bank of the Zambezi."*

McAdam also recalls flying many distinguished guests from the Falls Hotel, including Lady Baden-Powell in April 1936 (a regular visitor) and members of the Siamese (Thai) Royal Family in December the same year. Flights were not without the occasional problem, McAdam recalling an incident in October 1936 which nearly caused him to make an emergency landing on an island above the Falls:

*"Having dropped some passengers at Livingstone after a game trip, was half-way between the two landing grounds when, over the Zambezi, the engine slowed down and clouds of smoke poured out. Seriously considered attempting a landing on Long Island, but carried on and just made it into the Falls airfield. Upon inspection it was discovered that two of the four pistons in the engine had seized up in their cylinders due to defective lubrication caused, in turn, by a loose oil pipe connection between oil tank and pump."* (Stirling and House, 2014)

On another occasion in early 1937 McAdam recalled the propeller came off the single-engined Fox Moth mid-flight over the Falls and a hasty forced landing was made in the bush, incredibly without serious damage!

Spencer became something of a local legend in the Falls, and it is popularly believed that he was the first to fly a plane under the Victoria Falls Bridge, although McAdam is on record as discounting this story. There is, however, a photograph of him flying incredibly low over the Devil's Cataract.

*Spencer over the Devil's Cataract*

*"It is a part of old Falls legend that he was the first person to fly under the Victoria Falls Bridge early one morning in July 1938. However, there are some who say that* [Noel] *McGill, a bush pilot from Livingstone, was the first man to do it."* (Meadows, 2000)

# Power from the Falls

The BSAC had originally sold the contract to develop the hydro-electric potential of the Zambezi in the vicinity of the Victoria Falls in 1901 as a key part of the initial development of the region, but the project was not finally realised until the late 1930s. Surveys of the gorges for the project had been undertaken by the Bridge engineers Varian and Everard at the time of the construction of the Bridge.

Located in the bend of the third and forth gorges, known as the Silent Pool, construction of the plant was begun in June 1936 by the Victoria Falls and Transvaal Power Company. The power station was opened on 16th March 1938 by Sir Hubert Young, then Governor of Northern Rhodesia. The immediate scope of the scheme was to supply electricity to the neighbouring town of Livingstone, with power transmitted by underground cable, as well as serving the Falls Hotel and Railway Reserve on the south bank.

*View down to the Power Station*

*"At the request of the Government great care was taken to avoid spoiling the beauty of the Falls. The water inlet is some distance above the Falls and an* underground pipe-line leads to the top of a gorge some distance below them. An overhead power cable was necessary in one place [to cross the gorge and serve the Hotel], *but it was put as far from the Falls as possible and it will not be seen by tourists. Even in the dry season the quantity of water taken by the Power Station is negligible in comparison with the total flow over the Falls."* (Parsons, 1938)

In 1949 the then Northern Rhodesian Government acquired all interests in the Power Company for the sum of £104,000. The original capacity of 8 Megawatts (MW) was expanded in 1969 with the addition of six generators of 10 MW each (installed underground) and again in 1972 with an additional four units, increasing the total maximum capacity to 108 MW. The expansions and subsequent plant developments have significantly increased the infrastructure impacts both above and below the Falls, as well as increasing the volume of water diverted from the Eastern Cataract of the Falls.

## *World's Fair New York*

The World's Fair was held in 1939 with hopes of lifting New York City and the United States out of the continuing economic depression. Four years went into planning, building and promoting the Fair, which attracted over 44 million people over two years. The Southern Rhodesia exhibit included a 186 feet (56.7 m) by 22 feet (6.7 m) working replica diorama of the Victoria Falls, one of the feature attractions of the exhibition. The Southern Rhodesia Government Department of Publicity enthusiastically promoted tourism to Rhodesia and the Falls, 'the open air paradise of the world' and 'unspoilt playground of Africa.' In an increasingly competitive relationship, a 1941 publicity leaflet for the Livingstone Publicity and Travel Bureau positioned Livingstone as 'the Tourist Centre for the Victoria Falls' (Arrington, 2009).

# The Price of Paradise

The development of the Falls as a global tourism resort resulted in a steady process of eviction and exclusion of Africans from the immediate region of the Falls and the river, as evidenced on the southern bank during the establishment of the Victoria Falls Game Reserve.

*"The process of physical exclusion was most dramatic and most total on the south bank, from which the Leya population was completely removed between 1900 and 1940... The Leya on the south bank had initially been encouraged to move across the river to the north bank on their own accord, as taxes were more onerous and were implemented earlier south of the river. Evictions gathered pace in the 1920s and the last vestiges of Leya settlement on the south bank were totally cleared in the 1930s, when the Administration ordered them to 'return home' to the north bank, from which officials held they originated... Those who tried to resist were forced out by threats and the burning of their homes..."*

*"The former Leya inhabitants are still remembered in place names in the Victoria Falls National Park. Jafuta, for example, was an important Leya man who lived in what became the Park, and his name still appears on signposts to the luxury 'Jafuta Lodge.' He farmed a fertile vlei just south of the Falls at Chamawondo and owned a canoe and a sizeable herd of cattle. The village he headed was split by the evictions, some members went to Zambia as the state instructed, others moved onto the infertile lands of the increasingly crowded Hwange native reserve to the east and south of the Falls."* (McGregor, 2003)

Mubitana (1990) also records Leya presence on both sides of the river into the early 1930s, confirmed in a report by J Moffat Thomson, Secretary of Native Affairs in Northern Rhodesia. McGregor reflects in contemporary interviews:

*"Old people claim there were several rounds of evictions starting in the 1920s and continuing in the 1930s and 1940s. This seems plausible, although the archival record is scant, even at the height of the evictions in the 1930s. In 1935 the Native Commissioner Wankie noted: 'Most of the natives who resided in the Victoria Falls Game Reserve were removed in July to Northern Rhodesia'; in 1936 removing people 'from whence they came' is reported as almost completed; in 1937, a further 41 people were sent back to Northern Rhodesia..."*

*"Africans remaining in the vicinity of the Falls on the south bank in the wake of the 1930s evictions - most of whom were working at the resort itself and who included many Leya and Lozi - were 'removed to a central village away from the river' in 1940...*

*On the north bank, land alienation was also severe, and evictions also proceeded apace as Livingstone town grew, and as farms were pegged out along the river frontage and the line of rail, and as other prime sites for tourist development were reserved as crown land. Mukuni and Sekute's people were forced into the Leya and Toka reserves respectively, along with others, where soils were poor and where they lacked access to the river for gardens, fishing and grazing cattle. The justification for these restrictions was that African settlement and land use spoilt the view and undermined the area's tourist potential."* (McGregor, 2003)

## *Side by Side*

During the 1930s the Southern Rhodesian Government started laying down 'strip roads,' the early beginnings of a national road network. These consisted of two parallel strips of concrete or asphalt each about 60 centimetres wide and 80 centimetres apart, and allowing single file motor-vehicle traffic to run unhindered in one direction. When another, then occasional, car approached from the opposite direction, each pulled over to its respective side of the road, to the left, running the inside wheels on one side of the strip road and risking the others on the wide dirt margins that ran alongside either side of the road. The strip road from Bulawayo to the Victoria Falls was completed in 1941. Parts of the original strip road can still today be seen alongside the present-day highway from Hwange to the Falls in several sections where the modern road has diverted from its old route for a more direct pathway.

# Wings of War

During the Second World War (1939-45) the Falls Hotel played host to many Allied soldiers and airmen receiving their basic training in the country. Bulawayo was a major centre for the Royal Airforce Training Group with several Flying Training Schools for trainee airmen from across the British Commonwealth. An estimated 8,500 British Royal Air Force (RAF) crew were trained in Southern Rhodesia over the period of the war, and training continued into the post-war period. The Falls was one of several official recreational leave locations, and the Hotel offered special half-rates to RAF recruits.

*Viewed from above*

Towards the end of the war Spencer's Airways were operating a fleet of four different aircraft - the Avro Anson, de Havilland Fox Moth and a Tiger Moth to provide short pleasure trips over the Falls, and a larger Fairchild UC.61A for longer-distance safari flights. Ted Spencer died in a tragic accident at Croydon Airport, London, in early 1947. An advert in Flight Magazine records Spencer offering free passage from London for 16 married service men looking to emigrate to Rhodesia (Flight Magazine, Jan 1947). Spencer was piloting the newly purchased Dakota plane which stalled and crashed soon after take-off from London on the 25th January with 18 passengers, eleven of who also sadly died (Flight Magazine, July 1947).

Ted Spencer's nephew, Terrance, took over the family business.

*"His nephew, Terry, [who] took over the mantle of chief aviator for Spencer's Airways, had beat the odds flying a Lancaster through most of World War Two. His luck ran out almost two years after his uncle's. On 20 October 1948, whilst on a game flight, his plane caught fire somewhere over the Katambora Rapids. Turning for home on a burning wing and a prayer, Terry Spencer coaxed the Fairchild back towards Victoria Falls. Never made it. Crashed amongst the horizon-to-horizon teak forests... on the remote Westwood Farm. It was a long time, six weeks to the day, from the wristwatches of the crash victims, before the wreckage was found."* (Meadows, 2000)

# Royal Visit

In 1947 the British Royal Tour of the Union of South Africa included the Victoria Falls, with Their Majesties King George VI, Queen Elizabeth, and their two daughters, Their Royal Highnesses the Princess Elizabeth (now the reigning monarch, Her Majesty Queen Elizabeth II) and Princess Margaret, all staying at the Falls Hotel, which was reserved entirely for their use.

It was the first overseas state visit since 1939 and was celebrated with much pomp and fanfare. The young Princess Elizabeth also celebrated her 21st birthday during the tour. South African Railways provided a newly built Royal Train, the Garratt locomotives of which were painted deep royal blue and which were used throughout the tour of Rhodesia.

Staying at the Victoria Falls Hotel over the Easter weekend, the Royal party celebrated divine service in the Hotel chapel. The visit was a welcome break following many public engagements during the tour, and repeated visits were made to the Falls.

*The Royal Party view the Falls*

*"The Royal Family visited the Falls on two separate days. They saw them under the sun and under the moon, from the level of the upper river, and from that of the gorge. They walked through the so-called 'Rain Forest' opposite the Main Falls, where the spray forms a perpetual cloud, and where the King remarked that for the first time in his life he had been soaked even through his hat."* (Morrah, 1947)

Their Majesties' suite was on the first floor of the south wing 'hammerhead,' which for many years after was known as the Queen's Suite, and the Princesses suite located on the ground floor of the same wing.

On 11th April 1947, the day dubbed by the Livingstone Mail as the 'most important day in the history of the town,' the Royal Party visited Livingstone, for the afternoon at least, crossing the river in the Hotel's launch, Daphne. Flying the Royal Standard, the party sailed up to the Zambezi Boat Club on the northern bank, escorted upstream by the state barge of Barotseland Paramount Chief, Litunga Imwiko. The road from the river was resurfaced and re-named the Royal Mile in honour of the occasion.

*The Royal Party on the Hotel's launch, the 'Daphne'*

*"From the point of view of watchers on the northern bank, where Sir John Waddington, the Governor of Northern Rhodesia, was waiting, the launch flying the Royal Banner came into view round the eastern end of the largest of the many islands, called Long Island, and simultaneously, from the mouth of the tributary Maramba, appeared the state barge of Imwiko, Paramount Chief of the Barotse, the largest group of tribes in Northern Rhodesia."* (Morrah, 1947)

Several islands and special locations were named after the Royal visit:

*"His late Majesty, King George VI expressed a desire to have some of the islands in the Zambesi named after his family; Long Island [also known as Siloka or Loando Island] was renamed King George VI Island, Kalai Island became Queen Elizabeth Island, Siachikola Island became Princess Elizabeth Island... His Majesty also renamed Dale's Kopje, Queen Elizabeth Kopje."* (Clark, 1952)

Another island was also named after Princess Margaret. The Hotel's landing stage was renamed in honour of the visit, becoming known as the King's Landing Stage and Boat House. Her Royal Highness Princess Marie Louise, daughter of Princess Helena and grand-daughter to Queen Victoria, visited Livingstone and the Falls in 1955, also having an island named after her.

## *Contrasting Perspectives*

In 1947 the Northern Rhodesia Government invited the South African Tourist Corporation (SATC) to assess the country's tourism potential with the aim to develop the country as a prime tourism destination. The report highlighted the poor state of existing tourism infrastructure, urging improvements to Livingstone's roads, railway station and hotels (Moonga 1999).

Shortage of suitable standard hotel accommodation caused acute problems during the Royal Visit in 1947, and the Livingstone Mail of 24th January 1948 highlighted the poor state of the town's road network. In July the paper printed the contrasting experiences of one visiting tourist:

*"I was much struck by the difference between the gateway approaching to the Victoria Falls from Southern Rhodesia and that of Northern Rhodesia's neglect. On the Southern Rhodesia side the Victoria Falls station was clean... no wonder tourists hurried down the path to the nearby hotel... Livingstone station offers no such thrill... sordid is the word (which) best fits the entrance to Livingstone by railway... a shabby and miskept station."* (Livingstone Mail, July 1948)

In the year of the Royal visit, 1947, Southern Rhodesia recorded over 38,000 tourist arrivals. By contrast, Northern Rhodesia received less than half this number, recording 15,000 visitor arrivals.

In 1948 the Northern Rhodesia National Monuments Commission established the Victoria Falls Conservancy Committee to manage the area of the Falls on the northern bank. The protected area was extended downstream to Songwe Gorge (confirmed in legislation on 4th April 1949).

For a period in the 1950s tourists were allowed to descend down the Power Station rail-trolley to the bottom of the gorge.

*"The trolley service allows half an hour stay at the bottom of the gorge but visitors are not permitted into the power station itself… The trolley, which is really far more comfortable than it looks at first glance is hauled up and down a well set track by a winch. The track is 850 feet [259 m] long and descends a vertical height of 350 feet [106 m]. There are 406 steps at the side of the track which provides descent for about half of the way down the steepest drop, but the rest of the route is a sloping pathway."* (Woods, 1960)

# The Flying Boat Service

*Solent flying boat on the Zambezi*

In 1947 British Overseas Airways Corporation (BOAC) introduced the famous Short Solent S45 class of flying boat, based on the military Sunderland float planes, and a new trans-African airmail route was launched from Southampton to Vaaldam, Johannesburg, replacing the original Imperial Airways route and transporting mail across the world within days.

Operating the route twice-weekly (later increased to three services) the flying boat service evolved as an airmail service between England and South Africa, but also offered a unique mode of tourism travel, bringing more visitors to the Falls.

The low-flying Solents weighed 35 tons and were powered by four Bristol Hercules engines with a cruising speed of 210 mph (338 kmph). The aircraft carried a crew of seven, with up to 34 passengers plus mail and cargo. Tickets for the 6,350 mile (10,219 km) journey were advertised at £167 single and £300 12s return. There was no flying at night, and the route included overnight stops in Sicily, Luxor, Kampala and Victoria Falls. The flying boats landed on a wide flat stretch of the Zambezi River some seven kilometres upstream of the Falls, stretching 2,500 yards (2,286 m) in length, and 500 yards (457 m) wide. Passengers were serviced by a riverside reception terminal, landing stage and jetty, as well as a road linking with the Victoria Falls town and Hotel, constructed in late 1947.

*"Passenger reception buildings have been built on the banks of the Zambesi by the government of Southern Rhodesia, and a road was cut through the bush in 6 1/2 weeks from Victoria Falls to the hotel... Such co-operation from the government of Southern Rhodesia has saved BOAC considerable expense in opening and maintaining the base."* (Flight Magazine, May 1948)

The first Solent flying boat landed on a test flight on 11th December 1947, and the first commercial service was operated on 4th May 1948.

*"The BOAC Base comprised of a small group of buildings with the usual offices, workshops and passenger facilities on the southern river bank, with an unmade road some four miles* [6.4 km] *long connecting this to the Vic Falls 'village.' There was also a locally made bus 'garage' for a pair of passenger coaches owned by BOAC. This was a thatched roof spanning between several palm trees, just to keep the coaches cool, and which the local elephants took pleasure in knocking down periodically. There was a pier leading down to the river, with a hinged gangway from the pier down to a floating landing stage, which allowed for the rise and fall of the river, and from which passengers embarked into launches. On landing, the aircraft taxied to a large inflated buoy, which was moored to the river bed. The Radio Officer had the task of leaning out of a small hatch in the aircraft nose and hooking on to the buoy with a boat hook."* (Critchell, 2007)

The stopover at the Falls Hotel soon became one of the highlights of the route for those few lucky enough to experience the journey, and the stretch of river and terminal reception where the planes landed became affectionately known as the 'Jungle Junction,' a nickname apparently first given by a reporter from the Bulawayo Chronicle.

*"These wonderful aircraft... represented the best and most luxurious form of transport at that time. They were two decked, with comfortable seating, quite unlike today's aircraft, even providing a couple of four-seater cabins on the lower deck. There was a powder room for the ladies with a make up table, complete with illuminated mirror, and the top range of make up and accessories were provided free of charge. There was a cocktail lounge, complete with a well stocked bar where you could sit on a high bar stool and watch the ground slowly unroll below through large windows, whilst sipping the drink of your choice."*

*Take off from the river*

*"As these were unpressurised aircraft, they flew below 10,000 feet [3,048 m], or a little under two miles high, and frequently much lower. There being virtually no conflicting air traffic in those days in those places, pilots had more of a free hand as to whereabouts in the sky to go. It was not unusual to descend lower to afford passengers a first class view of a herd of animals below."* (Critchell, 2007)

The Hotel was responsible for providing the onboard catering for the return journey. Food rationing was still in force in England after the war and the passengers were apparently always impressed by the sumptuous catering.

## *Up the Junction*

Mr Andy Carlisle, engineer on Solent G-AHIR 'Sark,' recorded an incident-packed few days after landing at the Jungle Junction on 22nd November 1949:

*"[I was] on the wing after landing when we heard screams from one of the first passengers ashore... in the trees bordering the pathway up from the jetty a lady passenger had come face to face with darkest Africa. A mighty python was draped along an overhanging branch and in its mouth was a half-swallowed monkey! Rest of night uneventful at Falls Hotel. Take-off next morning was at 06:30 and downstream, just about to unstick when nasty, grinding noise brought proceedings to a halt.*

*"We had hit a rock and not done a lot of good to the keel. I shinned down the central ladder and beheld a strange sight. The passengers were still sitting, belted in, whilst around them floated a miscellaneous assortment of newspapers, handbags, magazines etc... [We] slowly proceeded to a sand-bar on the Northern Rhodesian bank and beached the waterlogged monster. Got the passengers clear, stripped off and did a bit of diving to try to find out by feel just how extensive the damage was. About a 12 foot [3.65 m] rent in the port keelson... [Later in] the hotel where we were downing a few 'Tuskers,' a tall, leathery individual approached and started giving us a hard time. It transpired that the sand-bar where we had beached was the one that he used to stake out goats to catch crocodiles! And after two days of disporting ourselves almost naked in these same waters, now he tells us."* (Stirling, 2015)

During the period from 1948 to 1950 when the flying boats operated, a BOAC emergency rescue team was stationed at the Jungle Junction. Raymond Critchell was one of the six man team based on the south bank of the Zambezi and records in his online memoirs:

*"Around this time, ...I met a chap, [Syd] Brown, who operated the Hotel tourist launch, which carries guests up the river. This was a very posh affair, all polished brass and varnish, with a shady canopy to keep the sun off. He had also been a signalman and used to call us up on his signal lamp to ask when the aircraft was due in so that he could pull well into the river bank. He would also pass on details of any dolly birds he had on board in case anyone from BOAC wanted to go down the pub that night to meet them."*

In the early 1950s the Victoria Falls settlement was still not much more than a village, Critchell continuing:

*"The community was centred around the hotel which had quite a large staff, the Railway station with an on-site Post Office, the Vic Falls Conservator who lived at the small government camping site, a Police/Customs/Immigration post, and of course, the ubiquitous Trading Store... The Police Post was manned by a Sergeant and two troopers of the British South African Police, plus a Customs and an Immigration Officer, and they controlled the to and fro traffic, such as it was, along the Great North Road... Livingstone over the river was building the first International Airport in Northern Rhodesia, equipped with all mod cons including an electric flarepath to accommodate the new generation of intercontinental machines coming off the drawing boards, such as the Comet."*
(Critchell, 2007)

The period of the flying boats was brief, operating for just over two-and-a-half years before being overtaken by the development of a new generation of pressurised aircraft. The Solent service ended in November 1950, replaced with the Hermes airliner which completed the journey between London and Johannesburg (via the new Livingstone Airport) in just under a day and a half. The flying boat service was commemorated by British Airways in December 1982 with the erection of a cairn and plaque dedicated to the flying boat service at the site of the Jungle Junction jetty, which still stretches into the river to this day:

*"Between 4 May 1948 and 7 November 1950 passengers and cargo to and from Rhodesia disembarked/embarked from this pier on the Short Solent flying boats of British Overseas Airways Corporation (BOAC) on the United Kingdom - South Africa trunk route. This concluded 26 years of continuous flying boat operation by British Airways' predecessors - Imperial Airways and BOAC."*

Flying boats returned to the Zambezi for a period in the late 1980s with a converted Catalina seaplane (Z-CAT), operated by the Catalina Safari Company, flying the route from Cairo to the Falls, landing at the old Jungle Junction on the Zambezi.

# Livingstone Joins the Jet-set

In 1950 Livingstone Airport was developed from the humble beginnings of the existing Aerodrome (previously not much more than a large open field) with a fully modernised control tower and tarmac runway. It was proudly reported that the spray from the Falls could be seen from the control tower. The opening ceremony for the new £1 million facility was performed by Lord Pakenham, Northern Rhodesia

*Livingstone control tower and buildings*

Minister of Civil Aviation, on 12th August 1950. Lord Pakenham himself chose to arrive by the Solent flying boat service (Stirling and House, 2014).

*"The inaugural flying display which followed caused immense interest; many of the spectators had never seen a jet aircraft, so it can be imagined that a fine exhibition of formation aerobatics by four South Africa Air Force Vampire pilots... caused something of a sensation."* (Flight Magazine, August 1950)

The airport served as the main international gateway for the region, including guests of the Falls Hotel, until the opening of Salisbury Airport in 1956 and the subsequent development of the Victoria Falls Airport in 1967. In the same year as the new Livingstone airport opened Mr H D Bridge was appointed Northern Rhodesia's first Tourist Officer as the country attempted to capitalise on its new aviation advantage. Based in Livingstone Mr Bridge's brief was to promote the country's tourism attractions at home and abroad.

*Four Vampire jet fighters fly in formation over the Falls*

## Growth of Commercial Airlines

The growth of long-haul commercial air travel opened up direct, and faster, travel to the Falls, further boosting tourism. International carriers serving Livingstone soon included BOAC, Air France and South Africa Airways. For a period all passengers disembarked at Livingstone Airport to stay overnight at the Falls Hotel before either continuing their flight to South Africa or travelling by land to many of the National Parks and other destinations within the region.

The introduction of regional aviation routes, including those of Central African Airways during the 1950s, marked a significant development in tourist travel, breaking nearly fifty years of railway dominance. Despite this, the railway-owned Falls Hotel continued to flourish during this period.

*"One of the most remarkably successful innovations has been a Sunday excursion trip from Salisbury to Victoria Falls and back, 680 miles [1,094 km] for a return fare of £10, which includes a box lunch, a boat trip up the Zambesi to see elephant, hippo and crocodile, a coach trip to the Falls, and tea at the Victoria Falls Hotel before returning to Salisbury."* (Flight Magazine, October 1951)

In order to integrate the arrival of passengers on commercial flights a new railway time-table was released and new routine established at the Falls Hotel.

*"The new train time tables now in operation have completely reversed the routine at the [Falls] hotel. Instead of the majority of passengers arriving at night they now get in before breakfast. All visitors from the south and from overseas are now making their reservations in good time rather than risk being disappointed."* (Rhodesia Railways Magazine, July 1952)

## First Commercial Jet Passenger Flight

On 2nd May 1952 the 'Yoke Peter' (G-ALYP), a de Havilland Comet Mark 1, took off from London Heathrow to Johannesburg carrying 36 passengers on the world's first commercial passenger jet flight, proudly operated by BOAC and heralding the new age of the jet airliner.

The flight stopped for refuelling at Rome (Italy), Beirut (Lebanon), Khartoum (Sudan), Entebbe (Uganda) and Livingstone before arriving in Johannesburg, a distance of 6,700 miles (10,782 km) in 18 hours 40 minutes flying time - and a total journey time of 23 hours 20 minutes. A single fare cost £175 and a return £315.

# Sky Safaris

After the war Mr Coleman Myers, from Bulawayo, purchased a surplus Tiger Moth (VP-YJN) and in 1946 started advertising scenic flips at £1 a head. He recouped the £160 cost of his investment in the first weekend of flying. Myers soon purchased a new Piper Cub (VP-YFK) and started his own charter company, expanding his business with the acquisition of Spencer Airways and operating under the name Victoria Falls Airways Ltd.

*Mr Coleman Myers of Victoria Falls Airways*

Through the 1950s Victoria Falls Airways operated tourism flights from the Victoria Falls Airfield on the south bank, now boasting a hard surface runway of 800 yards (730 m). The parent company, Air Carriers Ltd, continued to grow with the acquisition of smaller charter companies, ultimately resulting in the formation of Rhodesia United Air Carriers (RUAC) in 1957. In January 1955 a freak storm destroyed the hanger, two de Havilland Rapides and damaged several other aircraft. Six months later the company was back up and flying.

*"The Victoria Falls fleet comprises two Rapides, each seating eight passengers, and four Piper Tri-Pacers, each of which has accommodation for pilot and three passengers. There is a booking counter in the foyer of the nearby Falls Hotel where tickets are issued - £5 for a game flight or 25s for a trip round the Falls. Passengers are taken to the airfield in one of the ubiquitous Volkswagen Microbuses which are appearing in increasing numbers in all parts of Africa. The 'airport buildings' comprise one new hanger, which has risen beside the ruins of one blown down in a gale last January with the total loss of two Rapides and damage to other aircraft, and a smaller hangar - used by private owners...*

*"Back at the Falls Hotel, Mr Coleman Myers told me something of the background of the company as we relaxed over a refreshing glass. There are two other pilots - Mr J H Duplessis and Mr A E Rybicki - and the company flies about 10,000 passengers a year. Fifty percent of the work is accounted for by game flights, which continue throughout the year, and charter work makes up the other half."* (Flight Magazine, August 1955)

# Victoria Falls National Park

Changes on the south bank in 1952 amalgamated the Victoria Falls Reserve, including the Special Area immediately around the Falls, with the larger Victoria Falls Game Reserve, covering an area upstream of the Falls, to form the expanded Victoria Falls National Park under Proclamation 25 (1952) of the National Parks Act (1949). The protected area covered 60,000 hectares, with the town of Victoria Falls an excluded enclave, surrounded by the National Park and the main road from the Falls to Kazungula in neighbouring Botswana transecting the Park.

The Victoria Falls Special Area, including the river sections immediately above and below the Falls, was now effectively under the shared control of both the National Park Advisory Board (NPAB) and the Commission for the Preservation of Natural and Historical Monuments and Relics.

*"Although some duties were delegated to the NPAB in cases where the development of local amenities would be for the benefit of the visiting public, the Commission... by and large remained responsible for the management of the Special Area at Victoria Falls."* (Makuvaza, 2012)

Under the management of the NPAB tourism infrastructure and services on the south bank were developed, including the centrally-located Rest (or Main) Camp and the upstream Zambezi Camp, providing flexible accommodation options for independent travellers.

*"On the Southern Rhodesian bank, where a National Park has been established, there are two Rest Camps - Main Camp, which is close to the Victoria Falls village, and the Zambesi Camp, which is situated four miles [6.5 km] up river in shady surroundings and commanding magnificent views of the river and islands. The Zambesi Camp consists of a single building with a number of large double rooms, comfortably furnished, and with adequate bathing and sanitary arrangements... The huts at Main Camp are substantially built and comfortably furnished with beds, mattresses, chairs, table and toilet set. Each bed is fitted with a mosquito net and the windows are curtained and mosquito-proofed. Bedding is provided at the option of the visitor. Crockery and cutlery may be hired from the Falls Supply Store, where a full range of groceries is also stocked... Charges at Main Camp are 5s per day if no bedding is ordered and 6s per person per day with bedding. At Zambesi Camp the charge is 7s 6d. per person per day with bedding. Double and family huts are available at Main Camp."* (Southern Rhodesia Public Relations Department, c1955)

*National Park tourism chalets*

The Zambezi Camp offices and self-catering chalet facilities incorporated the abandoned BOAC buildings at the Jungle Junction.

*"The Zambezi Camp which is on the river bank was erected as offices and a staff residence for the BOAC during the time when flying boats were used on the London-Johannesburg flight. Holidaymakers not wishing to do their own catering will find the Impala Inn is very close to the Southern Rhodesian Rest Camp and the Falls Restaurant is only across the road from the Northern Rhodesian Rest Camp. For those people who prefer to sleep under canvas or use their own caravans, there are camping sites equipped with ablution and sanitary blocks near both the rest camps. Tents and marquees can be hired at the northern bank camping site."* (Woods, 1960)

A riverside drive was established running upstream along the scenic stretches of the Zambezi that had so enchanted Livingstone.

*"The main road in the Park is a gravel road and it has not been possible up to 1959 to make this an all-weather road, so during the rainy season this part of the park has unfortunately to be closed... Another 50 miles of loop roads were under construction in 1959 and these will give access to the country further away from the river and so open up new areas for the sightseer."* (Woods 1960)

The centrally located main Rest Camp would quickly grow to offer 30 self-catering chalets, caravan park and camping, set amongst shaded gardens and fine native trees. Increased tourism levels brought further development to the small town, with private stands and stores providing accommodation and services for the growing numbers of professional staff based at the Falls.

### Frost at the Falls

*"In winter icicles have been known to form on trees in the Rain Forest during an occasional heavy frost but theirs is a short-lived span once the sun appears in the heavens. Sir Peveril and Lady William-Powlett on their first visit to the Victoria Falls in 1953 were lucky to see and photograph this most unusual occurrence at dawn on 4th July that year."* (Woods, 1960)

# Formation of the Federation

A preliminary conference on the proposed unification of Southern and Northern Rhodesia, together with Nyasaland (Malawi), was held at Victoria Falls in 1947. A series of conferences were held in London during 1952/3 where the three African countries, with negotiators from the British government, finally agreed a complicated federal structure. The Federation of Rhodesia and Nyasaland, also known as Central African Federation (CAF), came into effect on 1st August 1953.

### Joint Publicity

*Touring the Rainforest*

Under the Federation, Northern Rhodesia, and Livingstone in particular, benefited from the experienced publicity knowledge of their Southern Rhodesian counterparts. Unified tourism information brochures publicised both sides of the Falls and the services available on each side of the river. A guidebook published by the Southern Rhodesian Public Relations Department promoted the Federal Tourist Centre in Livingstone, where *"the Federal Tourist Officer and a competent staff are available to give assistance to visitors"* (Southern Rhodesia Public Relations Department, c1955).

## *Victoria Falls Trust*

Another significant development on the northern bank was the formation of the Victoria Falls Trust, to oversee the preservation of the physical environment of the Falls from ecological damage and to encourage tourism, on 15th March 1954. Trustees were selected from the local Livingstone community and appointed by the Governor of Northern Rhodesia.

The wider area was de-gazetted as a National Monument but several smaller archaeological sites within the reserve were declared as National Monuments. The Historic Monument Commission continued to oversee the conservation and management of the Falls whilst the Trust concentrated on tourism management. The work of the Trust included overseeing the development and management of Rest Camp and Camping Site tourism facilities on the north bank of the river above the Falls, which now offered 36 self-catering chalets for visitors.

*"The Rest Huts in this Camp are equipped with electric light and adequate furniture, with separate bathrooms and outside fireplaces for cooking. Accommodation costs 3s per person per day (children under 12, 1s 6d) but tenants are expected to supply their own food and cooking utensils. Bedding is supplied, if required, at an extra charge of 2s 6d for the first night and 1s per night thereafter. A tearoom* [which became known by locals as 'Chippy Woods']... *is open until 10 pm where full meals are served and tinned goods stocked, is situated near the camp. It is advisable to book bungalows in advance, especially from May to August and over the Easter, Christmas and Rhodes and Founders holiday periods."* (Southern Rhodesia Public Relations Department, c1955)

In addition the Trust oversaw the development of tourism attractions such as the Maramba Cultural Village and the Livingstone Zoological Park (later the Mosi-oa-Tunya National Park), opened in 1955. The period saw rising tourism arrivals to the region, with 43,000 arrivals recorded for Livingstone in 1955 and over 47,000 in 1956, a fifty percent increase since 1953 (Economic Survey of Livingstone, 1957).

# Livingstone Centenary

On 16th November 1955 a ceremony was held to commemorate the centenary of Dr David Livingstone's first arrival at the Falls. Guests of honour at the ceremony and staying at the Falls Hotel included Dr Hubert Wilson, Livingstone's grandson, and Miss Dianna Livingstone-Bruce, his great grand-daughter.

A second plaque was unveiled at the Livingstone Statue on the southern bank by Lord Llewellin, Governor-General of the Federation of Rhodesia and Nyasaland. The dedication read:

*"On the occasion of the centenary of David Livingstone's discovery of the Victoria Falls men and women of all races in and from all parts of the Federation of Rhodesia and Nyasaland assembled solemnly to dedicate themselves and their country to carry on the high Christian aims and ideals which inspired David Livingstone in his mission here. Unveiled by his Excellency the right honourable the Lord Llewellin, GBE, MC, TD, DL Governor-General of the Federation of Rhodesia and Nyasaland and dedicated by his grace the Lord Archbishop of Central Africa, Edward Frances Paget, on 16 November 1955."*

Boat trips to Livingstone Island took guests to the very spot where Livingstone first saw the Falls, and some still claimed to know the tree upon which he carved his initials.

*"The African paddlers will point out to you a towering tree round which has been placed a circle of stones and will tell you this is the tree on which the famous explorer cut his initials, but there is now no proof that this is so and searches by the Museum authorities and others have so far failed to reveal a tree still bearing the initials."* (Woods, 1960)

The disputed 'Livingstone Tree' was still standing into the mid-sixties, and even featured in a BBC television series on the Zambezi made in 1965 by a young natural history presenter, David Attenborough (later Sir). Another 'Livingstone Tree,' located upstream at Old Sesheke, and under which Livingstone camped, had blown down in storms the previous year (Attenborough, 1965).

*Viewing the Falls*

# The Falls in the Fifties

Federation tourism brochures celebrated that one hundred years after Livingstone first reached the Falls tourists could still witness them unspoilt in their full natural splendour, promoting the Falls as the 'greatest river wonder of the world.'

> *"When you see the Victoria Falls today you see them as Dr Livingstone first saw them on November 16, 1855. With the exception of the great rail and road cantilever bridge which links Southern and Northern Rhodesia, nothing has been added to or taken from Nature."*

The extensive commercial development of the Falls envisaged by Leopold Moore fifty years earlier in the pages of the 1907 Christmas issue of the Livingstone Mail were thankfully still unrealised fantasies (although it could be argued he painted a realistic picture of the Falls today, over a hundred years later). A small visitor information centre had been developed at the entrance to the Falls on the south bank - curiously showcasing the construction of the Kariba Dam - and a chain-assisted path, known as the Chain Walk, descended down the western end into the gorge, enabling the visitor to experience the power of Devil's Cataract. Above the Falls a canoe could still be taken to Cataract Island, for the fee of one shilling, return.

> *"When you wish to return to the mainland go back to the landing stage where a rail will be seen hanging from a tree near the water. Striking this several times will call the canoe boys."*

Or the visitor could walk further along the riverbank to the Hotel Landing Stage, where tea was served on the banks of the Zambezi. Back at the Hotel scenic flights over the Falls could be booked for the price of 25 shillings.

> *"To see the Falls in proper relation to the river and surrounding country, see them from the air. For a charge of 25s you are assured of 20 minutes of glorious views. Not only is the river very picturesque but the Gorges are seen at their best from the air. Book your flights at the Falls Hotel."* (Southern Rhodesia Public Relations Department, c1955)

Whilst the period saw declining numbers arriving at the Falls by rail, there were growing overall visitor totals to the Falls Hotel with numbers boosted by increasing aviation arrivals. In 1957 the Hotel recorded over 21,000 visitors, staying an average of just over two nights, at the time a record for the Hotel.

## Trolley Service Terminated

The growth of motorised transport and development of local road infrastructure paved the way for a more flexible method of local transportation for visitors around the Falls and the Hotel trolley system was eventually decommissioned.

*"In 1957, the Southern Rhodesia Government built a road to the Boat House* [now known as Zambezi Drive]*, and in December of that year the hotel replaced the hand-pushed trolley by a service of nine-seat minibuses."* (Price, 1966)

*The Falls Hotel's new minibus service*

Dr William W Cowen, the railway medical officer based at the Falls and close friend of Mr Tones, the Hotel manager, recalled the passing of the trolley system:

*"This form of transport had been in used for many years without any denunciatory opinion being made, but in the latter part of the fifth decade the manager of the hotel and the general manager of the railways began to receive letters from guests complaining about the employment of human beings to propel the trolleys. The truth of the matter was that being 'trolley boys' was the most popular occupation of all hotel employees. The job was not nearly as physically taxing as they made out. The heavy panting was made audible in order to secure a good gratuity at the journey's end."* (Cowen, 1995)

One of the original trolleys, a reminder of days past, still waits under the shade of the mango trees in the Falls Hotel courtyard and offers a shady seat for quiet contemplation for today's visitors. A plaque records:

*"The Victoria Falls Hotel trolley service, which operated from the Hotel to the Bridge and the Boat House, was introduced in 1920. Before this date the Hotel guests were conveyed to various points of interest by means of rickshaws. During their life the trolleys were used by some 2 million guests, and were replaced by motor coaches in December, 1957, after 37 years of romantic, yet reliable service."*

# Falls in Flood

In 1957 and 1958, during the construction of the Kariba Dam, the Zambezi experienced unprecedented seasonal floods. In March 1957 the rising waters flooded part of the Power Station in the Gorge.

*"In 1957... the river rose higher than ever known before and reached, on the surge, a height of about 11 feet [3.3 m] above the level of the floor of the power station. All the windows by that time had been bricked in and practically all the main doorway was bricked in and reinforced with sandbags. No one knew how long the building could withstand the tremendous buffeting of the high waves of the Zambezi in spate and the power station staff with pumps going night and day cleared the building of water as it seeped in through many places in the walls. Access was gained by a temporary bridge of two steel pipes which swayed and swung as the mighty surges of water swept around the building like gigantic rollers on the sea shore.*

*"Profiting by the experience gained during this drama of man against nature, protective measures were taken and a reinforced concrete wall set in 2-3 feet [60-90 cm] of solid rock now surrounds the building to a height of 20 feet [6 m] above the floor level inside. An access bridge on concrete pillars now leads to an emergency doorway and the main entrance has been fitted with watertight doors... Again the Zambezi turned to fury in February and March 1958 and rose to an unprecedented high level, surging up to 15 feet [4.5 m] above the level of the floor inside the building with occasional waves splashing over the roof on the down-stream side. The power station staff were, however, the victors once again and marked yet another score against the Zambezi on the painted post at the side of the main entrance marking the highest levels reached by the turbulent water... It is estimated that with the heavy concrete protection now completed the building can withstand a river level of up to 10 inches [25 cm] more than the 1958 record flood."* (Woods, 1960)

*The flood-waters surround the Power Station*

Above the Falls on the northern bank of the Zambezi a stone monument erected by the National Monuments Commission marks the highest recorded level of the Zambezi in March 1958. On the south bank the barrel boom below the Hotel landing stage, installed to reassure passengers and act as a safety barrier in event of mechanical problems, was washed away in the floods (Woods, 1960).

The Kariba hydro-electric dam was constructed between 1955 and 1959 at a cost of $135 million, creating the largest man-made lake (by volume) in the world - holding an estimated capacity of 180.6 cubic kilometres of water - a title it still holds to this day. The formation of the lake displaced an estimated 57,000 Tonga people from their cultural homelands along both sides of the river valley.

## Millionaire's Playground?

In November 1957 the Northern Rhodesia Government invited bids for the lease of a site above the Falls for a new Hotel development, almost ten years after initially identifying the land for investors. In 1962 it was reported that an American investor, Mr Rendell Mabey (an ex-Senator and president of the Utah Industries Corporation), had been found for the development.

> "The Northern Rhodesia Government has approved plans for the building of a luxury hotel-casino on a 35-acre site close to the eastern cataract of the Victoria Falls in Northern Rhodesia. The total cost of the development, including furnishings, will be nearly £1,500,000. Approval was given after the Government had consulted the Victoria Fall Trust and the Commission for the Preservation of Natural and Historical Monuments and Relics. Building is expected to begin next year and hotel will open in 1965." (Northern News, April 1962)

Controversially the original plans for the 200-bedroom air-conditioned luxury hotel detailed a ten-storey building with rooftop gardens overlooking the Falls, described as a 'millionaire's playground' and 'the lap of luxury.'

At the same time the Railway Company was considering the possible sale of the Falls Hotel on the southern bank. News of the potential sale of the Hotel, now regarded a 'national asset,' reached the national press in April 1958, with the Minister of Transport confirming to the Bulawayo Chronicle that disposal of the Hotel was being considered whilst denying that a deal had already been done with an American financier. A South African millionaire with American business interests, Mr Schlesinger, was named in press reports at the time as looking to develop a 'drink-and-gamble-round-the-clock hotel on the south or north bank of the river' (Roberts, 2016b).

# Ripples at the Landing Stage

In the early 1960s the Falls Hotel had looked at expanding its facilities and services at the Boat House and Landing Stage. The site, a short distance upstream from the Falls was leased by the Railway Company on behalf of the Hotel. Over the years the facilities had developed to include a boat shed, launch slipway and an open-air tearoom for waiting passengers, serving 'the best tea and cream buns in the Falls.' In the early sixties the Hotel management seriously considered expanding this into a fully-fledged visitor restaurant with car-parking facilities. An internal Hotel report in 1963 concluded:

> *"After considering very carefully the provision of a restaurant at the boat house on the south bank of the Zambezi it was decided, that in view of the shortage of capital funds together with the fact that we were only able to obtain a very restricted liquor licence, the project should be abandoned."* (Victoria Falls Hotel Management Committee, March 1963)

Hotel management committee reports recorded that numerous delays were encountered in negotiations over the sublease of the Landing Stage site, and that during these delays, the launches and boat house were totally destroyed by a freak fire. Documents do not detail the cause of the fire and the site was abandoned. The Railway Company duly terminated the leases for the landing stage site and also the picnic-site on Kandahar Island, bringing to an end the Hotel's long association operating river launches and tours.

*The Falls Hotel boathouse on the river*

Requiring an immediate replacement for their launch services, the Hotel management turned to Livingstone based Greenway Launches & Taxi Services, operated by Mr A S Sussens from the north bank, the only operator with the capacity to deliver an adequate service for the Hotel. Whilst appreciating Mr Sussens cooperation in ensuring that the Hotel suffered no disruption to its launch services for its guests, the Hotel Management initially decided it unwise to pass all their clientele to a single operator, preferring to share their business among two or more companies and encouraging some healthy competition.

## Contract Competition

The Falls Hotel management committee eventually determined that the Hotel would *"benefit by allowing private enterprise to take over the launch services, under certain safeguards to the Management, on the understanding that the Hotel would be the sole booking agent for all trips, on a 10% commission basis"* (Victoria Falls Hotel Management Committee, March 1963).

The contract for the operation of the Hotel's vehicle transfers and boat tours was included in an invitation to private companies which appeared in the Livingstone Mail in September 1963. The call for tender appears to have sparked a scramble between Livingstone businesses, none of which appeared to have the existing capacity or quality of services the Hotel required. Partnerships were made, and broken, new companies formed and investors sought, all in the chase to land the Hotel's business.

Mr Harry Sossen, a businessman of some standing in Livingstone and manager of the Victoria Falls Garage on the south bank, originally agreed a partnership with the established Zambezi Safaris company, based on the southern bank and operated by Mr Jocelyn. However they were quickly to part company, for reasons unknown, with Mr Sossen setting himself up in the boating business on the north bank, and even going as far as to purchase the launches and buses necessary for the contract. Zambezi Safaris found themselves another financial investor, this time from Bulawayo, and together with several other companies, submitted proposals.

In 1964 the Hotel's transport and booking desk services were contracted to the United Touring Company, who were to exclusively manage and operate the Hotel's river cruises and local tours for many years. The Hotel's landing stage site, originally established by Giese and used by Clark until taken over by the Hotel, was abandoned and reclaimed by nature. New commercial jetty sites were developed further upstream, leased to a new wave of tour operators.

# Rail Overtaken

In 1962 the Falls were visited by a party of American and Canadian tourists on a luxury world cruise, travelling to the Cape on the S.S. Brasil. Instead of travelling by train to the Falls, the group toured South Africa before flying to the Falls via Livingstone, reflecting shifting travel preferences as aviation arrivals overtook those travelling to the Falls by train. Despite shorter travel times, stays at the Falls were still brief.

*"The passengers left the ship at Cape Town, and after touring the Republic they flew by charter 'plane to Livingstone. One party arrived on the Wednesday morning and left again on Thursday afternoon, ...while the other party arrived on the Friday afternoon and left the next morning...*

*"Many of them had recently visited the Iguaçu [Iguazú] Falls in South America, and they said that although these falls could boast greater volume of water, they were not so impressive as the Victoria Falls...*

*"Mrs Bernice Lynn, of Los Angeles, California, said that although her friends had often told her about the Victoria Falls, no one had told that there was a first-class hotel right on the spot. 'Now I am going to tell all my friends what a fine hotel you have here,' she said. 'It is unique; it is well managed, clean and the food is excellent. As a rule when one goes to see a natural wonder like the falls, the hotels do not bother too much about tourists.' Mr William Schaff, of New Jersey, said that the Falls Hotel could compare very favourably with most of the hotels in the United States."* (Rhodesia Railways Magazine, July 1962)

In response to an increasingly diverse tourism travel sector the Railway Company introduced Rainbow Tours in 1962, special packaged holiday deals including rail and accommodation at the Falls Hotel.

*"The colonial-style Victoria Falls Hotel, with its 120 bedrooms, also has a bank, hairdressing salons and shops, as well as a conference room. The national airline and United Touring Company (offering cars for hire) have their offices here. The hotel is famous for its multi-course table d'hôte menu. Many visitors come by rail, and there are all-exclusive Rainbow tours (by rail) from all centres in Rhodesia."* (Rhodesian National Tourism Board, 1967)

The 1962 census recorded the population of the small town as 1,601 (CSO, 1964). In an effort to attract arrivals, Livingstone Station was rebuilt and reopened in 1962 at a cost of £72,000 (Rhodesia Railways Magazine, May 1962).

*Modern luxury on the railway*

# Federation Folly

Increasing African nationalism, particularly in Northern Rhodesia and Nyasaland, persuaded Britain to agree to the organised dissolution of the failing Federation. The break-up negotiations, known as the Central Africa Conference, and involving delegates from five governments, were hosted in the Pullman Suite at the Falls Hotel over several days in July 1963. The Federation was officially dissolved on the 31st December 1963. Northern Rhodesia was granted independence on 24th October 1964, becoming the Republic of Zambia. Earlier in the same year Nyasaland had also gained independence as the Republic of Malawi.

Whilst the period of the Federation saw increased integration of tourism operations from opposite sides of the river, the break-up saw division with border control facilities developed on the southern bank in 1963 and on the northern bank soon after. Despite the inconvenience of passports and paperwork, however, Livingstone residents still regularly patronised the Falls Hotel for social events.

*"It was a bumper New Year's Eve at the Victoria Falls Hotel when some 650 people thronged the main lounge and verandas to see the Old Year out and the New Year in. Customs barriers certainly did not seem to have deterred the many merrymakers who had come over from Livingstone for celebrations. The enquiry counter in the foyer of the Victoria Falls Hotel has been taken*

*over by the United Touring Company which has acquired one of the two tourist and safari businesses in Livingstone... A new band is now in attendance at the hotel and is proving very popular. Known as the 'Rainbow Trio,' it was started by Mr Bob Webb, who was transferred to Livingstone some four months ago."* (Rhodesia Railways Magazine, Jan 1965)

Following the dissolution of the Federation, Central African Airways was divided into the national carriers of Zambia Airways, Air Malawi and Air Rhodesia.

## *Livingstone on the Offensive*

A June 1965 press release from the Zambia Information Department outlined another determined push to develop tourism in Livingstone.

*"The Ministry of Lands and Natural Resources, in close co-operation with the Ministry of Commerce and Industry and the Victoria Falls Trust, are going on to the offensive in their efforts to develop the Victoria Falls Trust Area and build up the tourist industry in competition with Rhodesia. To this end active steps are being taken to include in the proposed Four Year Development Plan extensive and co-ordinated projects to provide considerably greater facilities for tourists in the Falls area. At the same time, as the Minister of Lands and Natural Resources - Mr Kalulu - told a meeting of the Victoria Falls Trust in Livingstone last month, 'We must beware of the general mania for development of this area which would be at the expense of the natural beauty of the Victoria Falls Trust region'... He suggested that to most people development meant putting up wonderful buildings near and around the Falls, and said that it would be a sad thing if such a policy was implemented without discretion because once we lost our natural heritage it would be impossible to regain it... However, he was convinced that these matters need not militate against each other if properly planned and executed."* (Zambia Information Services, 1965)

With independence the National Museums Board was created in 1966 and the Rhodes-Livingstone Museum renamed the Livingstone Museum.

In 1965 a controversial experiment was held with floodlighting of the Falls from the northern bank.

*"The floodlighting of the Eastern Cataract of the Victoria Falls is proving a great attraction to residents and visitors alike, for a strange new beauty is being revealed in the delicately tinted rainbows which the floodlights throw into the*

*heavy spray... People who wondered whether artificial light would produce the lunar rainbows for which the falls are famous have been agreeably surprised, and since the lights were first switched on it is estimated that some thousands of people have made the nightly pilgrimage to view the fascinating spectacle."* (Rhodesia Railways Magazine, Feb 1965)

The experiment was, however, suspended soon after and the Falls returned to their natural nocturnal aspect. Woods, writing five years earlier in 1960, summarised the unspoilt magic of the Falls:

*"The great appeal of the Victoria Falls is its unspoilt beauty and natural surroundings. There are no peanut vendors, no grim rows of iron railings, no artificial floodlighting and no toll gates."* (Woods, 1960)

# Polarising Politics

The momentum for independent majority rule in Southern Rhodesia was growing. Against rising calls for democratic rule, however, the white-minority government under Ian Smith made its Unilateral Declaration of Independence (UDI) from Britain on 11th November 1965. Smith made the announcement after days of tense negotiations with British Prime Minister Harold Wilson, who was only prepared to permit Rhodesian independence on the basis of giving the black majority population a fair share of power. The British Government, Commonwealth, and United Nations condemned the declaration as illegal, leaving Rhodesia unrecognised by the international community. Economic sanctions were imposed on the breakaway colony. The Zambian customs and immigration post was built on the north bank soon after the declaration.

*"On the north bank, the area immediately before the approach of the bridge was cleared. It had a magnificent view down to the Boiling Pot and across the Knife Edge, and became known as 'scandal alley': Livingstone residents would go down there on Sunday afternoons to drink and revel in the week's gossip. The Zambian customs and immigration post was built on the... site soon after Ian Smith's Unilateral Declaration of Independence from Britain in 1965."* (Teede and Teede, 1994)

Strict visa regulations introduced by the Zambian immigration department in 1966 negatively affected tourism, with it being recorded that tourist arrivals declined by 18 percent in 1966 (Moonga 1999).

# South Bank Takes Off

On the south bank the Rhodesian Government announced a review of land tenure at the Falls, resulting in new areas being opened up for development. Land use policy up to this date had effectively restricted development and protected the natural environment of the Victoria Falls, but the changing geopolitical landscape made further infrastructure development inevitable. Victoria Falls town expanded rapidly during this period with the development of business stands and residential suburbs.

*"Little further development took place until the mid 1960s when major political changes caused significant growth in the village. Until this time, the residents of Victoria Falls were primarily railway or government employees with a few individuals involved in tourism. Financial, commercial and social services for the village were provided by Livingstone. Moreover, a large proportion of the visitors to the Falls arrived via the international airport at Livingstone and the majority of the tourist facilities were provided there."* (Heath, 1977)

In late 1965 Livingstone based businessman Harry Sossen approached the Falls Hotel for support in a bid to buy or acquire a revised long term lease for the Victoria Falls Garage, which he had managed since the death of Ted Spencer. Located on the turning to the approach road of the Falls Hotel, he hoped to expand his trade by negotiating around a lease clause which prevented him from operating a tourism agency.

Being part of the Railway Reserve, however, the land was deliberately leased on a short term basis (five years) with restrictions on 'taking bookings for, undertaking or arranging any excursions, boat trips or the like' specifically to protect the interests of the Hotel.

## *Victoria Falls Casino*

Growing tourism levels eventually saw the construction of the Victoria Falls Casino, later known as the Makasa Sun Hotel, in 1966 on the site immediately next to the Victoria Falls Hotel.

*"The modern, luxurious Casino Hotel was opened in 1966. It is air-conditioned throughout and has a bank, hairdressing salons, jewellery and other shops for the convenience of its patrons, besides a la carte restaurants serving breakfast 24 hours a day."* (Rhodesian National Tourism Board, 1967)

The casino was the first in the country and an added attraction advertised even by the Falls Hotel itself.

*The Victoria Falls Casino*

*"The [Falls] hotel is still as popular as ever with a steady flow of visitors in and out almost daily. The nearby Casino continues to prove a big attraction, especially in the evening, and there are the usual stories going the rounds of people managing to hit the 'jackpot.'"* (Rhodesia Railways Magazine, Nov 1967)

The Casino was extended in 1969 with the addition of a new wing comprising 54 bedrooms and three luxury suites, at a cost of £175,000, and by 1979 the Hotel boasted four luxury suites and 102 bedrooms all with private bathroom, shower, radio and telephone. Controversially the development broke the local skyline of the Falls, infringing a local council building requirement that no construction should be built above the tree-line, and so be visible from the river and Falls. A small section of the old trolley line down to the Falls was preserved in the grounds of the Hotel.

## *Airport Advances*

The Victoria Falls Airport was officially opened in 1967, allowing the growing town to service its own aviation arrivals and departures and avoiding the extra rigmarole of Zambian customs and immigration formalities. The new airport was built at some distance, 20 kilometres, from the Victoria Falls and the growing tourism town. The development of the Air Rhodesia Victoria Falls, Kariba and Hwange National Park domestic air routes boosted regional tourism.

*"From Johannesburg, Bulawayo, Salisbury, Kariba and Wankie, more than ten flights a week serve the new airport 15 miles [24 km] south of the Falls. Visitors from the north come via Livingstone airport, nine miles [14.5 km] north of the Falls, in Zambia. All exclusive Flame Lilly holidays starting from most centres in Southern Africa are on sale all over the world."* (Rhodesian National Tourism Board, 1967)

Despite all the new developments at the Falls, a late 1960s tourism information leaflet, produced by the Rhodesian National Tourism Board, still proudly presented the Falls as untouched by man and modern development.

> "Today the Falls are almost exactly as Livingstone first saw then, unspoilt in all their grandeur. Nothing has been allowed to mar the natural beauty of the surrounding; even the disfiguring precaution of guard rails has not been permitted. As Livingstone stood, lost in wonder, so do many thousands of visitors each year."

The town now boasted a modern Post Office and banks, including the distinctive Standard Bank building, opened in 1968. New tourist attractions included the Falls Craft Village (established in 1967), Snake Park and Curio Markets selling traditional carvings and tourism souvenirs.

*"The African Craft Village is unique in its conception. It is an exact replica of a nineteenth-century Matabele kraal, representing the home of one Matabele man and his three wives. A guided tour takes about 40 minutes and is a 'must' for every visitor to the Victoria Falls."*
(Harris, 1969)

*The Victoria Falls Craft Village*

The Falls Hotel saw another record year in 1967 with close to 22,000 visitors. The record numbers were largely credited to the new airport and growth of international and regional air travel, including Air Rhodesia's Flame Lilly holiday packages.

## A Birds-eye View

Scenic flights from the romantically renamed Sprayview Aerodrome offered by Rhodesian United Air Carriers now included two hour and 200 mile (321 km) flying safaris.

*Over the Falls (RUAC publicity image)*

*"Highlight of your stay is your flight over the Victoria Falls and surrounding countryside in search of the untamed game which roams this still primitive part of Africa. Not only do these dawn and sunset patrols offer glorious birds-eye views of the great Zambezi river, its zig-zag gorges and the mighty Falls themselves but, even more thrilling, your low flights over the broad savannah grasslands bordering Botswana and Zambia reveal great herds of stately sable antelope, zebra, tsessebe, waterbuck and many other types of antelope. As the vegetation patterns change below you, herds of buffalo are seen in the dense bush, giraffe wander browsing in the sparsely-treed lands and along the luxuriant river banks the elephant, giant of them all, drink and cool themselves in the sluggish water. Nearby the hippo wallow and crocodile bask. Throughout your 200 mile air safari you swoop low, seeming to pirouette on one wing, for a closer view of these rare and magnificent beasts, at home in their natural habitat but undismayed by the low-flying aircraft."* (Harris, 1969)

## On the Road

The reconstruction of the main Bulawayo to Victoria Falls strip road as a fully-tarred highway began in 1963 and took several years. The new road largely followed the route of the old strip road, although re-aligned to a more direct route in places.

The freedom of movement offered by the expanding road network attracted increasing overland travellers from regional markets, in particular South Africa, on self-drive safaris. The South African traveller and writer Lawrence G Green visited the Falls in the late 1960s on a road journey through Southern Rhodesia and published his writings in his 1968 travel book 'Full Many A Glorious Morning.' Green was not enamoured by the new breed of safari goers and relaxed clientele of the Falls Hotel, whose dress style he felt was at odds with the Hotel's grand setting:

*"People enter the Victoria Falls Hotel looking like dusty bands of dog-robbers. They simply have not got the sort of clothes that fit into a background of sophistication and elegance. Shorts do not go with chandeliers; bush shirts form a strange contrast with soft rugs and polished furniture. The final shock comes when you read this notice in the lounge: 'Gentlemen are requested to wear jackets and ties in the evening.' No doubt it is a necessary reminder though I have never encountered such a warning at a five star hotel."*

Green records an unfortunate incident which had occurred shortly before his visit:

*"I voyaged up the Zambesi to Kandahar Island in a large steel launch, hippo-proof and crocodile-proof, with powerful outboard motors. As we tied up on the island the girl in charge of the excursion led a party of natives on shore and called back: 'No one is to land until I give the word.' They searched the island and then allowed us to walk up to the tea shelter. These precautions were taken as a result of a tragedy earlier in the year. Mr Charles Graeme Young, a visitor from Durban, was standing on Kandahar Island when a hippo rushed out of the water and made for him... Mr Young stood his ground and tried to photograph the hippo. A few seconds later he was dead."* (Green, 1968)

## *Divided Viewpoints*

Controversy over the increasing development at the Falls rose to new heights with the proposed construction of an observation tower and restaurant on the southern bank overlooking the western end of the Falls:

*"In 1968, a company called African Panorama Limited applied for three acres of land to erect a 320 ft (95 m) observation tower and a restaurant about 100 ft (30 m) from the western end of the Devil's Cataract and adjacent to the railway line... The Victoria Falls Tower was to be modelled on the London Post Office Tower, with a restaurant below it to serve tourists."*

Despite being located within the core Special Area of the Falls, government ministers supported the development which was subsequently passed to parliament for approval.

*"During the debate some parliamentarians argued that the construction of the tower would promote tourism in the country while others strongly asserted that the tower would ruin the beauty of the Victoria Falls. After a considerable debate the parliamentarians eventually voted against its construction."*

In a separate proposal put forward in the same year the Railway Company applied for 4.5 acres of land to develop a tourist recreational facility including chip-and-putt golf course, bowling greens, tennis courts, a discotheque, a refreshments bar, and an amusement centre for children. These and other development pressures resulted in the decision to reduce to size of the Special Area to concentrate protection on the core area around the Falls.

*"In order to preserve the beauty of the natural and cultural surroundings of the site, the Commission* [for the Preservation of Natural and Historical Monuments and Relics] *made a decision in 1968 to reduce the size of the original boundaries of the Special Area. Accordingly, in order to change the boundaries of the national monument, the original site was deproclaimed as a national monument, cancelling the previous Government Notices no. 318 of 1937, no. 922 of 1947 and no. 453 of 1970. A smaller area was reproclaimed* [under of the Monuments and Relics Act] *as a national monument by Government Notice 640 of 1970."* (Makuvaza, 2012)

## Across the River

After decades of inviting investors to develop the site adjoining the Falls on the north bank, the Mosi-oa-Tunya InterContinental Hotel was finally opened in 1968. The hotel consisted of 95 rooms in two double-story blocks, set out at angles to the main building, housing the public areas and hotel administration. Developed by InterContinental Hotels & Resorts, part of Pan American Airways, the Hotel was operated in conjunction with the InterContinental Hotel in Lusaka. Many mourned the development of a site so close to the Falls, Teede and Teede recording:

*"Lights from the Mosi-oa-Tunya Hotel in Zambia interfere with moonlight viewing of the Main Falls from Zimbabwe and have ruined the spectacular series of lunar rainbows visible over the Rainbow Falls. Any more lights and the almost transcendental experience of seeing the Falls by moonlight would be totally lost."* (Teede and Teede, 1994)

The population of Livingstone was recorded at 49,063 in the census of 1969.

## Knife-Edge Bridge

In 1969 improvements were made to the tourism infrastructure on the northern bank with the construction of the Knife-Edge Bridge. The footbridge opened up access to views of the Falls which tourists had previously struggled to reach, resulting in many minor injuries over the years.

# Under a Southern Sun

On 1st February 1970 operation of the Falls Hotel was leased by the Rhodesia Railways to external management, marking the end of over fifty years of direct management by the Railway Company. Through its new managers, Rhodesian Breweries (Rhobrew), the Hotel was operated under the umbrella of the Southern Sun Hotel Corporation of Rhodesia Limited (known as Southern Sun), and part of a portfolio of hotels across the country - including its neighbour the Makasa Sun - and resulting in significant operational benefits and commercial opportunities, especially in the South African market. The group also had plans for another modern new hotel complex on the southern bank, which would result in the development of the Elephant Hills Country Club, opened in 1974.

The early seventies saw a continuing period of growth in the development of the town, with the construction of new infrastructure and tourism facilities, including housing suburbs, commercial centres, industrial premises, office and staff accommodation blocks and a diversification of new hotels. Local construction company Gardini & Sons, under the skilled guidance of Carlo Gardini, were responsible for a large percentage of the construction projects (including the previously constructed Casino and soon to be built Elephant Hills), with Carlo becoming known as 'the man who built Victoria Falls' (Meadows, 2000).

The fully air-conditioned, 40-room Peter's Motel opened in 1969 (later renamed the Victoria Falls Motel and later still the Sprayview Hotel), built, owned and operated by the Gardini family. The riverside A'Zambezi River Lodge, with 65 double and 15 family rooms, opened in 1972, and the centrally located 44-room Rainbow Hotel in 1974 - both again constructed by Gardini & Sons.

The Spencer Creek Crocodile Ranch was established in 1971, operating as both a commercial crocodile farm and tourist attraction. The ranch has grown into a major employer in the predominantly tourism based town. The old Sprayview Restaurant was demolished in 1970.

By 1969 the population of Victoria Falls town had grown to 3,450 (CSO, 1969). National annual tourism arrivals reached 270,000 in 1970, up from 250,000 the previous year. Arrivals peaked at 360,000 in 1972. In 1972 the town management board was upgraded into a Town Council, and the Victoria Falls Main Camp accommodation, camping and caravanning facilities located in the town centre were taken under the Council's management in 1974. By the mid seventies new visitor pathways had been developed running through the Rainforest and to the various viewpoints on the south bank.

*The Victoria Falls Rest Camp*

Dr Cowen, railway medical officer at the Falls during the 1950s, recalls returning after a long absence of many years, recording mixed feelings over the many new developments and changes in the town and surroundings.

*"On arrival we noticed that a large international airport had been constructed a short distance from the falls alongside the road leading south, no longer a picturesque strip road but now a 22-foot [6.7 m] wide macadamized highway. Apart from the Victoria Falls Hotel, the village used to consist of a small police and customs post, a curio shop, a general store and a few huts for visitors. It now boasted another hotel, a large pretentious casino, bank, building society, numerous shops and a large tourist area where African arts and crafts were displayed and African woodcarvers and dancers performed... New wide roads and paths had been constructed in the vicinity of the falls, which were artificially lit up at night. The Victoria Falls Hotel had been enlarged and modernized and, in our opinion, had lost its elegant charm. When we were stationed there the Falls and the area immediately around them were left as Livingstone had discovered them and we were distressed to find all the new development. Some might see it as progress, but for us it was an appallingly retrogressive step!"* (Cowen, 1995)

## *End of the Line*

The development of the Boeing 747 in the early 1970s and subsequent growth of economy air travel made the Union Castle Line passenger service increasingly uneconomical. The company ended its mail and other shipping services altogether in September 1977. Specialist long-distance and luxury cruises, however, would remain a mainstay of the tourism industry into the new millennium.

## *Mosi-oa-Tunya National Park*

On the north bank the Victoria Falls Trust was dissolved and the Zoological Game Park redesignated as the expanded Mosi-oa-Tunya National Park on 25th February 1972, managed by the National Parks and Wildlife Services (now the Zambia Wildlife Authority). The Natural Heritage Commission (now the National Heritage Conservation Commission) continued to manage the Falls and historic cultural sites within the National Park, including the Old Drift settlement.

# Seventies Struggles

Following the declaration of independence life in white-ruled Rhodesia initially carried on much as before, despite being unrecognised on the international stage and the imposition of trading sanctions. But with the ruling white elite representing less than ten percent of the national population the call for a popular representative government was steadily gaining momentum. In an effort to establish international recognition Rhodesia broke its last ties to Britain and declared itself a republic on 2nd March 1970, yet still found itself in international limbo.

Political relationships between independent Zambia and white-controlled Rhodesia deteriorated and the Bridge was frequently closed to goods and passenger services. In 1969 the passenger service over the Bridge was indefinitely suspended, with Rhodesian trains terminating at the Falls.

The early 1970s saw an escalation in the struggle, with independence fighters based in Zambia launching strategic incursions and attacks against communication and

*Ian Smith at the Falls*

infrastructure targets on the southern side of the river. On the night of the 16th January 1970 the Police Camp and Sprayview Hotel were attacked and shots were also fired at the Victoria Falls Airport buildings. During the subsequent operation to capture the insurgents the railway line south of Victoria Falls was blown up.

Land mine incidents and train derailments occurred over subsequent months as the conflict intensified. The following year, on 3rd August 1971, a train was derailed on the line to the Falls.

Eventually, on 9th January 1973, Smith announced the closure of border posts with Zambia, including Victoria Falls, until he received satisfactory assurances from the Zambian Government that it would no longer permit terrorists to operate and launch attacks against Rhodesia from within its territory. In response Zambia closed their side of the border with Rhodesia on 1st February 1973. The river border remained tense, with the Falls Bridge again closely watched from observation bunkers.

On 15th May 1973 a tragic incident occurred resulting in the death of two Canadian tourists. Whilst exploring the gorges below the Falls Hotel with friends, Marjan Iduna Drijber and Christine Louise Sinclair (both 19) were both shot and killed by rifle fire from the north bank (Terpstra, 2008). Tourism collapsed on both sides of the river, with national tourism arrivals to Rhodesia decreasing to 250,000 in 1975.

Despite the official closure of the border, freight was still transported over the Falls Bridge. A Rhodesian engine would shunt a string of freight trucks out on to the middle of the Bridge, and a Zambian Rail diesel would back onto its end of the Bridge and pull them into Zambia, and vice-versa, several times a day. The closure of the border had significant impacts on tourism, preventing tourists from the south crossing into Zambia and cutting off the south bank from the services provided in Livingstone, further stimulating the growth of the small town on the south bank.

*"With the closure of the border between Rhodesia and Zambia, Victoria Falls was forced to become self-sufficient and also to provide a far wider ranger of tourist facilities if the tourist market was not to be lost to Zambia."* (Heath, 1977)

In 1973 the town was estimated to cover 310 hectares (PlanAfric, 2001). Heath records the population of Victoria Falls Town in the mid-seventies at around 3,000, and highlighted the increasing tourism pressures during the 1970s.

*"The rapid growth of Victoria Falls during the last decade has caused considerable planning problems. It is of paramount importance that the immediate vicinity of the Falls should be altered as little as possible if its natural qualities are to be preserved. Conservation needs, however, may conflict with the need to provide facilities for tourists and in recent years there has been a proliferation of tourist services along the river bank upstream from the Falls."* (Heath, 1977)

## Elephant Hills Country Club

The Elephant Hills Country Club was opened in 1974, located a short distance upstream of the Falls on the high ridge Percy Clark had named Dale's Kopje. The development included a golf course designed by South African golfer Gary Player and opened in 1975.

The course became known among golfers as 'more like a wildlife reserve than a golf course,' famed for its wildlife hazards - including interruptions by elephant, hippopotami and ball-stealing baboons - and giving rise to some rather curious local rule variations. Charlie the crocodile was well known for leaving his water-hazard home on the eighth hole to roam the fairways. The club rules clarified that 'a ball striking or deflected by a wild animal may be replayed from as near as possible to the spot from which the original ball was played.'

## Bridge Over Troubled Water

On 25th August 1975 the Bridge was the site of unsuccessful peace talks, known as the 1975 Constitutional Conference. The talks, lasting nine and a half hours, took place aboard a South African Railways coach from the 'White Train,' used in the 1947 Royal Tour, positioned across the middle of the Bridge.

Supervised by South African Prime Minister John Vorster, the tense negotiations included Rhodesian Prime Minister Ian Smith, Zambian President Kenneth Kaunda, and representatives of the African National Council, led by Bishop Abel Muzorewa. The Rhodesian delegation sat on their side of the coach whilst nationalist representatives sat on the Zambian side. One account records the staff were apparently rather too liberal with the bar service and two members became intoxicated and disruptive, helping talks to continue throughout the day. The talks failed to reconcile the representatives divergent viewpoints and the independence war gained intensity.

On 12th December 1976 a passenger train travelling south of Victoria Falls detonated a landmine. The locomotive and four passenger coaches were lifted from the track but did not overturn and no serious injuries were sustained. The passenger service to the Falls was subsequently suspended until after the war.

By 1977 hotels and campsites were closing in the face of security concerns, including the Rainbow Hotel, mothballed until more favourable tourism conditions returned. Upstream of the Falls the Zambezi Camp was closed and access to the river controlled as a cordon of security surrounded the tourism resort.

## Elephant Hills Burns

The original Elephant Hills was destroyed by a fire caused by a SAM 7 heat-seeking missile launched from Zambia on 2nd November 1977. Apparently fired at a Rhodesia United Air Carriers light tourist aircraft which was circulating above the Falls, it missed its target and by chance landed on the thatched roof of the Hotel. The explosion was reportedly heard as far away as the Falls Airport.

*Elephant Hills burns*

*"It was the day after the conclusion of the Elephant Hills Golf Classic, and the luxury hotel, full to capacity the day before, was 'recuperating' from the excitement of the famous golfing tournament...The guests had all left the evening before, on the daily Air Rhodesia flight back to Salisbury, and the hotel was empty, apart from hotel staff busy cleaning and preparing for the next expected influx of guests. The terrorist rocket, fired at the hotel from Zambia, hit the top floor Gary Player Suite, vacated just the evening before by Commander, Combined Operations, Lt General Peter Walls, a guest of the golfing classic.*

*"The missile, attracted by the heat of the air-conditioning unit, caused extensive damage, and an uncontrollable fire soon raged throughout the building with staff running in and out of the stricken hotel trying to retrieve prized furnishings and equipment. There was no fire brigade in the Victoria Falls village, and the nearest fire engine was at the Airport, some 13 kms away. Used only for the occasional slow run along the runway, the fire engine now raced at top speed along the main road from the airport to the hotel. The first problem encountered was to find that the electricity to the hotel had been switched off in the village, presumably as a precaution, and the fire engine was unable to pump water; it was quickly decided to pump water from the swimming pool and it was then that the fire engine, overheating from its rush to the scene, seized with a loud bang! Everyone on the scene then had to help manually pump water from the pool.*

*The hotel was destroyed, and remained a shell for the next five or six years, with only a squash court and a bar still operating."* (Moore, 2012)

Luckily there were no casualties, but the hotel was completely gutted by the fire. The passengers from the light aircraft, piloted by Eddie Marucchi, apparently took it all in their stride. One, Mr Lief Bjorseth, was recorded as saying: *"It's not every day you get shot at - I got something extra for my money"* (Teede and Teede, 1994).

## Emergency Procedures

With the ongoing independence struggle and closure of the border Victoria Falls was the scene of heightened military activity, and the cause of much concern for the managers of Falls Hotel.

*"There was no particular reason to suspect that there might be an attack on the hotel as the Victoria Falls area was a hive of Security Force activity from the outset, although precautions were taken after the destruction of the Elephant Hills. Care had always to be taken not to alarm guests, nor to scare off would-be visitors, and after a failed mortar attack on the Victoria Falls area, with one off-target shell narrowly missing the laundry outbuilding, causing slight damage, it was decided to warn guests by sticking notices onto their bathroom mirrors. The hotel quickly found that the stickers were being removed by guests as souvenirs, and new stocks had to be constantly reprinted!"* (Moore, 2012)

*Hotel emergency notice*

Mitch Stirling, a pilot with Rhodesia United Air Carriers recalls the incident at the Falls Hotel:

*"One evening a mortar bomb landed in the tea garden of the world-famous Victoria Falls hotel. Nobody was injured, fortunately, but the Grand old Lady of the Falls... suffered great indignity. Dicky Bradshaw was the Rhodesia United Air Carriers engineer at the time and the two of us were enjoying a few*

*bitterly cold ales in the nearby Motel pub when the explosion occurred. Dicky didn't even spill a drop, but one of the customers, later nicknamed 'Sooty,' disappeared up the chimney where he hid. He later paid a severe penalty from the other patrons - drinks for the rest of the evening were on Sooty's account!"* (Stirling, 2015)

In the early 1970s annual tourist arrivals to the country had reached 360,000. By 1979 there were only 79,000 recorded - the lowest total since 1963. Over sixty percent of guests at the Falls Hotel came from South Africa, as international arrivals evaporated.

*"Tourism was badly affected by the war and the country's hotels survived only because of support from Government in the form of subsidies and subsidised travel by local and international visitors. To help the battered tourism sector, the national airline and hotel groups introduced the Super Six scheme, in which guests went on air and road packages for up to six nights at significantly discounted prices. The scheme met with reasonable success and the number of visitors to hotels, including the Victoria Falls Hotel, was remarkable given the overall situation in the country."* (Creewel, 2004)

## Minefield Menace

To prevent opposition forces crossing into Rhodesia the road surface of the Falls Bridge was removed and in late 1978 and the Bridge set with explosives, ready to blow a critical section should it be necessary (Burrett and Murray, 2013).

Extensive anti-personnel minefields were laid along 220 kilometres of border between Victoria Falls and downstream to Mlibizi during the period of the war. The minefields would continue to pose a serious threat to people and wildlife for decades after the war. It would take until 2015 before the vast majority of these minefields would be cleared, with the removal of over 50,000 land mines (Victoria Falls Bits and Blogs, June 2015).

## Flights Suspended

*"South African Airways has suspended Salisbury stopovers on its Johannesburg-London services, cutting the last direct air link between Britain and Rhodesia... It is also reported that SAA has suspended services from Johannesburg to Victoria Falls and has stopped selling inclusive tours to Rhodesia's northern border resorts."* (Flight International Magazine, Feb 1979)

## Zambezi National Park

Under the Parks and Wildlife Act (1975) the Victoria Falls National Park was subdivided in 1979 to form Zambezi National Park, covering 56,000 hectares upstream of the Falls, and the smaller Victoria Falls National Park, covering 1,900 hectares, under the management of the Parks and Wildlife Management Authority. Today the Falls Park includes the immediate area of the Falls, Rainforest and gorges stretching some 12 kilometres downstream, with a narrow strip of riverine fringe extending six kilometres upstream connecting with the Zambezi National Park. The redrawing of the park boundaries degazetted some 3,000 hectares surrounding the expanding town of Victoria Falls.

# Eighties Independence

Towards the end of 1979 the first steps towards peace and normality showed with the re-opening of the Falls Bridge in November. Divided Rhodesia became united independent Zimbabwe on 18th April 1980 in accordance with the Lancaster House Agreement, negotiated between the British government, independence leaders and the Rhodesian government, and signed on 21st December 1979.

Rail services to the Victoria Falls resumed from 6th July 1980 and the Bridge reopened to road and rail transport, although passenger services have remained suspended to this day. Rhodesia Railways became the renamed National Railways of Zimbabwe in May 1980.

The total number of international visitors to Zimbabwe in 1980 rebounded to 238,000 - triple those of the previous year - rising to 314,000 in 1981. The Zambezi Park reopened as normality returned to the region. By 1982 the population of Victoria Falls Town had grown to 8,126 (CSO, 1989).

Despite the formal end of hostilities, divisions between independence factions positioning themselves within the new political power structure resulted in violent flashpoints. On 23rd July 1982 another tragic incident occurred when a group of six international tourists were kidnapped and murdered by political dissidents whilst travelling between Victoria Falls and Bulawayo. Two of the group were Americans (Kevin Ellis, 24 years old, and Brett Baldwin, 23); two were Australians (Tony Bajzelz, 25, and William Butler, 31); and two were British (James Greenwell, 18, and Martyn Hodgson, 35). Tourism again slumped in the shadow of negative international headlines and travel warnings. National tourism arrivals dropped to 276,000 in 1982 and a low of 230,000 in 1983.

## Freedom of the Skies

Following independence in 1980 Rhodesia United Air Carriers evolved into United Air Carriers Ltd, later United Air Ltd. At the Falls the company offered the 15-minute 'Flight of Angels' in one of their twin-engined Piper Aztecs:

*The Falls from the air*

*"Winging low over the Falls and gorges, one thrills at the grandeur of this magnificent sight that can only be truly absorbed from the air. No traveller can claim to have viewed this natural wonder of the world in its entirety without seeing it from the air. This aptly named flight in a twin-engined Piper Aztec is designed for the keen photographer and adventurous traveller, giving a bird's eye view of Africa's greatest geological feature - Victoria Falls."*

Operating from the Sprayview Aerodrome the Sprayview Air Safari (30 minutes) and Zambesi Sky Safari (75 min) offered extended game viewing opportunities:

*"Departures from Sprayview are in the early morning or late afternoon, the ideal time to view Africa's paradise of wildlife. Your journey takes you along the Chamabonda Vlei, across thickly forested areas to Chundu Loop on the mighty Zambesi, then down the south bank to the Falls. You circle the mist of Mosi-oa-Tunya and capture the brilliance of one of nature's miracles."* (UAC, 1980s)

## Visit of Princess Anne

Her Royal Highness Princess Anne visited Zimbabwe in 1982 as part of a tour of six African countries in her capacity as President of the Save the Children Fund, staying in the Queen's Suite of the Victoria Falls Hotel (now renamed the Livingstone Suite) for two nights at the end of October 1982. The Princess undertook a tour of the Falls and Zambezi boat cruise - brief breaks in a busy official schedule which included visiting the local Jairos Jiri centre for severely handicapped children.

## Rising Fortunes

In an attempt to encourage tourism north of the river a Zambian Ministry of Tourism was formed in 1980. Tourism in Livingstone was still in the doldrums after decades of neglect and unsupportive government policies. In the national census of 1980 Livingstone's population was recorded as 71,521 (Moonga, 1999).

Positive results showed in 1981 with Zambia receiving close to 150,000 tourist arrivals, compared to just over 50,000 in 1979. The turnaround came too late to save the town's oldest hotel, the North-Western Hotel, which closed in 1984.

Zimbabwe was also on the rise, with the total number of recorded tourism arrivals in 1984 at 255,000. Figures steadily increased to 303,000 in 1985, 319,000 in 1986 and 339,000 in 1987.

In 1986 the Zimbabwe Tourist Development Corporation (ZTDC), a parastatal organisation, reopened the two-star Rainbow Hotel (closed during the late seventies) and later in the same year took over the three-star A'Zambezi River Lodge. ZTDC later became the government owned Rainbow Tourism Group (RTG).

The site of the old Sprayview Restaurant (demolished in 1970) was redeveloped as the family-run 16-room Ilala Lodge Hotel, opened in 1988. In the mid nineties the Hotel was expanded to 34 rooms.

By 1988 the total number of international visitors to Zimbabwe had jumped to record levels of 412,000, followed by 436,000 in 1989.

## On Location

Hollywood came to the Falls with the filming of the Cannon/Paramount Pictures action adventure films 'King Solomon's Mines' (released in 1985) and its sequel 'Allan Quatermain and the Lost City of Gold' (1986). Staring Richard Chamberlain and Sharon Stone the films were shot simultaneously on location in Zimbabwe during 1985.

The empty ruins of the burnt out Elephant Hills Country Club were used as a focal filming location for the second film - transformed into an 'opulent location set.' Stone received a nomination for a Golden Raspberry Worst Actress Award for her performance. Chamberlain is remembered by location crew for thoroughly hating his time in Africa and spending most of his spare time back at the sanctuary of the Falls Hotel.

# Africa's Adrenalin Capital

During the late 1980s and early 1990s Victoria Falls saw the development of thrill-seeking adventure activities, earning the town a new reputation as the 'adrenalin capital of Africa.' In addition to the traditional tourism activities of game drives and river safaris, new 'high-intensity' activities, such as white-water rafting and bungee jumping attracted a younger generation of travellers to the Falls. The section of river running through the narrow zigzagging Batoka Gorge offers some of the most extreme commercially operated white-water rafting in the world, with nearly half of the rapids classified as Grade 5 - the highest commercially runnable grading (Grade 6 is 'unrunnable').

White-water rafting on the Zambezi was pioneered by American company Sobek with the first expedition to traverse the rapids of the river below the Falls to Lake Kariba undertaken in October 1981 using specialist inflatable rafts. Eight of Sobek's most experienced guides, accompanied by an ABC 'The American Sportsman' film crew with actor LeVar Burton as presenter, took up the challenge.

The first raft capsized in the first rapid. The Zambian President, Kenneth Kaunda, watching from the Bridge above, turned to a reporter and asked, 'Is that how they do it?' As they progressed the expedition planned to number the rapids running downstream from the Falls, but lost count after 11! The group had to do precautionary sweeps for mines before camping on sandbanks, and half-way down one of the rafts was attacked by a crocodile. After several close shaves enough was enough for Burton and a helicopter air-evacuation soon followed.

*White-water thrills and spills*

Sobek started commercial white-water rafting with day trips covering the first 10 rapids and week-long expeditions downstream in mid 1982, operating from the northern bank and breathing life into Livingstone's struggling tourism sector.

The fact that they had no specialist inflatable rafts did not stop the first Zimbabwean group to raft

157

the rapids a couple of years later, notably completing the trip in home-made rafts comprised of tractor wheel inner tubes and bamboo frames (Pitman, 1984).

Home-grown Zimbabwe based companies followed, pioneered in similar infallible spirit, with the formation of the Zambezi Wildwater Rafting Company, founded in 1982 by Paul Connolly, a lawyer with a passion for canoeing and kayaking the river, the first to start commercial operations in 1985. The company quickly evolved into the Shearwater Adventures Group, specialising in canoeing safaris on the upper and middle Zambezi and rafting the rapids below the Falls.

Other companies, such as Frontiers, Adrift and Hi-Siders soon followed. Over the first decade of rafting it was estimated that some 50,000 tourists had experienced the thrill of the rapids, the majority with either Sobek or Shearwater. In 1991 alone Shearwater handled over 12,500 rafters. From 1996 to 1999 it was estimated that 50,000 tourists rafted the rapids below the Falls each year, and at its peak in popularity saw 60 rafts containing 420 people transit down the 18 sets of raging rapids in one day (Meadows, 2000).

The Zimbabwe based tourism operator Safari Par Excellence, established in 1988, started operating rafting trips on the south bank from 1994.

## *3, 2, 1 Bungee!*

Bungee jumping from the Victoria Falls Bridge, the first commercial jump in Africa, was started by Kiwi Extreme in the early 1990s. With a free-fall of 111 metres and the dramatic background of the Falls, it is without doubt one of the most spectacular and breath-taking commercial jumps in the world.

*"'How much do they pay you to do that?' asked an elderly Zambian incredulously, as he put down his groceries to stare at the extraordinary spectacle. When told that they actually paid for the privilege of thus risking their skins, he went off shaking his head. White men were a strange breed, as everyone knew, but this was too much!"* (Teede and Teede, 1994)

*Bridge bungee*

Noteable 'jumpers' include the current Chief Mukuni Siloka III, who appeared on the Bridge in full ceremonial regalia and accompanied by many followers, who were all in festive mood. Having come this far, the pressure on him to jump was intense, and after a brief hesitation he toppled into the void, to the accompaniment of wild cheers from the onlookers.

## Champagne Cruises and Dance Spectaculars

With the changing demographics of tourists to the Falls, and increase in young independent travellers attracted by adrenalin activities, sedate late afternoon Zambezi river cruises with complimentary sundowners evolved into party boats with free drinks - the 'booze cruise.'

*"Late afternoon found us on a sunset riverboat cruise quaintly called the Champagne Cruise, possibly so-named because the amount of wildlife was less than we would have like to have seen. But there were champagne, wine, and beer; and two of the passengers were four sheets to the wind before we returned to shore. Nevertheless, we did watch numerous hippos playing in the water... The sunset itself was beautiful, and our skipper got us back to shore in time to go to the 'dance spectacular' at the Victoria Falls Hotel."* (Boer, 2011)

## World Heritage Site

The core area of the Victoria Falls, covering some 6,860 hectares and including the river corridor upstream and downstream of the waterfall on both sides of the river, was designated by the United Nations Educational, Scientific and Cultural Organization (UNESCO) as a World Heritage Site on 15th December 1989, inscribed for both its outstanding geological and ecological value under the World Heritage Convention (1972), of which both countries are signatories. The listing described the Falls as *"the world's greatest sheet of falling water and significant worldwide for its exceptional geological and geomorphological features and active land formation processes with outstanding beauty attributed to the falls"* (UNESCO, 1989).

The Victoria Falls/Mosi-oa-Tunya World Heritage Site lies entirely within the protected areas of the Victoria Falls (741 ha) and Zambezi (2,340 ha) National Parks in Zimbabwe and the Mosi-oa-Tunya (3,779 ha) National Park on the Zambian side of the river. The site is protected under the Zimbabwe Parks and Wildlife Act (1975, revised 2008) on the southern bank, and the National Heritage Conservation Act (1998) and Zambia Wildlife Act (1998, revised 2015) on the northern bank.

# Boom Town

During the early 1990s tourism arrivals and hotel occupancy on the Zimbabwe side of the Falls was booming, leading to a rapid increase in tourism infrastructure development. Tourism operators and products diversified and accommodation providers flourished.

*"The years 1988 to 1999 were to become known as the boom years for Zimbabwean tourism. Large numbers of visitors arrived and demand for accommodation reached unprecedented levels, especially in Victoria Falls. New hotels and lodges were built, including Ilala Lodge, and air services to the local airport expanded to include up to three flights from Johannesburg each day, two flights from Harare, one from Bulawayo and various others from Botswana and Namibia. At one point a Harare-London service from Air Zimbabwe included a stop at Victoria Falls, making it a direct destination for international travellers from abroad for the first time."* (Creewel, 2004)

The re-invention of the destination as an adventure and adrenalin activity hub resulted in a boom in the town's night-life, with the famous Explorer Bar the centre of the late night scene, and earning the town a 24-hour, seven days a week, non-stop party reputation. Video presentations of the days' rafting, with all the thrills and spills, flips, and perhaps a few flops, drew people to the bars, followed by late-night DJ parties at Downtime, an underground bar within the Ilala Lodge development. Long-distance trans-Africa overland truck routes all led to the Falls, delivering thirsty thrill-seeking backpackers on 'round the world' gap-year adventures.

Annual international arrivals to Zimbabwe rose steadily to successive records of 583,000 in 1990, 607,000 in 1991 and 675,000 in 1992. In 1993 arrivals increased significantly to 879,500, followed by new record highs of 1,039,000 in 1994 and 1,415,500 in 1995.

The 1992 population census showed that Victoria Falls Town had grown to 16,826 (CSO, 1994) and by 1995 the town had expanded to cover an estimated 758 hectares (PlanAfric, 2001). By comparison Livingstone's population was recorded at over 82,500 in the 1990 national census (Moonga, 1999).

The high numbers of visitors raised concerns over the integrity of the Falls site. In 1986 the author Heath concluded the Rainforest had already reached its peak-season carrying capacity (Heath, 1986). Ten years later a World Conservation Union report raised similar concerns over the impacts of high visitor numbers, calculated to be close to the carrying capacity for the infrastructure facilities available (World Conservation Union, 1996).

## Elephant Hills Redeveloped

The Elephant Hills Intercontinental Resort and Conference Centre rose from the ashes of the old Country Club in 1991. The new 276-room hotel was developed by Zimbabwe Sun Hotels at a cost of $150 million.

The resort served as the exclusive retreat for the Commonwealth Heads of Government Meeting (CHOGM), hosted in Harare in October 1991, before being officially opened by President Robert Mugabe in February in 1993. The completed building, looking more like a fortress than a tourism resort, dominates the local landscape and has been described as a 'grey monolith' and in one famous travel guide series as a 'hideously obtrusive white elephant' (Pinchuck, 2000).

> *"For years the crumbling ruin sat atop Dale's Kopje, a forlorn, unwanted war victim. Then came the tourist boom of the late 1980s, and a new hotel rose like a hideous phoenix from the ashes of the old. It towered above the treeline, its dull granite walls capped with a ridiculous thatch bonnet. Visible for many kilometres upstream on the Zimbabwean side, it is virtually impossible to view the Eastern Cataract from Zambia without the new Elephant Hills decorating the skyline. A great swathe of trees was cleared for the new road, rubble was strewn throughout the surrounding bush, building sand was scoured out of the National Park; nothing was allowed to stand in the way of its completion in time for the Commonwealth Conference of 1991, in mockery of the very concept of world heritage."* (Teede and Teede, 1994)

The golf-course was restored to international standards, keeping close to Gary Player's original design, with a nine-hole course ready in time for the Commonwealth meeting, later expanded to a full 18-hole course. The resort also included tennis courts, casino and helipad - from which Southern Cross Aviation operated a Bell Long Range Helicopter for tourist flights from the mid 1990s, the first commercial helicopter flights over the Falls.

## Victoria Falls Safari Lodge

The 72-room Victoria Falls Safari Lodge complex, including the Lokuthula Lodges and The Boma - The Place of Eating, opened on the western edge of the growing town in December 1994. Developed by Africa Albida Tourism, the Lodge and surrounding estate complex is one of the largest new developments on the south bank since the construction of the original Elephant Hills complex in the mid 1970s.

During construction an environmental architect was employed to ensure minimal impact on the lodge's surroundings. No mature trees were

*Victoria Falls Safari Lodge*

felled during building work and 6,000 young trees were planted on and around the estate. These efforts were recognised when the Lodge was awarded the prestigious international Green Globe Distinction Award in 2000 for outstanding environmental practices in its construction. The development was, however, still criticised by conservationists for building on a natural site previously identified as an important wildlife corridor.

> *"In addition, the... Victoria Falls Safari Lodge... is built on land originally set aside as a wildlife corridor from the Zambezi National Park to the river. This has created a whole new problem - keeping potentially dangerous large animals at a safe distance from tourists. Electric fences have been erected to 'protect' the new Safari Lodge and the Elephant Hills Golf Course."* (Wynn, 1995)

The main lodge buildings are built on a natural ridge overlooking an artificial waterhole, pumped all year to maintain water levels and floodlit at night for nocturnal wildlife viewing. In 1995, its first full year of operation, the Lodge achieved an average occupancy of 72 percent.

## *Territorial Tensions*

News reports record that in September 1995 warning shots were fired over a Zimbabwean operated cruise boat from the Zambian side of the river. Business rivalries between cruise boat operators on either side of the river (and an ongoing dispute over the official line of the international border between the two countries), resulting in some over-zealous policing of territorial waters.

### Falls Hotel Reborn

During 1996 the Victoria Falls Hotel underwent a substantial redevelopment and full refurbishment, estimated at costing $6.5 million, upgrading and modernising the rooms and facilities to luxurious five-star standards, whilst recapturing the historical period feel of the original Hotel buildings. In 1997 the Hotel opened the 42-room Stables Wing, bringing the Hotel total to 161 rooms.

### Site for Sale

On the north bank of the Falls the site of the old InterContinental Hotel - derelict and decaying after many years in the tourist doldrums - was offered for redevelopment in 1997. The lease of the site, including the neighbouring Rainbow Lodge and additional connecting National Parks land, was bought by Sun International of South Africa. The agreement included a capital investment commitment of over $50 million for the redevelopment of the site and the building of a 250 room family hotel, 120 room luxury 5-star hotel and a 50 room bush lodge.

# Visitor Highs

Towards the end of the nineties Zimbabwe's tourism sector was riding high, with record arrivals and receipts. National annual international arrivals reached 1,596,500 in 1996, dropping slightly to 1,335,500 in 1997 before rising to 2,090,500 in 1998 and a new landmark of 2,249,500 in 1999.

> *"During the period 1989-99, the tourist arrivals increased at an average growth rate of 17.5 percent, whilst tourism receipts grew at an average annual growth rate of 18 percent in US dollar terms."* (Mugwati, Nkala and Mashiri, 2016)

Average room occupancy in the Falls rose from 59 percent in 1997 to 76 percent in 1998, dropping to 62 percent in 1999. The Falls Rainforest recorded 313,043 visitors in 1998, comprising 97,144 Zimbabwean and 215,899 international tourists (Nelson, 2000). In the same year 23,535 tourists visited the Zambezi National Park. Visitors to the Rainforest dropped to 190,000 in 1999.

The Elephant's Walk Shopping and Artists Village opened in 1997 on a site adjoining Soper's Curio's shop (and relocated to within the complex in 2016).

Responding to changing tourist demographics, the town's first backpackers, Shoestrings Backpackers Lodge, opened in 1997.

## Changing Face

During the late 1990s significant redevelopments and new ventures refreshed the image of the evolving tourist town.

The Makasa Sun Hotel site adjacent to the Falls Hotel was closed in 1998 with the Zimbabwe Sun Group investing $24 million in the complete redevelopment of the site. The 294-room The Kingdom at Victoria Falls was officially opened by President Robert Mugabe in July 1999. The architectural design of the hotel buildings were closely inspired and influenced by the ancient ruins of Great Zimbabwe. The complex includes 'The Great Enclosure,' an entertainment complex including the Makasa Casino, Quartermains (a stylish Edwardian themed bar), the Wild Thing 'action bar,' Panarotti's Italian pizza restaurant and the Thundercloud Spur steak-house.

The Stanley and Livingstone Safari Lodge was developed in 1999 by Rani Resorts, set amongst verdant grounds and adjoining a 6,000 acre private wildlife reserve on an out-of-town location. The five-star luxury lodge accommodates up to 32 in 16 suites. A separate private retreat, Old Ursula Camp, located on the Stanley and Livingstone Private Game Reserve, accommodates eight.

During the late 1990s Zimbabwe based operator Safari Par Excellence expanded operations into Zambia, developing the Zambezi Waterfront on the banks of the Zambezi River, four kilometres above the Falls. The development opened in December 1999 and includes riverside restaurant and bar with pool deck, 23 on-suite chalets, 24 permanent tents, camping for up to 100 clients and jetty sites for two cruise boats, the MV Makumbi and MV Mambushi.

In mid 1999 Cresta Hospitality announced plans to construct a five-star 80-room riverside hotel, Cresta River Lodge, on the site of the old Zambezi Caravan and Campsite, in a proposed joint venture with the town council. The proposed $30 million development failed to materialise.

## Victoria Falls Anti-Poaching Unit

Charles Brightman, a local safari operator and conservationist, together with support from the Victoria Falls Safari Lodge, established the Victoria Falls Anti-Poaching Unit (VFAPU) in January 1999. VFAPU works in close association with the National Park authorities undertaking regular anti-poaching patrols and supporting the arrest and prosecution of poachers, educating local communities, co-ordinating snare-removal operations and animal welfare interventions.

# Millennium Madness

The beginning of the new millennium was not an easy period for Zimbabwe or its tourism sector. State-sponsored land requisitions saw white-owned farms invaded and farmers intimidated, beaten and even murdered by mobs of liberation 'war veterans' in efforts to forcefully evict them from their land. Generating widespread international criticism and negative media headlines, tourism collapsed as international travellers turned instead to neighbouring countries. International visitors to Zimbabwe dropped from 2,249,500 in 1999 to 1,966,500 in 2000.

*"The Zimbabwe Tourist Authority offered free 'educationals' to international tour operators in a bid to coax them back to the country. An estimated 100 tour operators in Zimbabwe had closed since the crisis began, and tour operators catering for visitors to the Victoria Falls began transferring their bases across the Zambezi river to Livingstone."* (Murison, 2003)

In 2000 Rainbow Tourism Group doubled the capacity of their two-star Rainbow Hotel to 88 rooms, whilst also announcing plans for a new, eventually unrealised, five-star hotel development. Average room occupancy in the Falls fell from 62 percent in 1999 to 37 percent the following year, although recovering to 43 percent in 2001 (Mugwati, Nkala and Mashiri, 2016).

In 2001 the town's eight main hotels, several lodges and numerous guest houses were estimated to be able accommodate a capacity of about 3,000 visitor bed-nights, with the town calculated to cover an area of 2,212 hectares (PlanAfric, 2001). Victoria Falls Town attained municipality status in 1999 and by 2002 the population was recorded at 31,375 residents (CSO, 2002).

Despite the $81 million redevelopment of Harare International Airport terminal buildings in 2001, with a passenger capacity of 2.5 million per year, predicted increases in international tourism arrivals failed to materialise.

*"The number of airlines that linked Zimbabwe to one hundred international source markets in 1996 dropped from forty-five to fewer than ten."* (Mugwati, Nkala and Mashiri, 2016)

Political and economic difficulties continued in the build up to the Parliamentary and Presidential elections of 2002, resulting in a depreciating Zimbabwe dollar and shortages of fuel and basic food products. Following the election the European Union imposed 'targeted' sanctions on Zimbabwe for serious election irregularities

*The Victoria Falls from the western end*

and it was suspended from the Commonwealth of Nations. At the end of 2002 Zimbabwe introduced entry visa fees for British visitors.

International arrivals to Zimbabwe, which had recovered to 2,217,500 in 2001, dropped to 2,041,000 in 2002. Average room occupancy in the Falls fell from 43 percent in 2001 to 41 percent in 2002 (Mugwati, Nkala and Mashiri, 2016).

## Up, Up and Away

A short-lived attraction at the Falls was the establishment of a specialist tethered helium balloon, opened in early 2000. The balloon, rising to 120 metres, supported a circular gondola carrying up to 30 people and offering a 360 degree panoramic view of the town, Falls and river. Before long, however, the cost of the imported helium gas required to keep the balloon afloat apparently inflated some 600 percent (literally ballooning in cost), making the operation financially unviable. The attraction was suspended in June 2002.

## Elephant Hills Gutted

On 24th July 2001 a significant part of the Elephant Hills Hotel complex was, for the second time, gutted by fire. Following a major renovation (and insurance claim) the hotel officially reopened in June 2003 with improved and updated services and facilities, including a modern room-by-room fire alarm and emergency sprinkler system.

## Setting the Standard

Overlooking the Falls from the north bank, the redevelopment of the old InterContinental Hotel site established Livingstone as a serious competitor to Zimbabwe's traditional dominance in the tourism market. The Sun International development included the 173-room Royal Livingstone Hotel, opened in July 2001 to opulent five-star standards, and three-star sibling the 212-room Zambezi Sun.

The construction involved the controversial excavation and removal of stone and iron-age artefacts from prehistoric sites dating back 60,000 years. Together with other riverside lodges the majority of Livingstone's tourists were now accommodated outside of the town itself, in developments closer to the Falls.

The Mukuni Environmental, Cultural and Economic Development Trust was established in 2003 supported by contributions from local tourism activities and operations, with funds generated supporting community education and health projects.

## Veteran Vandalism

In December 2001, during a political party conference hosted at the Falls, a mob of 'liberation veterans' invaded the Rainforest and attacked the David Livingstone statue, apparently in the hope of tearing it from its plinth and hurling it into the gorge of the Falls. Frustrated in their efforts they turned to the metal plaques at the base of the statue, taking umbrage at their heralding of the Scottish missionary as the 'discoverer' of the Falls.

*"In December 2001, at a congress of the ruling party, a hundred veterans of the Zimbabwe liberation war began stoning the Livingstone Statue. Terrified tourists ran for cover, as the veterans smashed the historic markers describing Livingstone's 'discovery.' Riot police were forced to guard the statue for the remainder of the party congress."* (Robert, 2009)

Zambia subsequently requested in 2004 that the statue be moved to their side of the river, claiming the statue had been originally located on the northern bank before being relocated to its present location. The request was refused and Zambia commissioned its own statue of the Scottish missionary and explorer, unveiled on 16th November 2005 overlooking the Eastern Cataract to celebrate the 150th anniversary of the explorer's first sighting of the Falls. A second statue was also positioned in the front of the Livingstone Museum, together with a bust of Dr Emil Holub, unveiled in the same year.

## Looking East

In an effort to bolster tourism arrivals after the decline of arrivals from traditional source countries in Europe and North America, Zimbabwe turned to new, emerging tourism markets, looking especially towards Asia and the Middle East.

*"After losing export revenue from major tourist markets (UK and USA) due to travel warnings issued against Zimbabwe, the country had to look elsewhere to boost foreign tourist arrivals and generate the much needed foreign currency. During the period 2003 to 2005, the government focus shifted to targeting the Asian and Middle East* [markets]*, but the number could not surpass the loss from traditional source markets... Arrivals from Asia increased by 40 percent from 29,075 to 40,971 in 2003. The visitors were mainly from Japan, India and China."* (Abel and Mudzonga, 2016)

International arrivals recovered to 2,256,000 in 2003, falling to 1,854,500 in 2004, and average room occupancy in the Falls fell from 35 percent in 2003 to 29 percent in 2004. Visitors to the Falls Park dropped below 80,000 in 2003.

## Regatta Reborn

The Livingstone Regatta returned to the Zambezi in 2004 with an international invitation event sponsored by Sun International and pitching crews from Oxford, Cambridge and South Africa (from Rhodes and Rand Afrikaans Universities). Ernest Barry's grandson, Bill Barry, rowed in a special exhibition race. The regatta has been successfully held several times since.

## A Grand Old Lady

The Falls Hotel celebrated 100 hundred years of accommodating tourists and its pioneering role in the development of tourism to the Falls during 2004. From humble beginnings to modern five-star luxury, the Hotel has become an iconic symbol of the Falls, affectionately known by locals as 'The Grand Old Lady of the Falls.'

Meikles Africa Ltd and Zimbabwe Sun, now joint managers of the Falls Hotel, invested in a redevelopment of the tourist facilities at the Falls with an upgrade of the visitor car park at the entrance to the Rainforest. The new facility was officially opened in December 2003 and included the construction of permanent market facilities for licensed independent curio traders.

## *On Patrol*

A new initiative funded by tourism operators and supported by the Zimbabwe Republic Police saw the establishment of local community 'tourism police.' The tourism police patrol the main tourism areas around town, often enacting a daily game of cat-and-mouse with illegal street vendors. Tourists are encouraged to purchase arts and crafts only from licensed traders operating from the formal craft markets, stalls and shops and not to encourage informal traders who can plague visitors for their trade.

# In the Spotlight

In mid 2005 the Zimbabwe government launched the notorious Operation Murambatsvina ('Clear out the Rubbish'), also known as Operation Restore Order, forcibly clearing informally developed urban areas in major cities and towns, including Chinotimba, the African suburb at the Falls (Sokwanele, 2005).

Justified by officials as a legitimate operation to crackdown against illegal housing and an effort to control crime and the spread of infectious diseases, the areas targeted were incidentally also strongholds of political opposition against the government in recent elections. Homes were bulldozed and burned without notice as whole suburbs were raised to the ground. The United Nations estimated some 700,000 people were displaced from their homes nationwide.

Meanwhile the Zambian side of the river was operating at peak-season near-capacity, fuelling an increased growth in infrastructure development on the north bank. In 2004 visitors exploring the Zambian side of the Falls stood at 72,002. Political and economic uncertainty south of the river resulted in this figure jumping to 179,786 in 2005 (Zambian Ministry of Tourism and Arts, 2014).

The Zambian National Tourism Board (ZNTB) experimented with floodlighting of the Eastern Cataract during 2004, utilising lights which had been installed in 1989, but not used due to the controversy they caused. The development was short-lived, with the Environment Council of Zambia instructing the ZNTB terminate the project and remove the floodlights.

International arrivals to Zimbabwe fell to 1,558,500 in 2005. Visitors to the Falls Rainforest totalled 161,834 in 2005, declining to 134,010 in 2006. By 2006 average hotel occupancy on the Zimbabwean side of the Falls hovered to around 30 percent.

## Come to the Falls

In an effort to bypass negative perceptions of the country, tourism providers in Victoria Falls launched a campaign to directly market the destination.

*"Tourism activity dropped drastically from the period 2000-05... The improvement in output growth and receipts in the two years [2006 and 2007] was a result of the tourism and hospitality sectors efforts to manage the country's damaged image through a perception management campaign which was rolled out in overseas markets... However, the political instability in the country and the elections of 2008 resulted in the deterioration of the sector in the year, overpowering the image-building efforts that had been implemented in the previous two years."* (Mugwati, Nkala and Mashiri, 2016)

Official figures showed that international arrivals to Zimbabwe recovered to reach successive record highs of 2,286,500 in 2006 and 2,506,000 in 2007.

## Legacy Lunacy

In October 2006 it was announced that the Zambian Wildlife Authority (ZAWA) had awarded a concession to South Africa's Legacy Group Holdings for a major new tourism development within the World Heritage Site. The announcement stimulated a UNESCO monitoring mission to investigate the proposed development.

The proposed $200 million Mosi-oa-Tunya Hotel and Country Club Estate Project planned to develop a tourist resort on a 550 acre riverside site in the National Park. The plans included two five-star hotels, an 18-hole golf course, conference centre and a marina on the Zambezi, all a short distance above the Falls.

After widespread negative public reaction and strong local opposition to the proposals, Zambia abandoned the project in December 2006. A moratorium on development within the WHS was subsequently imposed by UNESCO, pending agreement and implementation of a joint management plan for the site.

*Lunar rainbow from the Eastern Cataract*

# World's Largest Conservation Area

The Kavango-Zambezi Transfrontier Conservation Area (KAZA TFCA) is a cooperative effort among five neighbouring countries - Angola, Botswana, Namibia, Zambia and Zimbabwe - to link protected wildlife areas across international boundaries. The Victoria Falls is at the heart of the TFCA, near the meeting point of four of the five participating countries on the Zambezi at Kazungula.

This vast wilderness and wildlife area is the world's largest transfrontier conservation project at approximately 520,000 square kilometres, a size rivalling that of France. Occupying the Okavango and Zambezi river basins, it includes 17 national parks and a host of game reserves, forest reserves, game management area, wildlife conservation and tourism concession reserves.

The region supports the largest contiguous population of African elephant, with more than 120,000 elephants recorded in recent aerial surveys from the Okavango/Chobe region, over 50,000 elephants in north-western Zimbabwe and 16,000 in north-eastern Namibia. Other focal species of conservation concern across the region include important populations of wild dog, lion and cheetah.

The TFCA was declared in 2006 with the signing of an Memorandum of Understanding between the five participating countries, followed by the signing of a formal Treaty in 2011 through which the park was legally established. The KAZA TFCA records its mission to 'establish a world-class transfrontier conservation area and tourism destination in the Okavango and Zambezi river basin regions of Angola, Botswana, Namibia, Zambia and Zimbabwe within the context of sustainable development.'

A survey of tourism accommodation provision in the KAZA region, undertaken over 2004, estimated a bed-night capacity of 8,312 and a total annual guest-night figure of 782,200. Tourism revenues were estimated at over $100 million, with $89.4 million generated within the accommodation sector and $10.8 million by tour operators. Of the available accommodation capacity, 35 percent was in Livingstone, 32 percent in Victoria Falls, 17 percent in northern Botswana, 12 percent in Caprivi and just four percent along the Upper Zambezi.

*"It is estimated that just over... 782,200 bednights were sold in the region. Livingstone made 39 percent of total KAZA TFCA sales, Victoria Falls made 25 percent, northern Botswana* [Chobe] *made 23 percent, Caprivi sold nine percent of total bednights and establishments along the Upper Zambezi sold the remaining four percent."* (Suich, Busch and Barbancho, 2005)

# Challenging Conditions

A new political landscape emerged in Zimbabwe after the disputed elections of March 2008, resulting the formation of the Government of National Unity, signed between the three main political parties (ZANU-PF and the two divided factions of the Movement for Democratic Change) on 15th September 2008.

Nationwide Zimbabwe received 1,956,000 tourism arrivals in 2008, rising slightly to 2,017,000 in 2009. Arrivals from South Africa declined 31 percent, attributed to negative media publicity of political violence during the build up to elections and a cholera outbreak in Harare in the second half of 2008 (Mugwati, Nkala and Mashiri, 2016). Annual average occupancy at the main Hotels in the Falls remained low, at 20 percent in 2007, 25 percent in 2008 and 24 percent in 2009 (USAID, 2013).

Difficult economic operating conditions made challenging work for the tourism sector. Years of quantitative easing and escalating hyper-inflation finally resulted in the collapse of the Zimbabwe dollar. At the height of the crisis in 2008 menu prices at the Falls Hotel had to be changed hourly to keep up with inflation. Staff salaries became virtually worthless and stores and stocks impossible to source.

> *"In 2008, when annual inflation peaked at 89.7 sextillion percent - that's roughly 9 followed by 22 zeros - a single egg could cost well over a billion dollars, assuming you could find one."* (Financial Times, 2016)

One casualty of the situation was the ultralight flight over the Falls originally established by Bush Birds Safaris in the 1990s and later part of the Shearwater portfolio of activities. Unable to secure the necessary international insurance cover the fleet of two ultralight planes and a specially customised ultralight float-plane (offering a uniquely breathtaking experience) was suspended in June 2007.

In 2009 Harare based tourism operator Safari Par Excellence pulled out of its south bank operations, concentrating its activities in Zambia, and resulting in the rebranding of the remaining Zimbabwe based operations as Adventure Zone.

The currency was redenominated three times (in 2006, 2008 and 2009), with banknotes of up to $100 trillion (one with 14 zeros), the highest numerical value legal tender ever issued in the world, issued in early 2009, and providing collectors and tourists a range of new novelty souvenirs. The US dollar was subsequently adopted in 2009 as the main trading currency within a multi-currency market, marking the turning point in the crisis with stability slowly returning to the national economy.

The global economic downturn of 2008-9 also negatively affected international tourism, with global figures for tourism arrivals down four percent and tourism receipts six percent in 2009 against the previous year. In 2010 the sector rebounded strongly, with international arrivals growing by 7 percent (Abel and Mudzonga, 2016).

The unity government ended in June 2013, with elections held in July under a new constitution returning ZANU-PF to full government. The Zimbabwe dollar was finally officially decommissioned in 2015 at a rate of 35 quadrillion (Z$35,000,000,000,000,000) to one US dollar (Reserve Bank of Zimbabwe, 2015).

## Wild Horizons

In 2007 Wild Horizons, originally established as Zambezi Fishing Safaris in 1982 and renamed in 1987, merged with white-water rafting company Adrift and African Sport and Leisure to form a single company offering a portfolio of tourism activities. The Wild Horizons Estate, a fenced privately managed wilderness concession within the Victoria Falls National Park, also opened operations in 2007. The Wild Horizons Wildlife Trust was formed in 2008 (renamed the Victoria Falls Wildlife Trust in 2012) to support local wildlife conservation management initiatives, including a flagship project establishing a specialist modern veterinary laboratory and wildlife rehabilitation facility.

## Making a Plan

A key landmark in the management of the Victoria Falls/Mosi-oa-Tunya World Heritage Site was the adoption of a joint five-year management plan, signed by Zambian and Zimbabwean counterparts in 2007, seventeen years after the designation of the site. The plan agreed a unified vision for the management of the site:

> "To ensure the integrity and long-term survival of the physical, natural and cultural resources of the Victoria Falls/Mosi-oa-Tunya World Heritage Site, and the water area around it, for the enjoyment and benefit of Zambia and Zimbabwe, the local urban and rural communities, and the national and international visitors." (Victoria Falls World Heritage Site, 2007)

The plan covers issues of transboundary coordination, management of urban and tourism facilities and funding schemes. The UNESCO imposed moratorium on development within the WHS was lifted in 2008 in response to the plans successful adoption.

A proposal for a tethered balloon located three kilometres northeast of the Falls on the north bank was rejected by UNESCO on the basis of its visual impact on the skyline. The project was resubmitted several times in subsequent years, on different potential sites, without success. A proposal for an amphibious vehicle ('amphicoach') was also rejected (UNESCO, 2012).

A new two storey 77-room four-star lodge, the David Livingstone Safari Lodge and Spa opened on the northern bank in April 2008, with rooms offering views of the river and including five luxury suites.

## Under an African Sun

Zimbabwe Sun Ltd, which was separated off from parent company Delta Corporation Ltd (the successor to Rhodesia Breweries) in 2003, was re-branded as African Sun Ltd in 2008, reflecting its pan-African holdings. Its portfolio of hotels included the Elephant Hills Resort and Conference Centre, and The Kingdom at Victoria Falls as well as The Victoria Falls Hotel, jointly managed with Meikles Africa Ltd since the late nineties.

## Reaching the Limit

In 2009 news reports highlighted concerns over noise pollution from helicopter flights over the Falls, stirred by proposals to issue further licenses to new operators, develop new helipad sites and increase the total number allowed to fly at any one time from five to up to 20. At the time eight helicopters were in operation at the Falls, five from Zambia, with Batoka Skies managing three helicopters and United Air Charters two, and the Zambezi Helicopter Company (part of the Shearwater portfolio of companies) operating three helicopters from the Elephant Hills helipad in Zimbabwe.

Guests at the Victoria Falls Safari Lodge, Elephant Hills, Kingdom and Falls Hotels often recorded the noise intrusions as 'a nuisance' and several major hotels formerly complained to the UNESCO World Heritage Commission regarding the high levels of disturbance already caused by excessive noise pollution levels over the town. Karl Snater, General Manager of the Victoria Falls Hotel, recorded:

*"On behalf of the Victoria Falls Hotel, I would like to register a complaint against the helicopters and the noise they produce which has a negative impact on the environment and likewise destroys the atmosphere in our hotel and grounds. Daily we have to endure the noise and constant irritation from these aircraft which fly directly over and above the Hotel. If one considers that current*

*hotel occupancies are running at approximately 20% of capacity surely when normal higher occupancies return the environment cannot sustain the impact of the increased flights, increased operators and increased frequency of the helicopters."* (Victoria Falls Bits and Blogs, June 2009)

A World Heritage Committee monitoring mission to the site in November 2006 confirmed the high aviation noise impacts, whilst also highlighting wider concerns over the volume of visitors to the resort and impacts on wildlife:

*"The World Heritage Centre and IUCN observed during the mission that high visitor rates are causing noise pollution from helicopters, microlight aircraft, and boats. In addition, aquatic wildlife is constantly disturbed by riparian activities."* (UNESCO, 2007)

A UNESCO approved plan to relocate flights from the Elephant Hills helipad and develop new facilities away from the main tourism areas - including adoption of new flight corridors to minimise disturbance over the town - has actually resulted in an overall increase in noise pollution impacts over a wider area of the Falls.

In 2012 a new operator, Bonisair, launched tourist flights with two helicopters operating from the newly developed Chamabondo helipad, located to the south of the town, with flight paths bypassing the town and approaching the Falls from the gorges. The new helipad has resulted in longer flying distances and shifted impacts of noise pollution over the natural areas downstream of the Falls - in addition to the existing flight paths above the Falls still being in operation. More recently a third company has started operations, further increasing the number of helicopters flying above the Falls and associated environmental impacts.

# Tourism on the Bounce

The Zimbabwe Tourism Authority (ZTA) reported a healthy increase in national tourist arrivals in 2010, with figures for the year reaching 2,239,000, largely credited to the regional benefits of the FIFA Football World Cup tournament hosted by South Africa. Of the total international arrivals received by Zimbabwe in 2010, Africa contributed 87 percent followed by Europe (six percent), the Americas (three percent) and Asia (two percent). Visitors from Oceania and the Middle East contributed less than two percent. Annual tourism receipts rose to $634 million from $523 million in 2009. Average annual hotel occupancy in the Falls, however, remained low at 28 percent in 2010 and 2011, reflecting the continuing high seasonality in tourism (USAID, 2013).

Visitors to the Falls Rainforest reached 141,113 during 2010, an increase from 116,223 the previous year. The Zambezi National Park received 58,598 visitors, up from 47,450 in 2009. The site of the old Falls Craft Village, another victim of the recent economic difficulties, was redeveloped with the construction of the N1 Hotel, opened with 15 rooms in December 2010 (now expanded to 30 rooms).

## *Rainforest Rumbles*

The Zimbabwe Parks and Wildlife Management Authority partnered with local activity provider Shearwater Adventures, trading through the Zambezi Helicopter Company, in a much needed, yet controversial, redevelopment of the Falls Park visitor reception facilities in 2010. The development included the conversion of the information centre into a modern commercial store selling high-value tourism souvenirs and the construction of a visitor restaurant and supporting facilities. An outdoor interpretation and information area was developed, with detailed displays on the natural history and formation of the Falls, as well as upgrading of toilets and other visitor facilities.

The project divided opinion and attracted a substantial amount negative publicity and media coverage. Stakeholders in the town's tourism sector argued that there had been no formal Environmental Impact Assessment undertaken, with no public notification or consultation ahead of the development. Even government authorities clashed, the development reigniting a long-running dispute over management the Rainforest. Sensing an opportunity, the National Museums and Monuments of Zimbabwe, with the support of Zimbabwe Republic Police, took control of the Falls Park visitor facilities, reclaiming their historic management of the Victoria Falls Special Area, and closing the restaurant. After a short period of impasse, and an eventual government ruling, the Rainforest returned to the control of the Parks and Wildlife Management Authority and the restaurant facilities reopened after receiving clearance from UNESCO.

Additional plans for a proposed $6 million development of the 'VIP Entrance' beside the Devil's Cataract, including restaurant, shopping and conference facilities overlooking the edge of the Falls, appear to have been quietly suspended (Victoria Falls Bits and Blogs, Nov 2010).

## *The Elephant Camp*

In 2010 Wild Horizons launched a new $1 million luxury safari camp, The Elephant Camp, located within the Wild Horizons Estate. The initial development consisted of 12 luxurious, tailor-made tented lodge units. A new extension, the Elephant

Camp West, opened in April 2015, consisting of four tented suites overlooking the gorges below the Falls.

## Stability and Growth

Hotel operators in the Falls recorded rising occupancy levels during 2011 with growth from new markets such as Eastern Europe, the Middle East and Asia. Occupancy rates for the seven largest hotels in the Falls, offering a combined total of just over 1,000 rooms, were up twenty percent in the first half of the year. Overall annual average occupancy, however, remained low at just over thirty percent (Victoria Falls Bits and Blogs, August 2011a). Ross Kennedy, director of Africa Albida Tourism and a director of the African Travel and Tourism Association recorded:

*"Victoria Falls Safari Lodge had the best July occupancy in 10 years at 70%. The Boma Place of Eating had its second best July ever. Only July 2007 saw more covers per night at an average of 183, while 2011 had on average 163 per night... The settling and stability of the economy since dollarisation in 2009 has meant that the supply chain has normalised and is thus operating to international standards. In addition it has meant that use of foreign currency, pricing and access to goods has normalised and we are once again a tourist-friendly destination."* (Victoria Falls Bits and Blogs, August 2011b)

Mr Kennedy noted that the UK market, along with other traditional markets that had been 'staying away' from Zimbabwe for the last decade, had started to return thanks to the success of local destination marketing campaigns such as the 'Go To Victoria Falls' initiative, and that many tourism operators and agents who had moved their business over the river to Zambia between 2000 and 2010 were also returning. Nationally tourism arrivals to Zimbabwe climbed to 2,423,000 in 2011, generating $662 million over the period. The upgraded four-star and 91-room A'Zambezi River Lodge reopened in May 2011 following a $4.5 million renovation programme, including development of a 100-seater Conference Centre.

During 2011 local tourism operator Wild Horizons investigated operating tours to Cataract Island from the south bank, having received permission to use the island for tourism purposes. The isolated island is a valuable refuge for the fragile flora sustained by the spray of the Falls - and highly impacted by visitor numbers across the rest of the site. After consulting local opinion on the proposal Wild Horizons withdrew their plans on the understanding that the island would continue to be protected in its pristine natural state.

The Bridge bungee briefly became worldwide news when a freak accident occurred on New Year Eve 2011. During 22-year-old Australian Erin Langworthy's jump the bungee cord snapped just short of its maximum extension and she dropped head-first into the Zambezi River. Miraculously she survived with just minor injuries (Victoria Falls Bits and Blogs, Jan 2012).

Zimbabwe recorded 767,250 tourist arrivals over the first half of 2012, and achieved a year end total of 1,794,000, earning $749 million in receipts. A combined total of 198,000 visitors toured the Falls on both sides of the river, a significant increase on 146,203 visitors recorded in 2011. Approximately half of these visitors were foreign tourists (Victoria Falls World Heritage Site Joint Report 2014). The Zambezi National Park received 70,980 visitors, up from 56,475 in 2011 (Victoria Falls Bits and Blogs, Jan 2013). The town's total population was estimated at 33,718 in 2012 (CSO, 2012).

In mid 2012 the Jafuta Heritage Centre opened at the Elephant's Walk complex, displaying a comprehensive private collection of local cultural artefacts and information on the human history of the Falls region. The Centre is managed by the Jafuta Foundation, a non-profit organisation with the aim of preserving the traditional culture and material history of the region.

# Centre Stage

The main accommodation providers in the Falls, now representing eight hotels, recorded combined revenues of over $23 million and 178,000 visitor room-nights in 2013, up from $19 million and 159,000 room bookings the previous year. A combined total of 252,800 tourists visited the Falls in 2013 (Victoria Falls World Heritage Site Joint Report, 2014). Tourism from Britain showed significant signs of recovery, with arrivals from the United Kingdom trebling against the previous year (Victoria Falls Bits and Blogs, April 2014). Nationally Zimbabwe recorded 1,833,500 tourism arrivals in 2013 and annual receipts of $856 million.

During the period the Zambian Government funded the extensive rehabilitation of tourism infrastructure at the Falls, including construction of a modern curio market buildings, car park, improved visitor facilities and upgrading of walkways.

## Zambezi Explorer

In mid 2013 a new luxury tourist cruise boat, the Zambezi Explorer, arrived on the Zambezi, having been built in Harare and transported to the Falls by road - no small task for a hull 27 metres in length, over seven metres wide and eight metres in height. The three-decked Zambezi Explorer accommodates 140 passengers and offers premium standards of service, complete with on board food galley. All of the vessel's state-of-the-art inboard facilities run exclusively on solar energy, which together with fuel-efficient engines, minimise the environmental impact of its operation and set new standards for the sector.

## *Riverside Lodges*

Private riverside safari concessions were developed upstream of the Falls within the Zambezi National Park with the opening several independent safari operations - the 26-bed Victoria Falls River Lodge (opened in April 2012) and the 12-bed tented Pioneers Camp (opened in mid 2013), located close to the site of the Old Drift river crossing. Zambezi Sands River Camp, opened in 2014 with a 16-bed tented lodge located in the western part of the Zambezi National Park.

## *Joint Hosts*

In August 2013 the Falls Hotel welcomed the opening reception of the 20th Session of the United Nations World Tourism Organisation General Assembly, jointly hosted by the towns of Livingstone and Victoria Falls. The event attracted more than a thousand delegates and VIP guests from across the world and provided a significant boost to local tourism, as well as giving both countries valuable international marketing exposure as a premier global tourism destination.

As nightfall gathered the Falls Bridge was illuminated as part of a new installation celebrating the joint event, with Telecel announcing a $100,000 sponsorship of the project over the next 15 years. In their inaugural addresses, President Robert Mugabe of Zimbabwe and President Michael Sata of Zambia called for increased support for sustainable tourism and capacity building that promotes environmental awareness and improves the welfare and livelihoods of local communities.

*The Bridge illuminated*

Addressing delegates at the opening session, the UNWTO Secretary General, Taleb Rifai, underscored the event as a *"timely opportunity for all of us to continue along an encouraging path to drive tourism towards its fullest potential in fostering sustainable economic growth, jobs and development, and what better backdrop to do so than here in Africa, a region where we believe tourism can be a true force for good"* (UNWTO, 2013).

## Selfie Slip-up

On 26th November 2013 a team of Livingstone Fire Brigade servicemen, together with Zambian Police and staff from the Victoria Falls Bridge Bungee, were called to rescue a tourist who fell into the gorge from the north bank. Wang ShunXue, a 45 year old Chinese national, fell into gorge near the Knife-Edge Bridge as he was taking pictures of himself with the Falls in the background, thus becoming the first person known to fall into the gorge whilst taking a 'selfie.' Fortunately he survived without serious injury (Victoria Falls Bits and Blogs, Nov 2013).

## Sprayview Redeveloped

In December 2013 Cresta Hotels launched the redeveloped Cresta Sprayview Hotel, after a $1.75 million investment of the old Sprayview Hotel, closed for many years. The reception area, 65 bedrooms, one restaurant, two bars and two conference rooms were completely remodelled and refurbished.

## Carnival Time

The Vic Falls Carnival, 'a three-day festival of music, performance, dance, adventure and fun' held over the New Year, soon became a significant annual event, attracting performers and visitors from across the region. Accommodation providers recorded 100 percent occupancies as thousands of revellers descended on the small town, swamping facilities and services. New Year festivals in the Falls started in 2009 with the 'Falls Fest,' operating from the central Victoria Falls Rest Camp, before the establishment of the Carnival in 2012 and which has been held annually since.

The Falls Rainforest recorded an incredible 16,573 visitors and entrance fee revenues in excess of $270,000 over a 10 day period to 2nd January 2014, with international visitor entrance fee receipts totalling over $147,500, regional receipts $75,400 and Zimbabwe nationals $49,700 (Victoria Falls Bits and Blogs, Jan 2014).

# Regeneration and Renewal

Recent years have seen encouraging signs of recovery in Zimbabwe's tourism industry, with 867,000 tourist visitors recorded in the first half of 2014 and year end arrivals of 1,880,000, despite the Ebola epidemic casting a shadow over travel to the continent. The country recorded a marginal decline in total annual tourism revenues to $827 million.

The tourism town of Victoria Falls was also experiencing regeneration, with several hotels investing in significant refurbishments and expansions. A long neglected corner, in the centre of town, the old Wimpy restaurant was redeveloped as the Shearwater Café, opened in August 2014.

Peak-season tourism arrivals were returning to the levels of the late 1990s, with the major hotels at Victoria Falls enjoying occupancy rates of 77 percent in August 2014, up from 62 percent in the same month in 2013. Mr Kennedy of Africa Albida Tourism reported a record month for their flagship property, the Victoria Falls Safari Lodge, achieving the highest occupancy figures since it opened in 1994.

Annual tourism visitors to the Falls Rainforest reached close to the 200,000 mark. Average annual room occupancy, however, fell to 49 percent from 53 percent in 2013 (Victoria Falls Bits and Blogs, March 2015).

## Safari Lodge Celebrates Twenty Years

Victoria Falls Safari Lodge celebrated twenty years of operation with a significant $1 million refurbishment, including an upgrade of all 72 rooms, completed in July 2014. The Africa Albida Tourism complex now included the six luxury Victoria Falls Safari Suites (converted from six of the existing Lokuthula Lodge units and opened in December 2013), the exclusive 20-room Victoria Falls Safari Club (development at a cost of $2.7 million and opened in August 2012), the as well as the original Victoria Falls Safari Lodge and six remaining Lokuthula Lodges.

## Gorge Lookout

In December 2014 Wild Horizons opened the new Lookout Café, part of a redevelopment of their gorge activity centre, perched overlooking the second and third gorges below the Falls. The development included a rebuild and expansion of the existing thatched structure, landscaped terraced gardens and the clearance of a large area of natural bush for customer car parking.

The gorge activity centre was originally developed in 2001 with the construction of a small thatched building and installation of high-wire infrastructure across the gorges, offering a bungee swing, zip-line and abseiling activities. The centre expanded its activities with the introduction of zip-line 'canopy tour' in the bend of the second and third gorges in mid 2013.

## *Development Dollars*

Pressure to develop new commercial tourism projects and products continued to drive the development of the local Falls environment, in many cases resulting in proposals inappropriate and unsuitable to its protected National Park status and UNESCO World Heritage listing. Proposals rejected by UNESCO in recent years including bids to operate tethered observation balloons, an amphibious vehicle, and, most recently, a viewing wheel development overlooking the Falls from the northern bank. The south side has also seen attempts to develop a cable car facility into the gorge and many other projects, including a recent proposal to reopen tours to Cataract Island, the last remaining fragment of the Rainforest untouched by modern tourism pressures (Victoria Falls Bits and Blogs, Nov 2016).

In late 2014 Zimbabwe Tourism Authority Chief Executive Officer, Karikoga Kaseke controversially proposed that Zimbabwe and Zambia should even forego the UNESCO listing of the Falls and instead maximise commercial revenues.

> *"We don't need the Falls to remain a natural world heritage site as stipulated by United Nations Educational, Scientific, and Cultural Organisation (UNESCO). We need to go the Niagara Falls way and make money for our people and our economies. We can gain a lot of benefits if we commercialise it... We need to electrify Victoria Falls and start running it on 24 hours basis instead of closing the premises in the night."* (Victoria Falls Bits and Blogs, Nov 2014)

Mr Kaseke said Niagara Falls attracted $30 billion annually, compared to less than $500,000 at the Victoria Falls for Zimbabwe and Zambia. Mr Kaseke expanded that Victoria Falls had potential to raise more revenue from tourists if the Falls Park had electric lighting to enable night-time visits, steady water flows, restaurants, accommodation facilities and other modern amenities like the case at Niagara Falls. Chief Mukuni countered that tourists around the world travelled to the Falls to see them in their natural form, undeveloped and untouched by commercial development.

> *"In my opinion, we should keep the Falls as natural as possible and not commercialise it."* (Victoria Falls Bits and Blogs, Nov 2014)

# Expanding Horizons

The first half of 2015 started strongly, with the Zimbabwe Tourism Authority recording 930,250 national tourism arrivals in the first six months of the year, with year-end figures reaching 2,056,500. African travellers contributed the majority - 1.76 million visitors - with overseas arrivals accounting for just 14 percent - the Americas 76,751, Asia 35,000, Europe 149,000, the Middle East 3,990 and Oceania 25,000 (Victoria Falls Bits and Blogs, Feb 2016).

Visitor figures for the Falls recorded significant increases in tourist numbers, with combined totals of 353,025 in 2014 and 544,104 and 2015 (Victoria Falls World Heritage Site Joint Report 2014). Occupancy levels from the ten leading tourism hotels on the south bank of the Falls recorded a small drop of two percent over the same period, and entry numbers to the Rainforest declined 2.6 percent (Victoria Falls Bits and Blogs, Feb 2016). Unfavourable government taxation policies, including a new 15 percent tax on hotel accommodation for foreign tourists, imposed at short notice at the beginning of the year, negatively affected predictions of increased growth.

In the face of challenging operating conditions Africa Sun Ltd shifted its business emphasis away from direct hotel operation toward a hotel investment and management model, resulting in the appointment of Legacy Hospitality Management Services Ltd to manage the operation of The Kingdom and Elephant Hills Hotel (Victoria Falls Bits and Blogs, Sept 2015).

## Ilala Lodge Spreads its Wings

Ilala Lodge began a significant extension in November 2014 with the development of a new three-storey wing (raising the profile of the previously two-storey building), adding an additional 20 deluxe rooms and two executive suites, and expanding the hotel to a total of 56 rooms. The new wing opened in October 2015.

## Going Green

Tourism operators in the Falls have in recent years increasingly adopted positive 'eco-tourism' principles, aiming to minimise environmental impacts and supporting conservation and community initiatives in the local area. From an emphasis on the 'green building' of new developments - minimising environmental impacts across all levels of the construction process - to the 'greening' of everyday operations, many tourism operators and accommodation providers have recognised the need to take active steps to reduce the impacts of their operations on the environment.

The Victoria Falls Green Fund, launched in February 2010 by Environment Africa, aims to encourage development of the Falls as a premier 'green destination' for tourism. Supported by contributions from local tourism operators the funds raised, including a $1 per bed-night contribution from participating hotels, are invested in local conservation and community based projects that promote sustainable development in an environmentally friendly manner.

In early 2016 several leading accommodation providers partnered with Green-Tourism.com in a trial project to encourage industry adoption of sustainable eco-tourism management practices. Cresta Sprayview, Pioneers Camp, The Victoria Falls Hotel, Victoria Falls Safari Lodge and Wild Horizons Elephant Camp are all working towards green tourism accreditation under the pioneering scheme.

## *Airport Expansion*

A new chapter in travel and transport to the Victoria Falls began in April 2013 with the commencement of significant $150 million redevelopment and expansion of the Victoria Falls International Airport, partially opened at the end of 2015 and officially opened by President Robert Mugabe on 18th November 2016. Works included the construction of an extended four kilometre runway and associated taxiways, the construction of new terminal buildings with air-traffic control tower and supporting emergency services.

The new airport runway, expanded from a length of 2,200 metres to 4,000 metres and doubled in width to 60 metres, and will allow international travellers to fly directly to Victoria Falls, accommodating the Boeing 747 and new generation of wide-bodied aircraft. The new terminal building has been designed to handle 1.2 million international travellers (compared to the previous capacity of 400,000) and 500,000 domestic passengers per annum. Concerns have been expressed, however, on the associated impacts of increased tourism numbers to the destination, with pressure to develop new accommodation facilities and services.

*The new terminal buildings under construction (May 2015)*

# The Falls Today

Provisional figures for the first half of 2016 showed Zimbabwe recorded 902,000 international tourist arrivals, a slight decline on the first half of 2015, rising to 2,167,500 by the year-end, up five percent and generating revenues of $819 million. Arrivals in Zimbabwe are projected to reach over 2.2 million by the close of 2017 and over 2.5 million by 2020 (Victoria Falls Bits and Blogs, April 2017b).

The Victoria Falls remain one of Africa's top tourism attractions, with the facilities and services on both sides of the river developing in recent decades into modern first-class destinations of global standing. The immediate area of the Falls survive, at first impression, preserved in their pristine and natural state - but look closely and the inevitable signs of 'progress' and development surround them.

Telephone towers can be seen on the skyline (rather unsuccessfully disguised as giant palm trees), hotel buildings lurk on the horizon and lodges crowd the river-frontage upstream of the Falls, where river cruise boats race upstream each evening, jostling for prime position as the sun sets over the Zambezi. Helicopters and microlight planes buzz overhead from dawn to dusk, the later often swooping low over the river and islands above the Falls, disturbing wildlife and people. Downstream power-lines cross the gorge and waste-water overflows drain into the river above and below the Falls.

Whilst wider infrastructure and utility services struggle to keep pace with ever increasing population demands, tourism developments continue to grow and expand, with increasing pressure and competition to develop new activities and services to attract yet more tourists and generate successively higher revenues.

In addition to the obvious direct impacts of development on the immediate environment of the Falls, larger, more complex and challenging issues threaten to change the very nature of the river and Falls themselves. Threats include deforestation, with illegal poaching for firewood, construction and curio carvings a significant local problem; water extraction and pollution, with the fragile habitat of the Falls Rainforest at threat from diminished volumes of localised rain and water quality threatened by sewage discharges from human settlements; the introduction and spread of non-native invasive plant species which again threaten the ecology of the Rainforest; and the spectre of the proposed Batoka Gorge dam development downstream, which threatens to flood the spectacular gorges below the Falls.

The protected area surrounding the Falls has been steadily eroded over the decades as the various reserves and protected areas have been redesignated.

Areas of human settlement have expanded, with increasing impacts on the surrounding buffer zones. The town of Victoria Falls is now home to 33,748 residents (ZIMSTAT, 2012), with the supporting suburban areas of Chinotimba and Mkhosana - developed on the site of the old Sprayview Aerodrome - expanding rapidly in recent years.

The Falls are, however, still surrounded by wildlife and wilderness areas. Elephant are often seen around - and sometimes even in - town, being attracted to well-watered suburban gardens for a feast of fruit trees and other seasonal favourites. In recent years they have become increasingly problematic for the town's human inhabitants, having learnt to lean on walls to break entry into the most desirable gardens and causing much damage (Victoria Falls Bits and Blogs, Feb 2013b).

In December 2014 warnings were issued around town after the local herd of buffalo, often to be found along Zambezi Drive and at the Safari Lodge waterhole, were chased into the suburbs of town by a visiting pride of lions. The herd were eventually ushered out of town by Park Authorities supported by VFAPU rangers, and the lions obligingly followed.

*"There has been a huge herd of Buffalo that has been chased into town by lions. This herd has now split up and half the herd is around the ZIMRA/Victoria Falls Court and the other herd is next to Cresta Sprayview. There have also been sightings of the lions in town."* (Victoria Falls Guide, 2015)

## *Memorable Names*

In June 2016 the town municipality announced a $6 million road regeneration project, including a proposal to rename many of the old roads originally named after key characters in the early history of the town's tourism development, including Clark, Dale, Giese, Hobson, Imbault, Soper, Spencer and others. After due consideration, and some shared research into the early history of tourism to the Falls, it was decided to retain the old street names. The two main roads in the town, however, Livingstone Way and Park Way, are due to be renamed Robert Mugabe Way and Joshua Nkomo Way respectively to honour the country's two main independence heroes.

Over the years there have been several attempts to encourage debate over the re-naming of the Falls, with some suggesting that their globally known English name should be abandoned, most recently in late 2013. The alternative name often suggested, 'Mosi-oa-Tunya,' is already strongly associated with tourism to the Zambian side of the river (Victoria Falls Bits and Blogs, Dec 2013).

## A Load of Rubbish

Management of the town's waste has long been problematic, with a large open landfill site on the outskirts of town the ultimate destination for the estimated 3,300 tonnes of rubbish generated annually by residents, tourists and supporting industries. The ingestion of plastic bags was linked to the death of at least eight elephants habituated to feeding on waste food found at the dump in early 2016, resulting in calls for the site to be properly fenced.

*Top of the pile - baboons sit atop mountains of rubbish at the town dumpsite*

A fundraising campaign was launched by concerned residents and local conservation organisations, and with the support of an online crowd funding campaign and input from the tourism sector (including significant financial support from Shearwater Adventures, who contributed fifty percent of the necessary funds), an electric fence was installed around the site at the end of 2016 (Victoria Falls Bits and Blogs, March 2016).

Increasing volumes of rubbish, from cans, bottles, fast-food wrappers and plastic bags to household and even business and industrial waste are, however, a regular feature in the open bush surrounding the town, promoting community groups and tourism operators to organise regular voluntary litter clearing collections.

## Explorers Village

The Shearwater Explorers Village opened in late 2016, a new $1.2 million development on the old tethered balloon site and providing camping for over 100 and 32 air-conditioned bedrooms, with plans to expand to 64 beds by the middle of 2017. Aimed at overland groups and independent travellers, the central complex includes restaurant, bar, pool and shop (Victoria Falls Bits and Blogs, April 2017a).

## Bridges and Borders

The Victoria Falls Bridge remains an essential transport and trade link connecting Zambia and Zimbabwe, the busy road, rail and foot crossing accessed through two border control posts on either bank. Recent upgrades to border facilities on both sides have increased light pollution impacts, negatively affecting the nocturnal viewing of the lunar rainbow on both sides of the river.

The development of the Kazungula Bridge, at an estimated construction cost of $259.3 million and linking Botswana and Zambia, will hopefully divert some of the high volume of freight and other heavy goods vehicles which currently queue daily to clear border controls and cross the Falls Bridge. The bridge is currently in the early stages of construction and is planned to open in December 2018.

Tourists and residents on either side of the Falls have to go through tedious border formalities, with associated visa restrictions and vehicle charges, to visit the other side of the river. The year-long introduction of a trial tourism 'Univisa' in December 2014, allowing unrestricted travel on both sides of the river, was welcomed as a success by tourists and industry. After a lapsed period following the trial the Univisa was finally re-introduced in late 2016 (Victoria Falls Bits and Blogs, July 2016). A resulting trend has been the growth of day trippers visiting the Falls in Zimbabwe from neighbouring countries of Botswana and Zambia.

## Running Dry?

Concerns over high levels of water extraction from the river were highlighted with news stories that the Falls were 'running dry,' with especially low water levels over the Eastern Cataract during recent dry seasons. An initiative to reduce extraction levels for the hydro-electric power station during these dry periods appears to have been abandoned. UNESCO reports estimate that to operate at full capacity the plant requires between 44-87 percent of the typical dry-season flow:

> "This level of water abstraction is clearly affecting the visual impact and aesthetic value of the property... and may be having other long-term impacts such as degradation of the adjacent rainforest as a result of reduced spray at critical times." (UNESCO, 2012)

Whilst energy demands require Zambian authorities to maintain extraction levels and power production during the dry season, generation is occasionally turned off for short periods. Often coinciding with visits of 'VIPs' to the Falls, the suspension in effect 'turns-on' the Falls, with noticeably higher flows over the eastern end.

*A section of the Main Falls*

# Into The Future

The Victoria Falls are often compared with those of Niagara, being viewed favourably in comparison by those who find the commercial development of the North American falls as detracting from their natural impact and beauty. With the search for ever increasing tourism arrivals, however, it appears inevitable that pressure will continue to develop further tourism infrastructure, facilities and services on both sides of the river.

The expansion of the Victoria Falls Airport has initiated a flurry of activity from the tourism sector. The increased handling capacity of the airport has resulted in predictions of an additional 80,000 tourism arrivals a year, with ZTA CEO Karikoga Kaseke highlighting the need for an additional 1,000 rooms at the resort by 2020. Arrivals, however, remain distinctly seasonal, and whilst new developments will increase overall capacity, average occupancies are likely to remain low.

Unsympathetic developments continue threaten the fragile nature of the Falls and its surroundings. Heath, writing in the late 1970s, highlighted that the growth of Victoria Falls town had followed a consistent pattern of planning adapting to, and following, development, rather than controlling and limiting it:

> *"It would be unfortunate if the trend, which has characterised the village throughout this century, of planning reflecting individual enterprise rather than guiding and controlling it, should be allowed to continue."* (Heath, 1977)

*The Victoria Falls from the western end*

It is, however, a pattern which continues to this day, with controversial developments seemingly often overriding environmental concerns and planning guidelines. Once developments are established they inevitably evolve and expand, creating far larger impacts than when originally planned.

Widespread concern was raised over the proposed Santonga development, first announced in 2007 and relaunched in late 2014 by Africa Albida Tourism as part of the expansion of their Victoria Falls Safari Lodge complex. The $12 million project, presented as an educational 'eco-park' attraction, will be one of the most significant new developments within the immediate vicinity of the Falls since the construction of the Safari Lodge itself - if allowed to go ahead (Victoria Falls Bits and Blogs, April 2015).

Commenting on the wider tourism development of the Falls, Ross Kennedy, Chief Executive of Africa Albida Tourism, highlighted the responsibility to manage growth in a balanced manner:

*"Some may believe Victoria Falls is better left as it is while others will embrace the counter argument that 'growth is necessary and good.' But what matters is that growth is inevitable, so both the public and the private sector must be responsible, accountable and caring in managing such expansion."* (Victoria Falls Bits and Blogs, Nov 2015)

Government plans, announced in 2013, for a proposed $460 million 'African Disneyland' on a 1,200 hectare site close to the airport have also received widespread criticism, with the proposals including the development of modern shopping malls, hotels, banks, and conference, exhibition and entertainment facilities aimed to attract major business conferences and events (Victoria Falls Bits and Blogs, Aug 2013).

In June 2016 the Zimbabwe Tourism and Hospitality Industry Minister, Walter Mzembi, was reported in the national press describing Victoria Falls as a potential $4.8 billion 'cash-cow,' quoting an average per tourist spend of $1,200 and predicting an incredible 4 million annual visitors to both sides of the river (Victoria Falls Bits and Blogs, June 2016).

Victoria Falls Municipality have also announced plans to develop a Civic Centre, shopping mall, convention centre, five-star hotel and theme park in the centre of Victoria Falls, redeveloping the substantial plots currently home to the Falls Rest Camp and Municipality offices. In September 2016 it was reported that a Memorandum of Understanding had been signed with a South African developer and a local construction company to develop plans for the multi-million dollar complex. The development threatens a significant area of green space within the town, with extensive grounds and many fine tree specimens under threat of being ripped up and replaced with concrete buildings and parking lots (Victoria Falls Bits and Blogs, Sept 2016).

The largest shadow, however, hanging over the future conservation of the Falls and its surrounds perhaps comes in the shape of the Batoka Gorge Hydro-Project, first proposed in the 1970s and currently undergoing a revised feasibility review. The proposed dam, some 50 kilometres downstream from the Falls, would flood the gorges below the Falls, forever changing their unique nature and bringing to an end commercial white-water rafting (Victoria Falls Bits and Blogs, Feb 2013a).

Despite its UNESCO World Heritage Site status, there is no doubt that the Victoria Falls and immediate surrounding areas are under sustained threat from the most intensive development pressures they have ever faced, on both sides of the river. Let us hope, however, that money does not do all the talking when it comes to the future development of the Falls, and that the priceless natural aspects of this global wonder, including the wilderness which surrounds them and wildlife that frequents them, are valued and preserved for future generations. There is a saying often applied to natural areas - 'take only photographs, leave only footprints.' We owe it to future generations to ensure the footprints we leave today at the Falls are as transient and ephemeral as possible.

# Acknowledgements

I am indebted to many people for their help and assistance in the production of this book. Thanks especially go to Gail van Jaarsveldt and the Jafuta Foundation (www.jafutafoundation.org) for supporting the research and publication of my second book, 'Corridors Through Time - A History of the Victoria Falls Hotel,' to which this companion book also owes its origins and is intended to compliment and support, providing much additional background material on the history of the Victoria Falls.

Thanks go to Gordon Murray of the Bulawayo Railway Museum, Zimbabwe, for his assistance and access to the railway archives under his responsibility. I am also grateful to Mr G S Mudenda, Director of the Livingstone Museum, Zambia, and his dedicated staff for their support, including Perrice Nkombwe and Kingsley Choongo. Sources from the Bulawayo Railway Museum Archive are marked 'BRMA' and Livingstone Museum Archive are marked 'LMA' within the References section.

Many of the historical images used are from the railway archives held in the Bulawayo Railway Museum, taken by unnamed publicity photographers over the years and digitally copied by the author. Thanks go to Tony Barnett (www.tonybarnettproductions.com) and the Victoria Falls Bungee Company (www.shearwaterbungee.com) for the use of the images on pages 158 and 170 and Gordon Shepherd/Stenlake Publishing for the use of the images on page 57. The photographs on pages 2, 166 and from 179 onwards are by the author.

Special thanks also go to those who share an interest in the history of the Victoria Falls for access to their precious archive reference material, knowledge and support, including among many others Graham Andrews, Andrea Arrington-Sirois, Ken Cowen, Larry Cumming, James Gavin (of the Rhodesian Study Circle, www.rhodesianstudycircle.org.uk), Peter Jones, David Moir, Hugh Macmillan, John Reid-Rowland, Mitch Stirling and again, Gail van Jaarsveldt.

Thanks also go to the Elephant Walk Shopping and Artists Village (www.elephantswalk.com) and Travellers Guest House (www.travellerszim.net) for hosting me during many visits to Victoria Falls and Bulawayo, and likewise others too many to mention on both sides of the river, for their hospitality and friendship over many visits over many years.

Final and biggest thanks go to friends and family for their support, help and advice during the development of this book.

# References

Abel, S. and Mudzonga, E. (2016) The Performance of the Tourism Sector in Zimbabwe during the 2000-08 Economic Crisis. [In Kararach, G. and Otieno, R. [Editors] (2016)]

Agate, W. (1912) Diary of a tour in South Africa. Holness, London.

Arrington, A. L. (2009) Competitive Labour: Divisions between Zambian and Zimbabwean Workers. African Studies, Vol.68 No.1.

Arrington, A. L. (2010) Competing for tourists at Victoria Falls: A historical consideration of the effects of government involvement. Development Southern Africa. Vol.27 No.5, December 2010.

Arrington-Sirois, A. L. (2017) Victoria Falls and Colonial Imagination in British Southern Africa: Turning Water into Gold. Palgrave Macmillan.

Attenborough, D. (1965) Zambezi: A Journey. Episode 3: Livingstone's River. British Broadcasting Corporation television film documentary.

Baines, T. (1864) Explorations in South-West Africa: Being an account of a journey in the years 1861 and 1862 from Walvisch Bay, on the Western Coast to Lake Ngami and the Victoria Falls. Longmans, Roberts and Green, London.

Baldwin, W. C. (1863) African Hunting and Adventure from Natal to the Zambesi. Bentley, London.

Balfour, H. (1905) Diaries of Henry Balfour (1863-1939) South Africa 1905. [Online source: www.prm.ox.ac.uk/manuscripts/balfourdiaries1905.html]

Balfour, H. (1929) Diaries of Henry Balfour (1863-1939) South and East Africa 1929. [Online source: www.prm.ox.ac.uk/manuscripts/balfourdiaries1929.html]

Beet. G. (1923) The Story of the Ox Wagon - The Story of a Famous Engineering Feat. [In Weinthal, L. (1923)]

Boer, F. P. (2011) Accounts of My Travels: Exploring a World Abroad.

British South Africa Company (1905) Annual Report.

British South Africa Company (1906) Annual Report.

British South Africa Company (1907). Rhodesia, A Book for Tourists and Sportsmen. BSAC.

Bulawayo Chronicle (September 1905) British Association at the Victoria Falls: Dinner and Speeches. 14 September 1905.

Burrett, R. and Murray, G. (2013) 'Iron Spine and Ribs' A brief history of the foundations of the railways of Zimbabwe and Zambia. Bulawayo.

Chapman, J. (1868) Travels in the Interior of South Africa, London.

Clark, J. D. [Editor] (1952) The Victoria Falls : A Handbook to the Victoria Falls, the Batoka Gorge, and part of the Upper Zambesi River Commission for the Preservation of Natural and Historical Monuments and Relics, Lusaka.

Clark, P. M. (c1911) Guide to the Victoria Falls.

Clark, P. M. (1936) Autobiography of an Old Drifter. Harrap, London.

Coillard, F. (1897) On the threshold of Africa - A Record of Twenty Years Pioneering among the Barotse of the Upper Zambezi. Hodder and Stoughton, London.

Cowen, W. W. (1995) A Central African Odyssey. Radcliffe Press.

Creewel, J. (2004) A history of the Victoria Falls Hotel - 100 years 1904-2004. [Edited and updated by Stan Higgins. Originally published in 1994 as 'A history of the Victoria Falls Hotel - 90 Glorious Years 1904-1994.']

Critchell, R. (2007) A Visiting Fireman in Africa. [Online source: www.greatnorthroad.org/boma/Fireman_in_Africa]

Croxton, A. H. (1982) Railways of Zimbabwe (Originally published in 1973 as Railways of Rhodesia). David & Charles.

CSO (1964) Final Report of the April/May 1962 Census of Africans in Southern Rhodesia, Central Statistics Office, Salisbury.

CSO (1969) Census Report, Central Statistics Office, Salisbury.

CSO (1989) 1982 Population: Main Demographic Features of the Population of Matabeland North Province, Central Statistics Office, Harare.

CSO (1994) Zimbabwe Census Report 1992, Central Statistics Office, Harare.

CSO (2002) Zimbabwe Census Report 2002, Central Statistics Office, Harare.

CSO (2012) Zimbabwe Census Report 2012, Central Statistics Office, Harare.


Decle, L. (1898) Three Years in Savage Africa. London.


Economic Survey of Livingstone (1957) Rhodesia and Nyasaland Prime Minister's Department.


Fagan, B, M. [Editor] (1963) The Victoria Falls : A Handbook to the Victoria Falls, the Batoka Gorge, and part of the Upper Zambesi River. Lusaka.

Financial Times (2016) Zimbabwe swaps hyperinflation for deflation with use of US dollar. 25 January 2016 - [Online source: http://www.ft.com/cms/s/0/9eb1c2d8-c341-11e5-b3b1-7b2481276e45.html#axzz46QonixAJ]

Flight Magazine (Feb 1929) Eddies. 28 February, 1929. p.162. [Online source, retrieved: www.flightglobal.com/pdfarchive/view/1929/1929%20-%200404.html]

Flight Magazine (Jan 1947) Sporting Offer. 16 January 1947. p.71 [Online source: www.flightglobal.com/pdfarchive/view/1947/1947%20-%200083.html]

Flight Magazine (July 1947) The Spencer Crash. 17 July 1947. p.67 [Online source: www.flightglobal.com/pdfarchive/view/1947/1947%20-%201181.html]

Flight Magazine (May 1948) Inaugural Flight to South Africa on the First Springbok Flying-boat Service. 27 May, 1948, p.381-3. [Online source: www.flightglobal.com/pdfarchive/view/1948/1948%20-%200765.html]

Flight Magazine (August 1950) Livingstone Airport Opened. 17 August 1950. p.188. [Online source, retrieved: www.flightglobal.com/pdfarchive/view/1950/1950%20-%201538.html]

Flight Magazine (October 1951) Not-so-dark Africa. 05 October 1951. p.446 [Online source: www.flightglobal.com/pdfarchive/view/1951/1951%20-%202003.html]

Flight Magazine (August 1955) Game-Watching from the Air in an African Rapide: Bush flying with a difference. 01 August 1955. p.20 [Online source: www.flightglobal.com/pdfarchive/view/1955/1955%20-%200910.html]

Flight International Magazine (Feb 1979) World news. 24 February, 1979, p.514.

Frew, A. A. (1934) Prince George's African Tour. Blackie & Sons.


Gibbons A. St. H. (1904) Africa from South to North through Marotseland. London.

Glyn, R. (1863) A diary of ten months in South Africa. Quoted by Clay, G in Fagan, B, M. [Editor] (1963)

Green, L. G. (1968) Full Many a Glorious Morning. Timmins.


Harris, D. (1969) Victoria Falls Souvenir Guide Book.

Heath, R. A. (1977) Victoria Falls. The Growth of a Rhodesian Village Proceedings of the Geographical Association of Rhodesia, No.10 p.15-29.

Heath, R. A. (1986) The national survey of outdoor recreation in Zimbabwe. Zambezia XII(1), 26-36.

Hlatywayo, L. and Mukono, A. (2014) An Evaluation of the Zimbabwean Government of National Unity (2008-2013) Volume 3 Issue 8, August 2014.

Hobson, G. (1923) The Great Zambezi Bridge - The Story of a Famous Engineering Feat. [In Weinthal, L. (1923)]

Holub, E. (1881) Seven Years in South Africa. Travels, Researches and Hunting Adventures, Between the Diamond-Fields and the Zambesi, 1872-1879.

Holub, E. (1890) Second Voyage to Southern Africa. From Cape Town to the Land of the Mashukulumbwe. Travels in Southern Africa in 1883-87.

Hoole, R. J. (undated) The First Photographs of Victoria Falls taken by Frank 'Zambezi' Watson. [Online source: www.hoole.easynet.co.uk/]

Hutchinson, G. D. (1905) From the Cape to the Zambesi. J Murray, London.


Jeal, T. (2007) Stanley: The Impossible Life of Africa's Greatest Explorer. Yale.

Kararach, G. and Otieno, R. [Editors] (2016) Economic Management in a Hyperinflationary Environment. Oxford University Press.

Lewis, J. (2018) Empire of Sentiment - The Death of Livingstone and the Myth of Victoria Imperialism. Cambridge University Press.

Livingstone, D. (1857) Missionary travels and researches in South Africa. London.

Livingstone, D. and Livingstone, C. (1865) Narrative of an expedition to the Zambesi and its tributaries and of the discovery of the lakes Shirwa and Nyassa, 1858-1864. John Murray, London.

Livingstone Mail (April 1906) 21 April, 1906. No.3 [Quoted in Arrington, 2010]

Livingstone Mail (Dec 1906) Livingstone in 1906 - A Retrospect. Christmas Edition, December 1906. [LMA]

Livingstone Mail (Jan 1907) Meeting with His Honour the Administrator. 19 January 1907. No.43. [LMA]

Livingstone Mail (Dec 1907) A Peep into the Future. Christmas Edition, December 1907. [LMA]

Livingstone Mail (Dec 1908) Retrospect. Christmas Edition, December 1908. [LMA]

Livingstone Mail (March 1909) Front page advertisement for the North-Western Hotel. 13 March 1909. No.155. [LMA]

Livingstone Mail (Dec 1909) Our Annual Retrospect. Christmas Edition. [LMA]

Livingstone Mail (Dec 1910) Our Annual Retrospect. Christmas Edition. [LMA]

Livingstone Mail (March 1911) Advertisement. 18 March 1911. No.260. [LMA]

Livingstone Mail (July 1948) Article. 16 July 1948. [Quoted in Moonga, 1999]

McAdams, J. (1969) Birth of an Airline - Establishment of Rhodesia and Nyasaland Airways [Online source: www.rhodesia.nl/Aviation/rana.htm]

McGregor, J. (2003) The Victoria Falls 1900-1940: Landscape, Tourism and the Geographical Imagination, Journal of Southern African Studies, Volume 29, Number 3, September 2003, p.717-737.

McGregor, J. (2009) Crossing the Zambezi : The Politics of Landscape on an African Frontier.

Mackintosh, C. W. (1922) The new Zambesi trail ; a record of two journeys to North-Western Rhodesia (1903 and 1920). Unwin, London.

Makuvaza, S. (2012) Who Owns the Special Area at Victoria Falls World Heritage Site? The Historic Environment, Vol.3 No.1, April, 2012, p42–63

Martin, D. (1997) Victoria Falls: Mosi-oa-Tunya African Publishing Group, Harare

Meadows, K. (2000) Sometimes when it rains: white Africans in black Africa. Thorntree Press.

Metcalfe, C. Sir, and Richarde-Seaver, F. I. (1889) The British Sphere of Influence in South Africa. Fortnightly Review, p.267. London.

Metcalfe, C. (1904) Cape to Cairo Railway. Dawson Daily News, 29 September 1904. [Online source: https://news.google.com/newspapers?nid=41&dat=1904 0922&id=TJ4jAAAAIBAJ&sjid=1DYDAAAAIBAJ&pg=4126,6068996&hl=en]

Mohr, E. (1876) To the Victoria Falls of the Zambesi, translated by N. D'Anvers. Sampson Low, Marston, Searle and Rivingston, London.

Moonga. K. (1999) The Development of Tourism in Livingstone District, 1945-1991. University of Zambia.

Moore, J. (2012) Hotels at War [Online source, retrieved: www. rhodesianassociation.com/armies-that-served-rhodesia]

Morrah, D. (1947) The Royal Family in Africa, Hutchinson.

Mubitana, K. (1990) The Traditional History and Ethnography. [In Phillipson D. W. [Editor] (1990) Mosi-oa-Tunya: a handbook to the Victoria Falls region.]

Mugwati, M, Nkala, D. and Mashiri, E. (2016) Experiences in the Zimbabwe Hotel Industry during Hyperinflation. [In Kararach, G. and Otieno, R. [Editors] (2016)]

Munokalya, M. (2013) The Mukuni Royal Dynasty's Short History and the Munokalya Mukuni Royal Establishment's Ritual and Political Sovereignty.

Murison, K. [Editor] (2003) Africa South of the Sahara 2003, 32nd Edition. Europa.


Nelson, R. H. (2000) Entrance and Lodging Fees in the National Park System: Options for Zimbabwe. University of Maryland and ICER.

Northern News (1962) Victoria Falls Hotel Casino Approved. 13 April 1962.

Northern Rhodesia Journal (July 1950) European Names of Geographical Features. Lancaster, D. and Brelsford, W. V. Vol.1 No.2 p.64-70.

Northern Rhodesia Journal (Jan 1953) The World Sculling Championship on the Zambezi, Vol.2 No.1 p.73.

Northern Rhodesia Journal (July 1953) Island Names. Vol.2 No.2 p.89.

Northern Rhodesia Journal (Jan 1956) A Country in Search of a Name. Gray, J. A. Vol.3 No.1 p.75-78.

Northern Rhodesia Journal (July 1964) The Livingstone Pioneer, The First Newspaper. Barnes, P. Vol.5 No.4 p.389.


Pare, V. B. (1926) One of God Almighty's Grandest Sermons - What Visitors Think of the Victoria Falls. The Rhodesia Annual.

Parsons, D. (1938) Harnessing the Victoria Falls. Discovery.

Phillipson, D. W. (1990) The Early History of the Town of Livingstone, in Phillipson D. W. [Editor] (1990) Mosi-oa-Tunya: a handbook to the Victoria Falls region. Salisbury: Longman, Zimbabwe. (First published 1975, Second edition 1990)

Pinto, S. (1881) How I crossed Africa; from the Atlantic to the Indian Ocean, through unknown countries. London.

Pirie, G. H. (2011) Elite Exoticism: Sea-rail Cruise Tourism to South Africa, 1926–1939). Journal of African Historical Review, Vol.43, p.73-99.

Pitman, D. (1984) Riding the Rapids. Africa Calls from Zimbabwe magazine, unknown month, 1984.

Pinchuck, T. (2000) Rough Guide to Zimbabwe. 4th Revised edition.

PlanAfric (2001) Victoria Falls Combination Master Plan, Victoria Falls Combination Master Plan Preparation Authority. Bulawayo.

Price, J. H. (1966) Behind the Headlines. Modern Tramway and Light Railway Review. Vol.29 No.338 p.48-49.


Reserve Bank of Zimbabwe (2015) Demonetization of the Zimbabwe Dollar.

Rhodesia Railways (1905) Minutes of Ordinary General Meeting.

Rhodesia Railways Magazine (July 1952) District notes, Victoria Falls, Vol.1, No.3, p.27. [BRMA]

Rhodesia Railways Magazine (Dec 1954) First Hotel Built in a Month. Vol.3, No.8, p.13. [BRMA]

Rhodesia Railway Magazine (May 1955) District Newsfront: Victoria Falls. Vol.4, No.1. p.32. [BRMA]

Rhodesia Railways Magazine (July 1955) Fifty Years - The Story of a Bridge (Part 1). Vol.4, No.3, p.21-23. [BRMA]

Rhodesia Railways Magazine (Aug 1955) Fifty Years - The Story of a Bridge (Part 2). Vol.4, No.3, p.21-23. [BRMA]

Rhodesia Railways Magazine (Sept 1957) Railway History In The Leaves of A Circular. Vol.6, No.5, p.67. [BRMA]

Rhodesia Railways Magazine (Nov 1957) Special Railway Diamond Jubilee Issue (various articles), Vol.6, No.7. [BRMA]

Rhodesia Railways Magazine (July 1958) Some Reminiscences of The Early Days at the Falls. Vol.7, No.3, p.15. [BRMA]

Rhodesia Railways Magazine (March 1962) The Falls Fifty Years Ago. Vol.10, No.11, p.15-17. [BRMA]

Rhodesia Railways Magazine (May 1962) Livingstone - A New Station. Vol.11 No.1, p.13 [BRMA]

Rhodesia Railways Magazine (July 1962) Luxury Cruise Tourists Visit The Falls. Vol.11 No.3, p.19 [BRMA]

Rhodesia Railways Magazine (Jan 1965) District notes, Victoria Falls, Vol.13 No.9, p.44. [BRMA]

Rhodesia Railways Magazine (Feb 1965) District notes, Victoria Falls, Vol.13 No.10, p.41. [BRMA]

Rhodesia Railways Magazine (Aug 1967) The bridge - Some reminiscences, Vol.16, No.4, p.19. [BRMA]

Rhodesia Railways Magazine (Oct 1967) A Message from the General Manager, Vol.16 No.6, p.4. [BRMA]

Rhodesia Railways Magazine (Nov 1967) District notes, Victoria Falls, Vol.16 No.7, p41. [BRMA]

Rhodesian National Tourism Board (1967) Victoria Falls. Publicity brochure.

Rice, T (2008) Great Victoria Falls, Zambesi River [Online source: www.colonialfilm.org.uk/node/503]

Robert, D. L. (2009) Christian Mission: How Christianity Became a World Religion. Wiley-Blackwell.

Roberts, P. (2016a) Sun, Steel & Spray - A History of the Victoria Falls Bridge. Second (Revised) Edition. Zambezi Book Company / CreateSpace Independent Publishing. (First published 2011, Victoria Falls Bridge Company).

Roberts, P. (2016b) Corridors Through Time - A History of the Victoria Falls Hotel. Second (Revised) Edition. Zambezi Book Company / CreateSpace Independent Publishing. (First published 2015, The Jafuta Foundation).

Rogerson, C. M. (2009) Tourism Development in Southern Africa: Patterns, Issues and Constraints. In Saarinen et al [Editors] (2009).

Ross, A. C. (2002) David Livingstone: Mission and Empire. Hambledon, London.


Saarinen, J, Becker, F, Manwa, H, Wilson, D. [Editors] (2009) Sustainable Tourism in Southern Africa: Local Communities and Natural Resources in Transition.

Scientific American Magazine (1905) Completion of the Victoria Falls Bridge. 22nd July, 1905, pages 68-69.

Selous, F. C. (1881) A Hunter's Wanderings in Africa.

Selous, F. C. (1893) Travel and Adventure in South-East Africa - Narrative of the Last Eleven Years Spent by the Author on the Zambesi and its Tributaries.

Shepherd, G. (2008) Old Livingstone and Victoria Falls. Stenlake Publishing.

Shepherd, G. (2013) Old Frontier Life in North-Western Rhodesia. Stenlake.

Sokwanele (2005) Clearing away the Trash. [Online source: www.archive.kubatana.net/html/archive/opin/050615sok.asp?sector=REFUG&year=2005&range_start=271]

South Africa Handbook, No.34 (1905) A Trip to the Victoria Falls and Rhodesia. Winchester House, London.

Southern Rhodesia Publicity Office (1938) The Victoria Falls of Southern Rhodesia. Government Stationery Office.

Southern Rhodesia Public Relations Department (c1955) Victoria Falls, Greatest River Wonder of the World. Public Relations Department of Southern Rhodesia.

Stanley, H. M. (1898) Through South Africa - His Visit to Rhodesia, the Transvaal, Cape Colony, Natal.

Stead, W. T. (1902) The Last Will and Testament of Cecil J Rhodes.

Stirling, W. G. M. and House, J. A. (2014) They Served Africa with Wings. E-book Edition (First published 2002).

Stirling, W. G. M. (2015) Angel's Wings. December 2015 [Online source: www.linkedin.com/pulse/angels-wings-mitch-stirling]

Stirling, W. G. M. (2016) Personal communication with author. June 2016.

Strage, M. (1973) Cape to Cairo. Jonathan Cape.

Suich, H, Busch, J. and Barbancho, N. (2005) Economic Impacts Of Transfrontier Conservation Areas: Baseline Of Tourism In The Kavango–Zambezi TFCA. Conservation International South Africa.

Sykes, F. W. (1905) Official Guide to the Victoria Falls. Bulawayo.


Teede, J. and Teede, F. (1994) African Thunder - The Victoria Falls. Zimbabwe.

Terpstra, P. (2008) Tuesday Afternoon [Online source: www.dinny.net/africa/home.html]


UAC (1980s) United Air Charters Advert, unknown publication.

UNESCO (1989) Mosi-oa-Tunya/Victoria Falls summary. [Online source: www.whc.unesco.org/en/list/509]

UNESCO (2007) State of Conservation summary report. [Online source: www.whc.unesco.org/en/soc/967]

UNESCO (2012) State of Conservation summary report. [Online source: www.whc.unesco.org/en/soc/137]

UNWTO (2014) UNWTO General Assembly Opens. [Online source: www.zw.one.un.org/newsroom/news/untwo-general-assembly-opens]

USAID (2013) Positioning The Zimbabwe Tourism Sector For Growth: Issues and Challenges. USAID Strategic Economic Research & Analysis – Zimbabwe.


van Riel , F. (2008) Walking with my uncles. Africa Geographic Magazine. Vol.16 No.5, July 2008.

Varian, H. F. (1953) Some African Milestones. Oxford.

Victoria Falls Bits and Blogs (June 2009) Vic Falls Heritage Status Threatened. 19 June 2009. [Online source: www.vicfallsbitsnblogs.blogspot.co.uk/2009/06/vic-falls-heritage-status-threatened.html]

Victoria Falls Bits and Blogs (Nov 2010) Urban sprawl threatens Vic Falls. 10 November 2010. [Online source: www.vicfallsbitsnblogs.blogspot.co.uk/2010/11/urban-sprawl-threatens-vic-falls.html]

Victoria Falls Bits and Blogs (Aug 2011a) Victoria Falls reports good occupancies. 30 August 2011. [Online source: www.vicfallsbitsnblogs.blogspot.co.uk/2011/08/victoria-falls-reports-good-occupancies.html]

Victoria Falls Bits and Blogs (Aug 2011b) Vic Falls reports an upswing in arrivals. 31 August 2011. [Online source: www.vicfallsbitsnblogs.blogspot.co.uk/2011/08/vic-falls-reports-upswing-in-arrivals.html]

Victoria Falls Bits and Blogs (Jan 2012) Australian woman Erin Langworthy survives 111m bungee fall into the Zambezi River. 15 January 2012. [Online source: www.vicfallsbitsnblogs.blogspot.co.uk/2012/01/australian-woman-erin-langworthy.html]

Victoria Falls Bits and Blogs (Jan 2013) Tourism industry on recovery path. 14 January 2013. [Online source: www.vicfallsbitsnblogs.blogspot.co.uk/2013/01/tourism-industry-on-recovery-path.html]

Victoria Falls Bits and Blogs (Feb 2013a) Batoka Dam Update. 05 February 2013. [Online source: www.vicfallsbitsnblogs.blogspot.co.uk/2013/02/batoka-dam-update.html]

Victoria Falls Bits and Blogs (Feb 2013b) On the elephant frontline. 24 February 2013. [Online source: www.vicfallsbitsnblogs.blogspot.co.uk/2013/02/on-elephants-frontline.html]

Victoria Falls Bits and Blogs (Aug 2013) Victoria Falls 'Disneyland' on the cards. 26 August 2013. [Online source: www.vicfallsbitsnblogs.blogspot.co.uk/2013/08/victoria-falls-disneyland-mooted.html]

Victoria Falls Bits and Blogs (Nov 2013) Chinese tourist rescued after falling into Falls. 28 November 2013. [Online source: www.vicfallsbitsnblogs.blogspot.co.uk/2013/11/chinese-tourist-rescued-after-falling.html]

Victoria Falls Bits and Blogs (Dec 2013) Victoria Falls no more? 20 December 2013. [Online source: www.vicfallsbitsnblogs.blogspot.co.uk/2013/12/victoria-falls-no-more.html]

Victoria Falls Bits and Blogs (Jan 2014) Vic Falls rainforest draws 17,000 visitors over festive period. 15 January 2014. [Online source: www.vicfallsbitsnblogs.blogspot.co.uk/2014/01/vic-falls-rainforest-draws-17000.html]

Victoria Falls Bits and Blogs (April 2014) Vic Falls hotels income up 20 percent. 04 April 2014. [Online source: www.vicfallsbitsnblogs.blogspot.co.uk/2014/04/vic-falls-hotels-income-up-20pct-on.html]

Victoria Falls Bits and Blogs (Nov 2014) Chief Mukuni opposes the commercialisation of Victoria Falls. 30 November 2014. [Online source: www.vicfallsbitsnblogs.blogspot.co.uk/2014/11/chief-mukuni-opposes-commercialisation.html]

Victoria Falls Bits and Blogs (March 2015) Tourism receipts down 3%. 30

March 2015. [Online source: www.vicfallsbitsnblogs.blogspot.co.uk/2015/03/tourism-receipts-down-3.html]

Victoria Falls Bits and Blogs (April 2015) $18m park set for Vic Falls. 27 April 2015. [Online source: www.vicfallsbitsnblogs.blogspot.co.uk/2015/05/18m-park-set-for-vic-falls.html]

Victoria Falls Bits and Blogs (June 2015) Zim struggling to clear landmines 35 years after independence. 19 June 2015. [Online source: www.vicfallsbitsnblogs.blogspot.co.uk/2015/06/zim-struggling-to-clear-landmines-35.html]

Victoria Falls Bits and Blogs (Sept 2015) Legacy partners African Sun in Victoria Falls. 22 September 2015. [Online source: www.vicfallsbitsnblogs.blogspot.co.uk/2015/09/legacy-partners-african-sun-in-victoria.html]

Victoria Falls Bits and Blogs (Nov 2015) Vic Falls set to go from a charming town to major hub. 28 November 2015. [Online source: www.vicfallsbitsnblogs.blogspot.co.uk/2015/10/vic-falls-set-to-go-from-charming-town.html]

Victoria Falls Bits and Blogs (Feb 2016) Victoria Falls to see recovery in 2016. 08 February 2016. [Online source: www.vicfallsbitsnblogs.blogspot.co.uk/2016/03/victoria-falls-to-see-recovery-in-2016.html]

Victoria Falls Bits and Blogs (March 2016) 6 elephants die from eating plastic bags in Vic Falls. 14 March 2016. [Online source: www.vicfallsbitsnblogs.blogspot.co.uk/2016/03/6-elephants-die-from-eating-plastic.html]

Victoria Falls Bits and Blogs (June 2016) Vic Falls a $4,8bn cash cow: Minister. 13 June 2016. [Online source: www.vicfallsbitsnblogs.blogspot.co.uk/2016/06/vic-falls-48bn-cash-cow-minister.html]

Victoria Falls Bits and Blogs (July 2016) Suspended Uni-Visa facility to bounce back. 01 July 2016. [Online source: www.vicfallsbitsnblogs.blogspot.co.uk/2016/06/suspended-uni-visa-facility-to-bounce.html]

Victoria Falls Bits and Blogs (Sept 2016) Multi-million dollar complex for Vic Falls? 15 September. [Online source: www.vicfallsbitsnblogs.blogspot.co.uk/2016/09/multi-million-dollar-complex-for-vic.html]

Victoria Falls Bits and Blogs (Nov 2016) Cataract Island threatened by tourism development. 06 December 2016. [Online source: www.vicfallsbitsnblogs.blogspot.co.uk/2016/12/cataract-island-threatened-by-tourism.html]

Victoria Falls Bits and Blogs (April 2017a) Shearwater News April 2017. 04 April 2017. [Online source: www.vicfallsbitsnblogs.blogspot.co.uk/2017/04/the-pioneering-spirit-shearwater.html]

Victoria Falls Bits and Blogs (April 2017b) Tourist arrivals to reach 2,2 million by year end. 18 April 2017. [Online source: www.vicfallsbitsnblogs.blogspot.co.uk/2017/04/tourist-arrivals-to-reach-22-million-by.html]

Victoria Falls Guide (2015) Lions & Buffaloes Come Into Town. [Online source: www.victoriafalls-guide.net/lions-buffaloes-come-into-town.html]

Victoria Falls Hotel Management Committee (1963) Report from General Manager, The Victoria Falls Hotel: Progress Report. 26 March 1963. [BRMA]

Victoria Falls World Heritage Site (2007) Joint Management Plan. Victoria Falls/ Mosi-oa-Tunya World Heritage Site, 2007-2012.

Victoria Falls World Heritage Site Joint Report (2014) Joint State of Conservation Report. Victoria Falls/Mosi-oa-Tunya World Heritage Site.

Victoria Falls World Heritage Site Joint Report (2016) Joint State of Conservation Report. Victoria Falls/Mosi-oa-Tunya World Heritage Site.


Ward Price, G. (1926) Through South Africa with Prince. Gill Publishing, London.

Weinthal, L. (1923) The Story of the Cape to Cairo Railway and River Route from 1887–1922. Pioneer Publishing Co.

White, B. (1973) The Trailmakers, The story of Rhodesia Railways. Supplement to Illustrated Life, Rhodesia, 31 May 1973.

Whitehead, D. (2014) Inspired by the Zambezi, Memories of Barotseland and a Royal River – the mighty Liambai. Goshawk, South Africa.

Woods, J. (1960) Guide book to the Victoria Falls, S. Manning.

World Conservation Union (1996) Strategic Environmental Assessment of Developments Around Victoria Falls. Regional Office for Southern Africa.

Wright, E. (2008) Lost Explorers: Adventurers who Disappeared Off the Face of the Earth. Murdock Books.

Wynn, S. (1995) The Victoria Falls : A Fragile Power. Africa Geographic Magazine, Vol.3, No.1, January 1995.


Zambia Information Services (1965) Press Release, June 1965.

Zambian Ministry of Tourism and Arts (2014) 2013 Tourism Statistical Digest.

ZIMSTAT (2012) National Population Census, Zimbabwe Statistics Agency, 2012.

# LIFE AND DEATH
# AT THE OLD DRIFT

## VICTORIA FALLS
## (1898-1905)

The Old Drift holds a pivotal place in the story of the modern development of the Victoria Falls region, marking the main crossing point on the Zambezi River above the Falls for travellers and traders heading north. Established in 1898 the crossing became the focal point for the beginnings of a small European community, before the development of the railway and opening of the Victoria Falls Bridge in 1905 shifted the focus of activity downstream.

With over 90 period photographs and fully referenced, 'Life and Death at the Old Drift' presents a detailed look at this period of great change along the banks of the Zambezi.

# Sun, Steel and Spray

## A History of the Victoria Falls Bridge

'Sun, Steel and Spray - A History of the Victoria Falls Bridge' presents a comprehensive look at the story of this iconic structure and engineering marvel. Built in 1904-5 as part of the extension of the envisaged Cape-to-Cairo railway north into central Africa, the spanning of the Zambezi pushed engineering knowledge and construction techniques to new heights, literally, for at the time the Bridge was the highest of its kind over water.

With over 100 period photographs and illustrations, 'Sun, Steel and Spray' is full of interesting facts, entertaining stories and information detailing the rich history of the Bridge, from conception and construction to its ongoing management and maintenance.

# CORRIDORS
# THROUGH TIME
## A HISTORY OF
## THE VICTORIA FALLS HOTEL

Established in 1904 the Victoria Falls Hotel has played a central role in the romance of a visit to the Falls for generations of travellers, its walls and gardens echoing with  a rich history covering the development of a modern global tourism icon.

Fully illustrated with over 100 period images and 30 modern photographs, 'Corridors Through Time' details the changing face of the 'Grand Old Lady of the Falls'  and growth of tourism to the Victoria Falls, from humble beginnings to luxury five-star elegance, from the arrival of the railway to the age of aviation, and through colonial administration to political independence.